Praise for **Artist's Pants**

"These prose paragraphs are as intricately structured as a sonnet and melodious as a rhythmic poem of rhyme beyond reason. This does not happen by accident, nor is it paced to complete in conformity to a calendar. This happens by the sweat of one man's brow and the spark of his unique, dare I say genius."

~ Mat Gleason, Editor of the Coagula Art Journal

"Mr. Wisecrack himself, Gordy Grundy offers insightful and humorous commentaries on the art world; especially relevant for readers who are considering jumping feet first into its treacherous waters."

~ Frances Colpitt, Art Writer and Professor of Art History

"His writing accomplishes exactly that to which serious fine art aspires yet rarely achieves: it makes us see the world in a different way."

~ Shana Nys Dambrot, Arts Writer, Huffington Post

"Grundy is a masterpiece that will go unrecognized in his own time. I stole that line from an unheralded artist named Mitchell Syrop and this makes perfect sense. As Grundy posits, anything goes: It's all luck or chance, anyway."

~ Michael Delgado, Executive Producer and Publisher

"It is with great enthusiasm that I recommend the works of Gordy Grundy."

~ Ronee Blakley, Academy Award Nominee and Singer

"Hold onto your cocktail and tighten your ascot: Gordy Grundy's prose takes you on a trippy cruise through the laughable bourgeois art-world, John Cheever-style. Is this guy for real?"

~ Tulsa Kinney, Editor of Artillery magazine

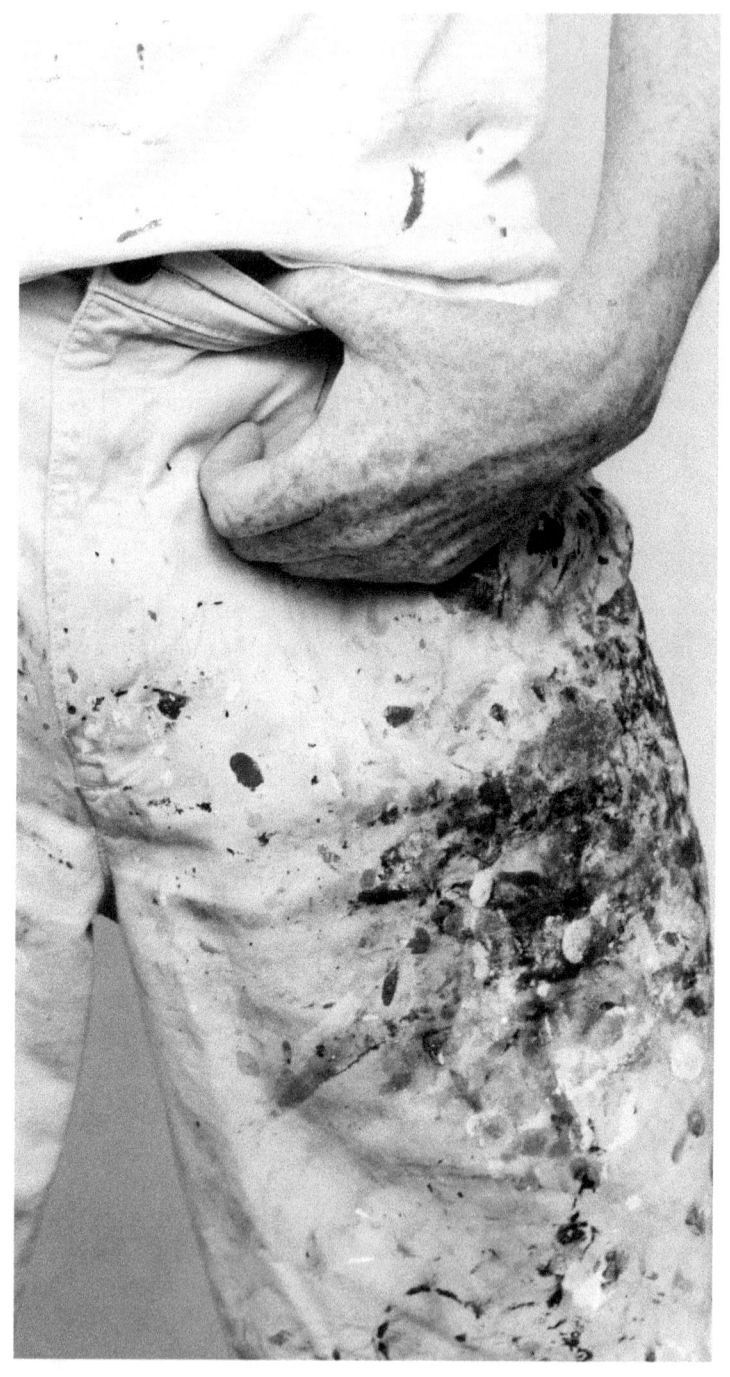

ARTIST'S PANTS

FORTUNA
EX LIBRIS

FORTUNA EX LIBRIS
CHANCE IS OUR COMPASS

This Book Belongs To

ARTIST'S PANTS

Words and Pictures by

GORDY GRUNDY

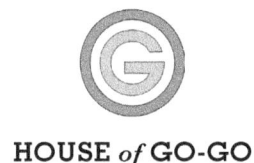

HOUSE *of* GO-GO

The author would like to thank those for
their help in this project:
John Tottenham, Chris Buzzini and Margel Nusbaumer

Published in the United States of America

Acknowledgment is made to the following, in which
various forms of this book's pieces first appeared.
~ *All but one piece first appeared in the Coagula Art Journal.*
~ *Catalogue Essay for Transit Projects: 'Survival L.A.' at
Raid Projects, Los Angeles "Strategies, Survival Skills And Guer-
rilla Tactics For The Fine Artist"*

Book Design and Artworks by the Author
Cover Photography by Meghann McCrory
Design Consultant: Wendy Furman

Visit our website at www.GordyGrundy.com

ISBN-13: 978-0692225257
ISBN 9780692225257

Library of Congress Control Number: 2014909401

Printed in the United States of America

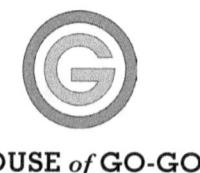

HOUSE *of* **GO-GO**

For Luck

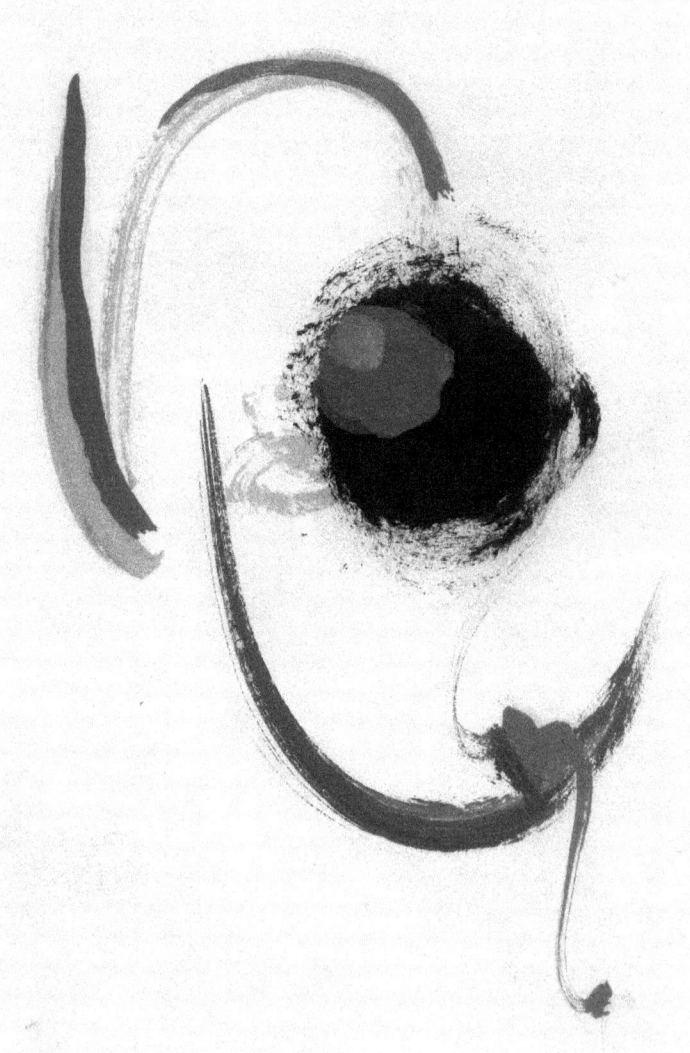

CONTENTS

n a GLASS
BOTTLE, mix 2
parts GASOLI
with 1 part OIL.
Stuff neck wit
a GAS SOAKE
RAG. Cork it.

Light fuse.
Toss 'n run.

INTRODUCTION

You never really know someone unless you've walked a mile in their pants. Howdy, friend. Thanks for cracking the spine.

Artist's Pants is a collection of selected work from my popular column Genuflect that appeared in the Coagula Art Journal, the notorious, must-read, Los Angeles art magazine. This book was first produced in 2007 as a limited edition, hardcover Artist's Proof of 100 copies.

Genuflect was one of the great joys and freedoms in my life. Editor Mat Gleason gave me permission to take chances, make mistakes and try anything and everything new. Over a decade, I never missed a glorious issue. As a result, I learned how to write. For that opportunity and education, I am eternally grateful.

This new edition has been revised. I have added several pieces that concern 9-11, for that event and the repercussive aftermath, has changed so many lives and lifestyles. In retrospect, it cannot be ignored or eagerly forgotten, hence the inclusion.

There is a madness to a life in the arts and in the beautiful fools who choose to live it. Artist's Pants is a madcap adventure, a mere glimpse, into that world. Enjoy! There is more to come.

~ Gordy Grundy

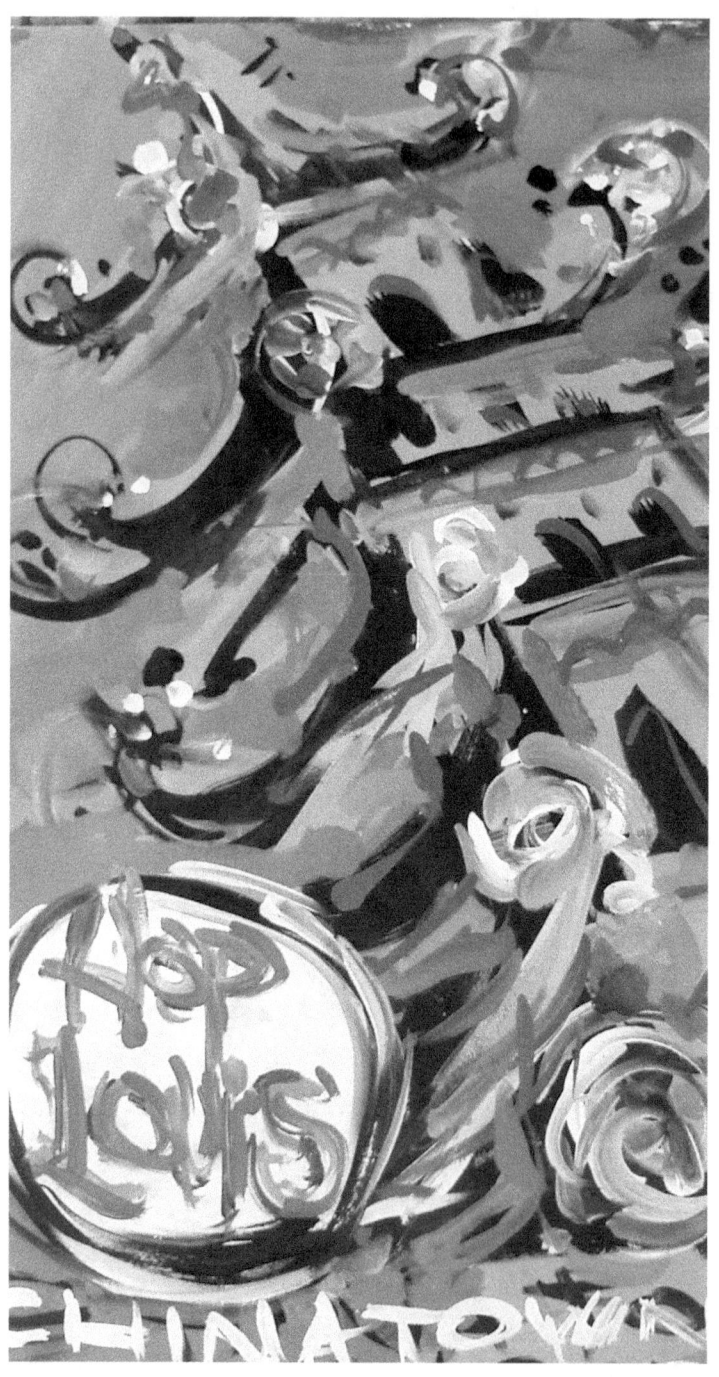

MAT GLEASON

It used to anger me when Gordy Grundy would be late for his deadline. Perhaps you heard a strange scream while driving through downtown Los Angeles over the past dozen years? That might have been me, ready to go to the printer's *(a quaint notion in the era of the internet)*, still without a *Genuflect* column, held hostage by a popular columnist.

My readers wouldn't pick up the rag if there was no Grundy and so I waited, in between howls.

It took many years to get it through my thick skull that these essays were taking so long not out of disregard for my impositions of time. No, these seemingly effortless essays on the simple expectations one man has in regards to the quality of life, these prose paragraphs are as intricately structured as a sonnet and melodious as a rhythmic poem of rhyme beyond reason.

This does not happen by accident, nor is it paced to complete in conformity to a calendar. This happens

15

Mat Gleason

by the sweat of one man's brow and the spark of his unique, dare I say genius.

The occasional sophisticate will pull me aside at an art world affair and ask, with great consistency in curiosity over the years and among the personalities so interested, the question will be "Tell me just who this fabulous Gordy Grundy is…" In any line of work, when you are asked the same question enough times, you prepare a fallback answer. Mine has become, "He wears an ascot, never spills his drink, and falls in love with whomever he makes eye contact. Think twice before assuming you can keep up with him."

I could hardly add anything to complement the words he has authored, except to gloat that I finally made him wait for this essay until after the deadline on which he had insisted.

As you read this compilation, you'll soon genuflect with joy, and to get you to do so is why Gordy Grundy was put on this earth.

MAT GLEASON *is the Founder and Publisher of the Coagula Art Journal and curator at gallery Coagula Projects in Chinatown, Los Angeles.*

SHANA NYS DAMBROT

A MILE IN HIS PANTS

Gordy Grundy is one of my favorite art writers in Los Angeles, despite the fact that he rarely actually writes about art. It's not his opinions he shares with his loyal readers, though lord knows he's got plenty of them, it's himself. Or rather a version of himself, a character based on himself; close enough to the real thing to ring true. The first person narrator in his work is a looking glass version of Gordy, distorted the way painted self-portraits are distorted; trading verisimilitude for deeper insight, but not telling the whole story.

Grundy is at heart I think a conceptual artist whose work in visual art and the written word each express the evolution of his gold-plated freefall, using whatever means seems most suited to the task that day. He once told me he has written a post-Modern neo-

Shana Nys Dambrot

vaudeville nightclub review, *The Blackouts*.

He has a flair for the dramatic, he's picky when it comes to martinis, and most of his confessions are as fictional as surrealist paintings.

He floats in and out of his own dream states at will, but rather than disorienting the reader, he leads us by example to do the same, demonstrating time and again just how easily breached the walls of perception actually are.

His writing accomplishes exactly that to which serious fine art aspires yet rarely achieves: it makes us see the world in a different way.

He exaggerates, he embellishes, picks scabs and flirts with disaster. He practices stylish gonzo art criticism like Hunter S. Thompson mashed up with Susan Sontag. He manages to always embrace the present moment completely while simultaneously pondering its meaning.

Like a beatnik Gatsby, a Rat Pack Clem Greenberg, he's a holy fool, always willing to put his own comfort level at risk in the service of something larger. Like me, and maybe this is why we're friends, serendipity is the organizing principle of his life and he makes decisions based on what he feels will make the better story later.

In one essay he asserts, "I am a man divided. My soul cries for salvation, yet my body seeks sin. I am straddling the double yellow line of change. One foot is firmly placed on the sizzling asphalt of hellfire while the other is set on the path of righteousness."

Bullshit, Gordy. You're one of the happiest people I know. Anyway, nice pants.

SHANA NYS DAMBROT *is an art critic and editor based in Los Angeles. Her work appears in Flaunt, Scene, the Huffington Post, the LA Weekly, ArtNews, Juxtapoz, Flavorpill.net, Artkrush.com, Art Review, Modern Painters, Uber.com/art, and, once upon a time, The Coagula Art Journal.*

PASSION OF
A VOODOO
PRIESTESS.
WALK
IN
DANCE
OUT.
TRYST
AND
SHOUT

MICHAEL DELGADO

Artist Gordy Grundy is the quintessential Angeleno. He's not sure if salvation comes from physical and spiritual discourse or pagan hedonism. It's THINK-ING about a soul cleansing dip in the Pacific ocean and instead snapping your fingers for another martini. Simultaneously Prophet and Philistine, Grundy proclaims that the gravelly road to salvation may just as well be paved with the asphalt that has little gold flakes ground into it, as only Hollywood can lay down. (In Grundy's dogma: self expression= emancipation)

'Artist's Pants', is a compendium of articles and musings from 1997 to the present day and at once lays bare an unchecked romanticism for a LA that might have never existed, while also serving up darkly humorous anecdotes from a contemporary tale of self-destruction. This is not a bad thing; at least we get mayhem and confession with style and laughs.

21

Michael Delgado

As a barefoot acolyte in the temple of Warhol, Grundy puts a particularly Los Angeles, nay, Southern Californian scent into the incense of a regional self-journalism. You can recognize the hard-boiled rat-a-tat-tat of Raymond Chandler, the poetry of Nathaniel West, the dreamy feel-good of the Beach Boys as well as the "Why can't we all just get along" desperation of the Rodney King legacy.

Grundy of course understands none of this--or does he? Like Warhol, he plays dumb and hangs with questionable company.

Gordy Grundy is a masterpiece that will go unrecognized in his own time. I stole that line from an unheralded artist named Mitchell Syrop and this makes perfect sense. As Grundy posits, anything goes: its all luck or chance, anyway.

MICHAEL DELGADO *made art, then wrote about others as an art writer for the LA Weekly, before moving to Minneapolis to produce television as if there was none in Los Angeles. After producing specials for MTV, he was back in print as the Associate Publisher of METRO, a Twin Cities lifestyle monthly. He's thinking about just making art in LA again.*

22

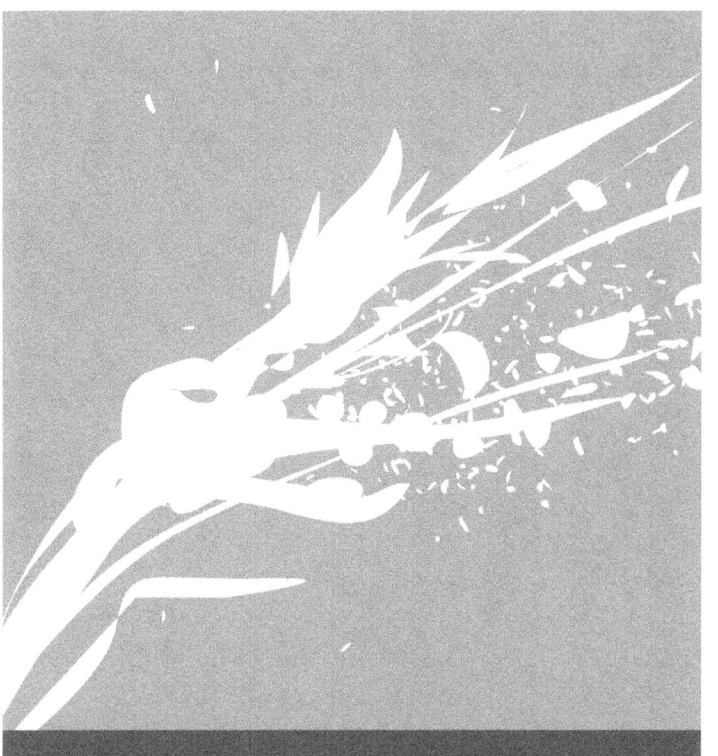

All Wheat. No Chaff

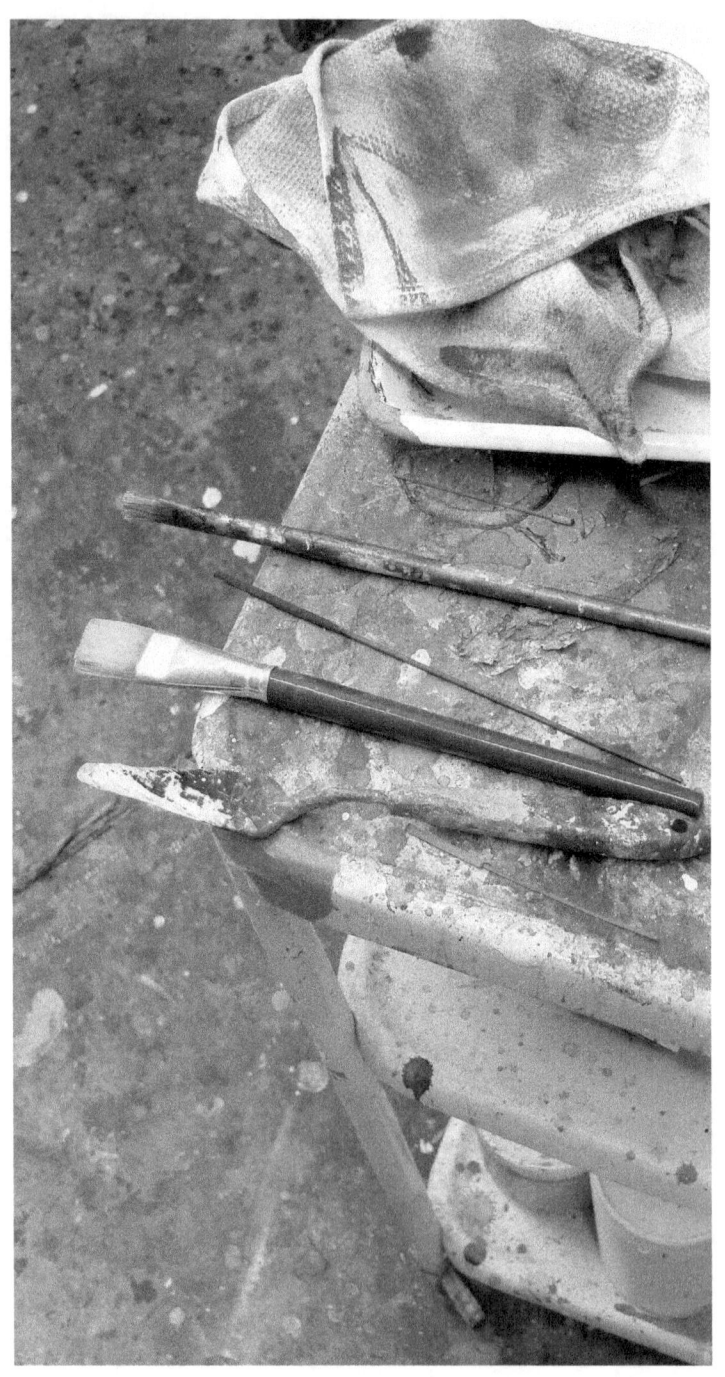

ARTIST'S PANTS

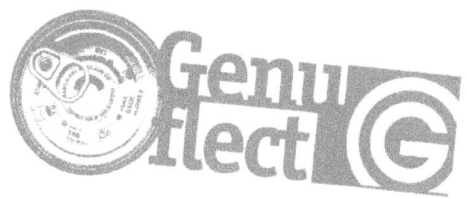

GORDY GRUNDY

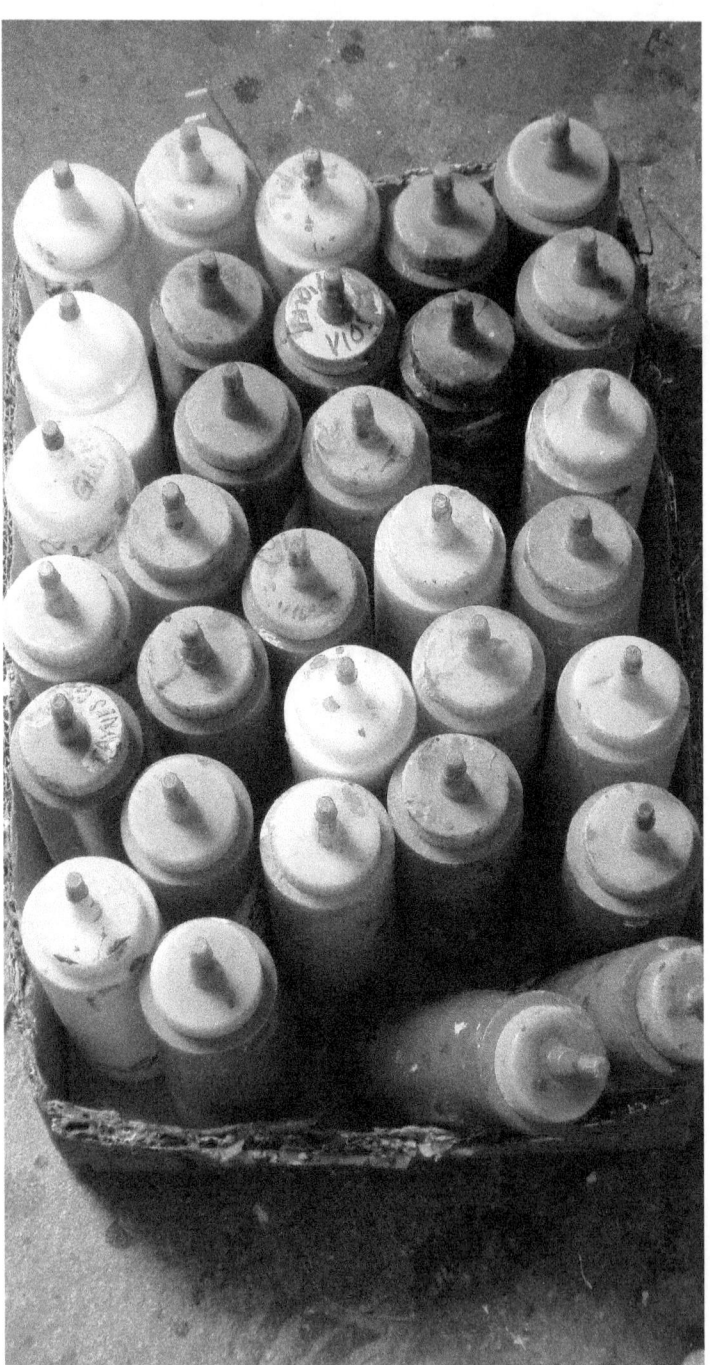

SURVIVAL SKILLS, STRATEGIES AND GUERRILLA TACTICS FOR THE FINE ARTIST

I can't imagine why anyone would want to become an artist.

The hours are long, the benefits are few and the pay is lousy. Even worse, it's a lonely place; most folks cannot fathom our what and why of it. 'Success' in the arts cannot be quantified nor is the pursuit easily explained.

I don't know why I make art, but every day I'm trying to figure out how to make more. In a true American style, I have sought to find a system of survival that will allow more time and greater resources to do what I do best. My Design for Living is constantly being amended and it shall never be perfected, but I believe the basic structure shall benefit my fellow artists everywhere.

Following is a list of survival skills and guerrilla

Gordy Grundy

tactics in order of greatest importance:

I) MORAL SUPPORT

Find a bartender with an MFA. If everyone needs a shoulder to cry on, then you might as well make it an empathetic and educated one. I highly suggest that you conscript several. Should you ever get 86'd, it's good to have a back-up.

II) LEGAL SUPPORT

Find a good criminal attorney. I am not suggesting that you keep one on retainer, but I do advocate a relationship that you can count on. Plug that phone number into Speed Dial. The hair on your chinny chin-chin is rather thin and easily plucked. Your lives are limited to nine. The American penal system does not provide art supplies. Natch.

III) FINANCIAL INDEMNIFICATION

Money, or rather the lack of it, may be one of the greatest and most vexing roadblocks to the free-flowing life force of an artist.

The following Flow Chart is a simple one: Art demands time. Time is money. Money is earned through time spent anywhere but in your studio.

As you can see, it is a vicious and endless cycle that does not offer many opportunities for relief. I shall endeavor to list several venues of escape.

In order of greatest convenience and benefit:

III: A) The ultimate fantasy is an aggressive, dynamic and global gallerist who pays the artist at fifty-fifty, net fifteen. Their devotion to you and your aesthetic is absolute and held more dearly than their own lives.

As previously stated, this is the fantasy. The reality is generally so ugly that I prefer to wear blinders. Attaining a gallerist engenders a descent into an eighth and ninth level of Hell that Dante never imagined. Unconditionally trusting a dealer would test the compassion of Christ and the intellect of Forrest Gump.

This road is fraught with much grief and is not conducive to making art. Move on.

III: B) An adequate trust fund is not as suitable as a bountiful one, but I would refuse neither. An inheritance is, by far, the most preferable financial opportunity for an artist. You are beholden to no one except the dead. The demands of time and effort are limited to endorsing a check once a month.

Unfortunately, *my* prospects of a trust fund are nil. This unforgivable and cruel fact has often driven me to shake my fist at the moon and loudly curse the Gods, much to the dismay of my neighbors.

III: C) Marry well. Many suggest that marriage is a wise and valuable option. I like the idea that sex is included in the package but I have my reservations.

Often times, 'to marry well' can demand more emotional grief and time at hard labor than a counter job at McDonalds.

III: D) Go Third World. The coffee is better and the rent is cheaper.

III: E) A favorable day job. This is easier hoped for than found. If time is money, then you want to make the most money in the least amount of time. (See Figure 23.1, Page 266)

Gordy Grundy

Unfortunately, a law degree yields a higher hourly wage than an art degree. Fortunately, most states offer a minimum wage, which unfortunately does not buy spit.

Ideally, you will be lucky to serve your time under a sympathetic boss who has a love, appreciation and a support for the fine arts. He or she will be inspired (or at least amused) by your singular passion and lend assistance and resources in every way.

This is the exception to the rule. Most employers will view your artistry with suspicion, sneer at your 'misguided' values and do everything they can to thwart your quest.

"I don't care if you are debuting in Belgium--Sweep the f***ing floor!"

IV) THE MINDSET OF THE ARTIST

From Aristotle to Anthony Robbins, every smart mind concludes, "Attitude is everything." That cup can be sadly half empty or gleefully *half full!* Unfortunately, artists tend to dig a bit deeper and ask, "Full of *what?*"

The cranial synapses of an artist are not wired like that of a civilian. There are quirks and contradictions to most of us that make life as carefree as dancing on a minefield. The world is marching one way and we are blithely skipping in another. How do we endure?

Attitude. The artist must foster and nurture a mindset to survive.

IV: A) NO ABSOLUTES: FAD AND FASHION

I like to think there is a Valhalla of Beauty, an absolute in Art. I prefer to believe that there will be an epiphany or a revelation, a destination to any artistic journey. Such a glory does not exist.

The art world that I want to believe in is merely a concoction of a fantastic mind and my preference for the HyperReal. The actual art world has as much resolve as next season's wallpaper. It is a victim *and* a proponent of fad and fashion.

When I first realized this, I felt like a Believer who suddenly learns that the parish priest is a pederast. My devastation has since mellowed and aged into a steadfast resolve: *Stay the course, lads. Stay true to your aesthetic. This is our integrity. This is our power and our strength. The dedication and perseverance to our Form becomes our ultimate joy.*

IV: B) TRUE REWARD

As artists, we seek recognition for our work, yet this is a slippery slope to climb. It demands an investment into a judicial authority whose demeanor can only be described as capricious.

The work of Jackson Pollack was hailed as genius and slaughtered as stale, all within a very short period of time. A gnawing hunger for external recognition can never be fed. It is an emotional hole than will never be filled because the appetite grows larger and demands more.

A gaggle of psychologists will tell you that self-worth is the only panacea and they are right. The reward is in the work. As much as I bitch and moan about the storage, maintenance and preservation of my inventory, I am damn proud of that pile.

This private joy is our pay dirt.

IV: C) RECOGNITION

Your efforts are not wasted. Your time will come. You will be recognized. Your dedication guarantees it.

As fad and fashion gallop and leap like horses on

a slow moving merry-go-round, your turn to snatch a brass ring will come.

We must show graciousness for any attention that is thrown our way. We must be humble before every gesture. You may never show your work at MOMA, but you can be damn sure you'll have a retrospective somewhere awesome before you turn seventy-five. That will be a glorious honor.

IV: D) PATIENCE AND LONGEVITY

Like aging hookers and old buildings, artists become respectable over time. Great success in the arts comes from the courage and single-mindedness of your durability.

The true reward is in your daily journey and the daring, impractical belief in your quest. Given the high attrition rate of artists, you will be ultimately honored for your longevity. Keep making art.

IV: E) BALANCE

A sailor's legs are the greatest survival skill an artist can possess and the most difficult to acquire. We need to keep both feet on a pitching deck.

Artists are a species of anxious and warring contradictions. We are giants and we are dwarves. We are Ying and we are Yang. We are sorely selfish and genuinely generous. No one can beat their chest and roar in triumph as loud as we. Conversely, no one can lock themselves into a closet as black, insular and deep as ours. In the mind's own eye, no light shines as bright and there is no darker hell. We are invincible and we are worthless. We see the sadness in beauty and the genius in madness.

Long ago I proffered that 'artists are the astronauts of our sociology.' Test pilot Chuck Yeager may have nicked the sound barrier, but artists push the frontiers of human experience. We laugh more and we cry more. We feel more and we see more; I believe that is what motivates us to make the choices that we make and the actions that we take.

We seem to embody *all* of the contradictions of humanity. This is the gasoline of our fire. The trick and the skill is to singe ourselves without self-immolating. To triumph with humility. To fade with dignity. To lose graciously and congratulate whole-heartedly. To pursue our own individual aesthetic with a plausible and steadfast integrity.

This is the balance. This is our self-worth. This is our life.

V) BE PRACTICAL

Don't drink and drive. Plein Aire painters should use a good sunscreen. Try to find a cold water flat with a water heater.

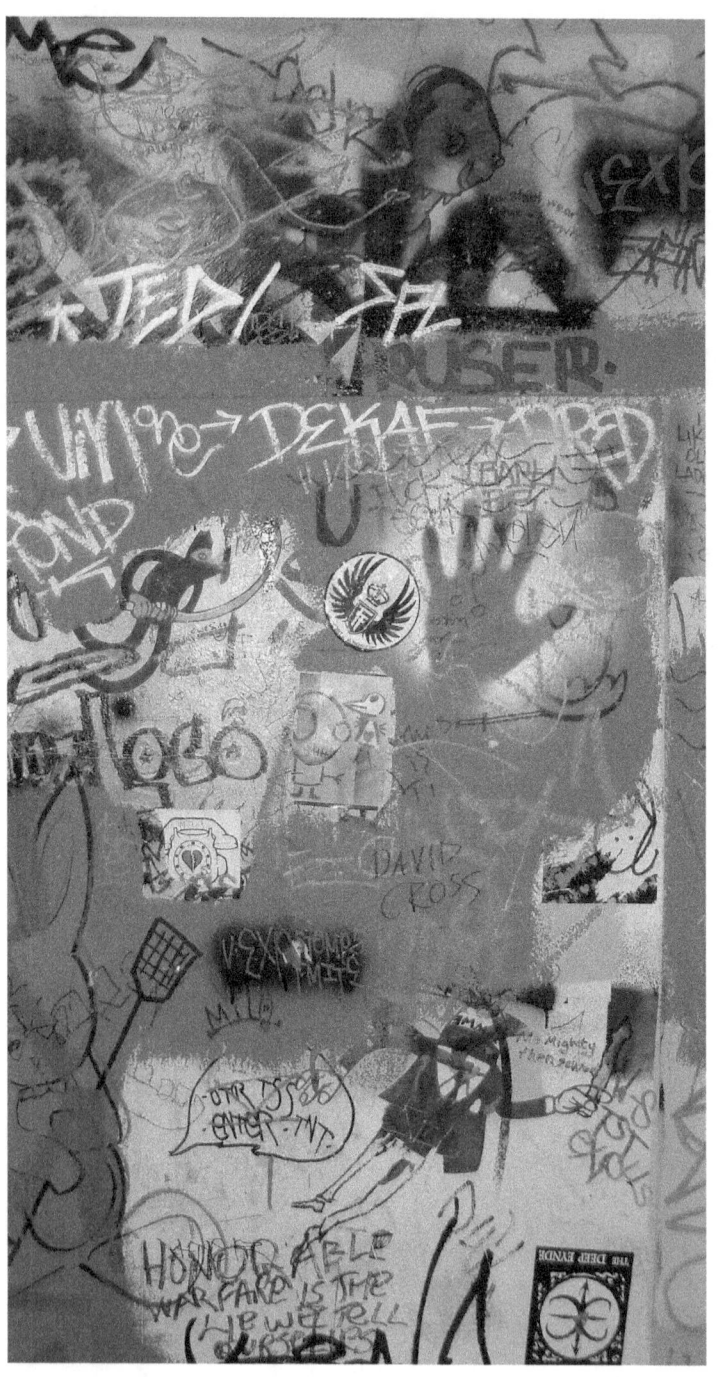

LIVING IN WARTIME, PART ONE

HELL IS OTHER PEOPLE

Many of you don't know that I own an island in the South Pacific where I spend a great deal of my time. When I'm not dogging it in Los Angeles, Walihi is the place I call home. It is a refuge—it *was* a refuge, a place of tranquility and beauty far, far away from the many humanities of our world.

Walihi lies north of Tahiti and southwest of the Hawaiian Islands. Far from the shipping lanes, it is a small island that has been charted by only a few seafarers throughout history. Walihi (pronounced 'volley-high') roughly translates as 'The Island of Limitless Love and Endless Beauty to the Edge of Time.'

Despite its size, the island affords several lush green valleys and seven distinct beaches where long rollers, perfectly shaped, caress the wide shores of fine white sand. The surf is always up on my *moku*, my island.

The *hale nui* or Plantation House was built in the mid-nineteenth century by a reclusive whaling captain who had a startlingly contemporary eye for architecture. It was his passion to spend the cocktail hour facing West in a comfy chaise on a wide lanai. The few guests that I've brought to the island cannot witness a sunset without sobbing, for the beauty is so intense that it invokes a private and personal catharsis.

I don't mean to brag but there are two painting studios on the island, the smallest offering five thousand square feet of workspace and a motorized roof. Lack of storage is an ill wind of the past.

When I go 'figurative' there are plenty of models, ready and willing. Walihi is populated with dark eyed men and women, none of whom are virginal. This is just one of the many reasons why nightclub Mocambo at Bacchus Beach on the North Shore is always hoppin'.

Life on Walihi is idyllic, but the island is not a utopia. Even though the team of gardeners will snip the thorns from every rose and comb the thistles off a Koa tree, the Realities of Life are not ignored for they are accepted judiciously and rationally.

Red ants battle black ants and jellyfish invade the shores after every full moon. Orchids blossom and die. Cows are murdered, tarred with marinade, then sacrificed upon my barbecue grill. A bartender may screw up a cocktail proportion. *Haole* guests will get a sunburn and a coconut occasionally falls upon my head.

Artist's Pants

Prominently placed on a rise in the 'Valley of Higher Thought,' there is a small but tastefully designed temple dedicated to Aristotle. A long reflecting pool edged with lotus blossoms mirrors the bright light of 'The Eternal Flame of Reason and Objectivity.' On nights when dark clouds obscure the ever-present full moon, the Eternal Flame fills the valley and glows like a volcanic beacon.

Nicknamed Led Zep, *Haleakala* or 'Mount Stairway to Heaven' is the island's highest peak. The purple and black lava rock rises abruptly and dramatically to an elevation of 5,280 feet above sea level. The summit is narrow and affords a spectacular and unobstructed view.

When a Chinese junk crashed upon the 'Reef of Irresponsibility,' I salvaged the lazy susan from the galley and brought it to the plateau of Led Zep. The lazy susan was big enough to sit on and allowed me to spin slowly and view the world in 360 degrees.

There I have witnessed seven solar eclipses. I have seen the umbra, the shadow of the Moon, cross the Pacific and darken the blue waters like the hand of a God. I have seen the fire of Bailey's Beads, the flare of the Diamond Ring, and the horizon bleeding red in an endless sunset.

I rarely tell anyone about Walihi because such beauty is too hard to put into communicable words. I try with, "Life on the island is as easy as a fond memory. It is as soft as the Castillian leather in a SUV. It is as warm and constant as an electric blanket. It has the forceful power of a 9.3-liter engine, the refreshment of a sports drink and the sensuality of a stripper dancing on a velvet pole." Walihi was all these good things, but so much, much more.

Early on the morning of Tuesday, September Eleventh, I was collecting seashells in the 'Lagoon of Romantic Love' on the southwestern shore of the island. The water I was standing in was such a translucent blue green that no artist's palette could ever capture it. Ka'ne, my pet dolphin, was leaping and playing just a few yards away. The tradewinds cooled the early sun, crisp on my neck and shoulders.

Suddenly the seashell basket that was floating beside me drifted seaward so fast that I could not grab it. At first, I thought the tide was simply changing. Then I noticed an increasing pull upon my legs. The pull became a surge.

The water was draining from the lagoon with such force that I was knocked off my feet. The sea was leaving the shore. I staggered to stand upright. Ka'ne leapt high but his powerful tail could not propel him forward and he was swept away.

Any escape was useless. The outer reef, which just a minute before had been invisible and submerged, now stood exposed. Fish, suddenly stranded, flip-flopped their useless tails in puddles of wet sand.

The water from the lagoon had fed the growing surge offshore. It was not a wave but a wall of water moving incredibly fast and forcefully. The reef was consumed and the lagoon was filled instantly. It lifted me up, gently at first, and shoved me along at increasing speeds. Suddenly I was thrown over the beach, across the park, over roads and through the fields.

Palms were ripped from their shallow roots. The

Plantation House splintered into shards of glass, mahogany and sandalwood. Wild-eyed livestock thrashed to keep their heads above water. The wave carried us relentlessly forward. I could make no resistance nor offer help as friends flailed past me. The red striped walls of nightclub Mocambo zigzagged to abstract expression. Books were torn from their shelves and the shelves ripped from the walls in the 'Library of Progress and Modernity.' The bleachers in the volleyball stadium dissolved into splinters of broken bamboo. Onward the waters pushed over the island.

The great surge began to slow as the wave ran up the 'Valley of Higher Thought' and destroyed the temple. The 'Eternal Flame of Reason' was snuffed instantly.

Usually caused by the sudden displacement of land in an undersea quake, a tsunami (or *kai e`e*) is a rhythmic wave of kinetic energy. As it crosses the ocean at speeds over five hundred miles per hour, a tsunami often passes under a ship at sea unnoticed, for the wave averages a height of only three to five inches. When it meets an island, a tsunami does not collide but rather envelopes. Water is piled upon the land kinetically.

This is not the source of its great destruction; the advance of the water destroys little. The devastation is wrought when the waters are sucked back to sea with a hellish force and uncontrollable fury; its retreat carries everything and everyone away with it.

THE GOOD, THE BAD AND THE UGLY

With the quiet power and speed of a tsunami, our American way of life has changed. The waters have

39

just begun to recede and it is too early to determine the breadth of the destruction. All we can feel now is the shock and sting of the slap. Like the beauty that accompanies great sadness, there is opportunity in our tragedy.

These events have kicked open a fresh window into our sensibilities. We have been given a new chance to think deliberately. This situation is forcing us to determine value, to find what truly matters and what does not.

Life is not the same. Our channel has been changed. The Refresh Button has been hit. Some of what we see is good, some of it is bad and some of it is ugly.

THE HOLLOW

There is a sound that sometimes reverberates in my head. It haunts me often and fascinates me endlessly. The Hollow, as I call it, lives deep in my ear. It is as horrific as it is beguiling. I am seduced by it.

The sound is hard to describe. It is the cacophony of formed metal as it is forced into another shape. It is the howl of a car flipping over and over across a boulevard. It is the moan of a ship as it tears into an uncharted reef. It could even be the sound of an airplane as it enters a skyscraper.

The Hollow's screeching high treble is murdered by it's hellishly low, pounding, and unforgettable bass.

The Hollow is a trigger to survival. It produces a unique, instinctive reaction. When faced with danger, the human animal will assess a situation and react accordingly. We judge the threat against our defensive capabilities, list our options and scan for venues of escape before we make the decision to fight or flee.

The Hollow is a representative sound of a peril so fierce, so ungodly and incomprehensible that there is no retreat from it. Its force is so devastating and its path is so unpredictable that any fight is futile and all escape is impossible. Logic demands that we relent to its great and unknown power. To survive, one's muscles must go lax and follow the flow of the turbulence.

The Hollow demands that we lose our control and abandon our will, for that is the only survival option. Given the current threats to Civilization, all we can do is give a little blood, strengthen our vision and try to keep an even keel while the Hollow screams and howls in our ears.

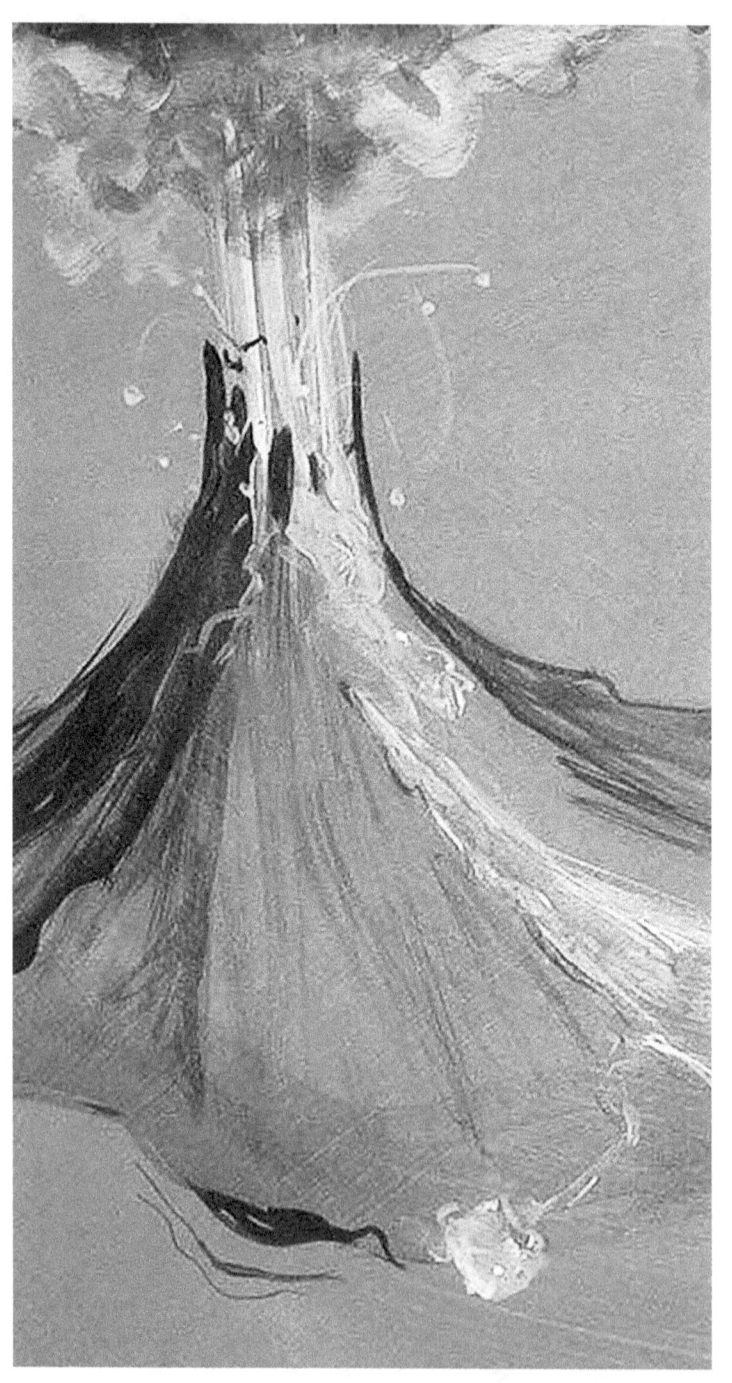

THE WARM, CHILLY
WINDS OF CHANGE

I am a man divided. My soul cries for salvation, yet my body seeks sin. I am straddling the double yellow line of change. One foot is firmly placed on the sizzling asphalt of hellfire while the other is set on the path of righteousness.

And the gap is widening. I'm afraid it might split the seam in my trousers.

Change is absolute. We, and the world around us, are always changing. I am older than I was five minutes ago. I get better looking every day. I know less than I did yesterday.

Change is good. Change is fresh, exciting and zesty. Yet the winds of change feel rather chilly, coming through the hole in my pants.

Many believe you can change your habits in twenty-one days. I believe this to be true for I have picked up many bad habits in far less time.

I want change. I need change. I want to change my artwork, my day job, my home life and my love life. I'd like to be more physically fit. I'd like more dough.

Hell, I'd like to change just about everything. Except for my truck. I love my truck.

A DINNER PARTY

Artists have many influences. When an artist comes to a crossroad and seeks guidance, those influences can get pretty loud arguing for attention.

Maybe I've seen too many detective films. Just like Nick and Nora Charles or a game of *Clue*, I decided to invite all of my Influences to a swank dinner party. Good food and loose booze would get them talking. In no time, we'd see who the most influential of the Influences was.

Recently, a group of my top twenty came over for drinks, dinner and my divinity. My metaphysicalist Lily Larraleaf sat next to the Duke Kahanamoku. Madine DuPreen, an art curator, was drinking heavily with author Jack Kerouac and painter Jackson Pollock. 50 Cent was hashing fashion tips with Cary Grant. Captain Jack Sparrow sauntered out of the bathroom in a cloud of smoke and Sir Richard Branson was chatting it up with Don Diego de la Vega in the living room.

It was an odd, wide-ranging mix.

Hoping for a denouement, I had turned my painting studio into a dining room. I installed Grandma's antique mahogany twelve footer and extended it with a few card tables. It was still a tight fit. Cocktail glasses competed with elbows. We didn't mind.

Trading artwork for services, I had L.A. art collector-caterer Tom Peters kick it out. The seven-course menu was inspired by the great chefs of the Renaissance. Or maybe it was the Bauhaus. It didn't matter; I wasn't eating. Not only did we have a bartender, but the cocktail waitress was a kitten with a whip.

In the background, a string quartet quietly played Arcade Fire covers. We even had an ice sculpture that towered over the seafood spread. It was a bacchanalia.

One guest was represented electronically. A flat-screen monitor topped with a web cam occupied a chair. Since I could not afford a plane ticket for my Viennese psychiatrist, he agreed to participate via video web link.

On the huge screen, Dr. Burstebagge was standing in a pastel colored room and was speaking rapidly and gesturing wildly to someone out of camera range. In the background, an accordionist in lederhosen was playing a zippy polka. My elderly, pear-shaped shrink wasn't wearing his usual plaid, tweed suit. He was bare-chested, which made me nervous. Onscreen, I couldn't see what he was wearing from the waist down, but I was afraid he might stand up.

Editor's Note: Long time readers will recall the misadventures of the esteemed Austrian psychiatrist Dr. Emile Von Burstebagge, a staunch Freudian with a penchant for Las Vegas. Due to an HMO insurance foul up, Grundy was able to fly the bestselling author of 'Id's It!' to Los Angeles on a weekly basis over a period of several years. With his thick and incomprehensible accent, the

Gordy Grundy

*advice of this great man was easily misinterpreted.
The resulting confusion led to the first of Grundy's
many adventures and arrests.*

I tapped a spoon on a wine glass to get the attention of the assembly.

"Ladies. Gentlemen. I'd like to thank you for coming. To get to the point, how in the hell do I affect a new course?"

There was silence, a moment's pause. Andy Warhol raised his finger for permission to the floor but everyone started speaking at once. Andy retreated, embarrassed.

When everyone started yelling over each other, the string quartet stopped playing in protest.

I ting-ting'd the wine glass once again.

All eyes met mine. Before I could say anything, all eyes turned to something far more compelling.

On the flat-screen, a young woman, nude, was serving Dr. Burstebagge a large martini. She then disappeared from view. The accordion was leaping merrily.

"I'll have what he's having," said Cary Grant, pointing to the screen.

Everyone laughed.

Oblivious to his Los Angeles audience, Dr. Von Burstebagge was clapping his hands and bobbing his head to the polka beat.

I leaned into the monitor and gently barked, *"Doc Von! We're on!"*

It startled the hell out of him. As Burstebagge snapped to the screen, his thick round glasses flew off his head. He yanked a bed sheet across his shoulders.

"Vat?! Vat?!" exclaimed the Doctor as he fished for his glasses.

The accordion music wheezed to a stop.

" I thought ve vere having ah party."

I tapped the wine glass once again and addressed the general assembly.

"Alright," I coughed. "Change? How do we find new horizons?"

50 Cent, my thug-life advisor, was the first to speak. "Phuck-dat. Why you wanna change, when change gonna bite you in da ass anyway?"

"*Is* change going to *'bite you'* in the fanny?"

The forceful yet lilting voice came from a silver translucent glow seated at the end of the table. Fortuna, purveyor of Luck, pointed her sword at 50 Cent. "Maybe change will *kiss* your butt."

Clark Gable started to say something but caught himself. He just grinned and scratched his jaw.

Fortuna continued, "Take the chance. Make a change. Either way you're lucky. Good or bad, it's all luck."

Gable leaned over to 50 Cent and quietly asked, "You play cards?"

"Change. It's kinda simple, really," said Kerouac, "The hitchhiker who doesn't put his thumb out isn't gonna get a ride. I know."

Keeping to himself, Bas Jan Ader was folding a sailboat out of a sheet of newspaper.

"You must *prepare* for the voyage!" said Lily Larraleaf enthusiastically, "You need to pack a bag."

47

Gordy Grundy

My Metaphysicalist folded her hands together and closed her eyes as she spoke. "Before you take a journey, you must pack your satchel. Change will come whether you are ready, or not."

She lowered her voice into a husky, bedroom octave. "Now remember, Gordy…"

Instantly my eyes closed and I started to feel drowsy.

"Deeper into the Blue. Remember the archetypes. The wise wizard who will beckon to your call. Remember the safety and security of the monkeys. Think of the golden key and the blue light bulb."

"Horseshit," said Clark Gable.

"No. No. I can dig it!" Gene Krupa, my bongo teacher, jammed a cigarillo between his lips and slapped the table with a fast riff. "It's all in the beat, baby. Listen to your natural rhythm! Find your downbeat. Find your strength. The melody follows." Then he turned to Gable and said archly, "Horseshit? It takes a jackass to know it."

Gable grinned at him and winked. Ed Ruscha laughed.

"It's part of the flow." Duke Kahanamoku, the ambassador of surfing, shook his water glass, making waves in the goblet. The Duke said, "Wait for the swell. You don't paddle until you got-ta wave. *Chill.* Whatever it is, whenever it is, waves happen."

"*Shit* happens," said 50 Cent.

A wine glass screamed above my head and exploded against the wall. Everyone turned to see Hunter S. Thompson, sweaty, pale-faced and wild-eyed. He was

48

wagging a boney finger at me, raging.

"CHANGE IS FOR THE WEAK *AND DE-PRAVED!*" Thompson screamed. His erect cigarette holder was clenched between bared teeth. He stomped his foot and stormed from the room.

A minute later, we heard glass break and the front door slam.

Gable smiled, "There goes the authority on depravity."

"We have no shortage of *that*," laughed Cary Grant.

Charles Bukowski got the attention of my houseboy, who was serving drinks and dessert. "Hey-Hey, bring me whatever Thompson had. Really."

I tapped the table. "Ladies. Gentlemen. Let's stay on point."

John Wayne punched the table with his forefinger, then at me, "Quit moanin' and belly-achin'. Change? *Change!* You ride at dawn."

"He's not ridin' nunny-where."

It was Madine DuPreen, my personal curator and art critic. She was drunk.

"Nuthin's gonna change until you go back to your earlier work and throw it all out. Ya gotta shtart— start over."

A loud hiccup seemed to perk her up for a second, but, like a champagne bubble, Madine popped. She fell face first into a plate of tiramisu.

Cary Grant neatly folded his napkin and said, "Well put."

Gordy Grundy

I addressed the crowd. "If *Greatness* is thrust upon you, then therefore must not *Change* also require an external motivation?"

"Abso*lutely*, dear boy," said Thurston Howell III. "Self-induced heroics smell like an unused country club membership."

"Adventure is a reaction to the physical world," intoned Lord Bagby.

My parole officer, Ernest B. Dick, snorted, "Yeah. Nothin' like a steel toe'd kick in the ass."

Captain Jack Sparrow arched a wide suspicious eye at the officer. Hiding his face with his cap, he stood and casually sauntered through the exit.

Madine DuPreen was snoring loudly in her plate of tiramisu. Gene Krupa leaned in with a spoon and dug a little trench around Madine's mouth so the curator wouldn't suffocate. Gene patted her back and whispered, "I *never* liked his earlier work either."

A *harrumph* trumpeted from the flat-screen. The polka band played a fanfare. Dr. Emile Von Burstebagge, the great man, was standing bare chested with a towel around his waist. As he was starting to speak of something greatly serious, "I zink zee true treasure...," the topless bar maid snuck up behind him. She was carrying a tray with drinks and a shaker. Giggling, she took the icy cocktail shaker and pressed it against his bare back.

Gesturing wildly, Doc Von howled with fright and shock. The towel around his waist fell. As the doctor scrambled to cover himself, the European half of the broadcast devolved into pandemonium to a polka beat.

Madine DuPreen sat up with her eyes still closed and her face half-frosted with tiramisu. "Hold it down in there!" she shouted, "I'm trying t'get some *shleep*!"

I couldn't take any more advice. Life comes as it comes, when it comes.

I signaled for the attention of my hypnotist Lily Larraleaf. Silently I mouthed, "Get-me-outta-here."

She walked over and leaned into my ear. Lowering her voice an octave, she spoke deliberately. "Gordy. Take a deep, full breath… And another… You are at the top of a staircase. Take a step down. Twelve. Down another, eleven. Ten..."

My eyelids got heavy, very heavy.

The caterwaul in the room faded until I could hear it no longer.

"Nine…Down the stairs…Eight…"

By the time she said, "Seven," I was out.

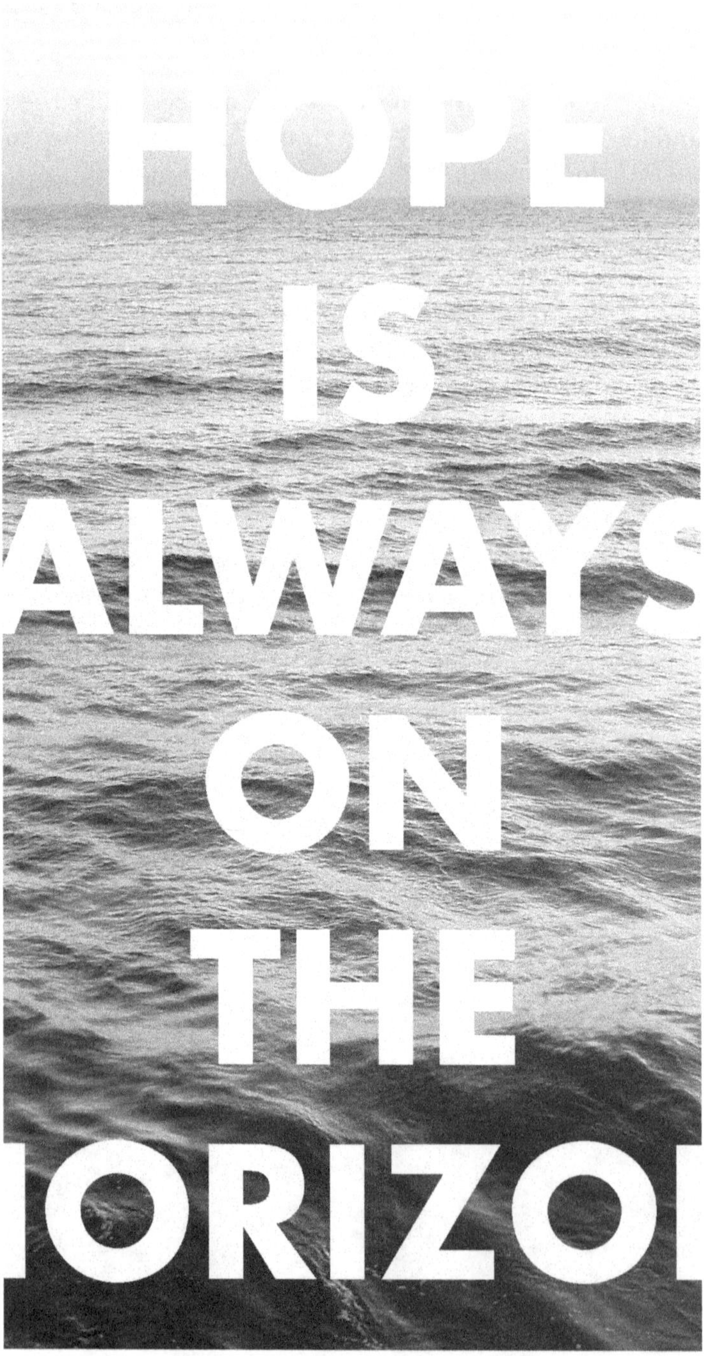

HOPE
IS
ALWAYS
ON
THE
ORIZO

SOUTH OF SURREAL, PART ONE

ADVICE MY FATHER NEVER TOLD ME

"Always drink liquor that they can smell on your breath. That way they won't think you're stupid."

EARLY WARNING SIGN

When the supermarket cashier rings up your purchases and cheerfully remarks, "I hope you have a nice party!"

Confused and embarrassed, you mumble, "Thanks," rather than correct her. There is no party. You're just buying staples.

Gordy Grundy

QUE COLOR?

If it is a thin *blue* line between order and anarchy and a thin *red* line between sanity and madness, what is the color of the line between art and commerce?

FOUND

Outside Art LA in Santa Monica, a xeroxed flier was pasted to select lamp posts and electrical boxes. It read "Mormon Artist" and listed a phone number.

THE BOOK, STUPID, NOT THE MOVIE

A swank cocktail party has once again ignited the friendly fire between literature and film. It seems that novelist Ian Fleming had concocted a martini for his hero James Bond that is very different from the drink recipe of the movies. Fleming didn't care if it was shaken or stirred.

I remember a swank drink-fest hosted by curator Kim Light in her suite at the Chateau Marmont. She served the authentic "James Bond" martini. It packed a greater punch than Odd Job's hat trick.

Despite a hefty room rate, the Chateau Marmont does not allow parties in their suites. Our hostess had to create an elaborate ruse to get provisions and guests past the evil eye of management. Liquor, glasses, ice and caviar were packed in boxes and gift-wrapped to look like birthday presents. Our hostess also managed to smuggle in a bar, bartender and customized drink menu.

Everyone was given a different M.O. The studio executive and the CEO were given a false name and room number should they be detained and questioned. The sunglass designer, the Butoh master and the urban novelist were given another. The jewelry designer said she was making a diamond delivery. The cinematographer said he was a gallery assistant and carted a fresh Kim Dingle just to look official. Fearing that I may crack under the pressure of a fierce interrogation, my little petunia and I played it safe and took the Service Elevator.

Only after a coupla "James Bonds" was I able to see straight enough to read the fine type on the cocktail menu. It explained why people were dancing on the table tops. These babies packed gin *and* vodka. Smart drinkers know never to mix your liquors, yet these "James Bonds" have proven to speed a party from 33 to 78 RPMs in a hurry.

The JAMES BOND
(Literature, not Cinema)
3 parts Bombay Sapphire Gin (*)
1 part Blue Ice Vodka (*)
Half part blonde vermouth
Half part dry vermouth
Drown a lemon peel
　　　(*) This author's recommendation

ETIQUETTE

It's an easy sin to commit, yet the consequences can be damaging and severe. What do you do when your invitation reads "and guest" but you're hanging with six?

Gordy Grundy

When attending any hosted function, introduce your guests to the ringleader when you arrive. It is the only way you can bring your uninvited friends to a party and get away with it.

Whether it is your dealer, your boss or a good friend, this little courtesy, like all courtesies, goes a *long* way.

BALANCE AND PERSPECTIVE

Jackson Pollack did his best work when he was sober.

POETRY

"There's a tear in my beer;
'Cause I'm crying for you, dear;
You are on my lonely mind;
Into these last nine beers;
I have shed a million tears;
You are on my lonely mind;
I'm gonna keep drinkin' until I'm petrified;
And then maybe these tears will leave my eyes..."

(From "There's A Tear In My Beer" by Hank Williams Sr., courtesy of Rightsong Music, Inc.)

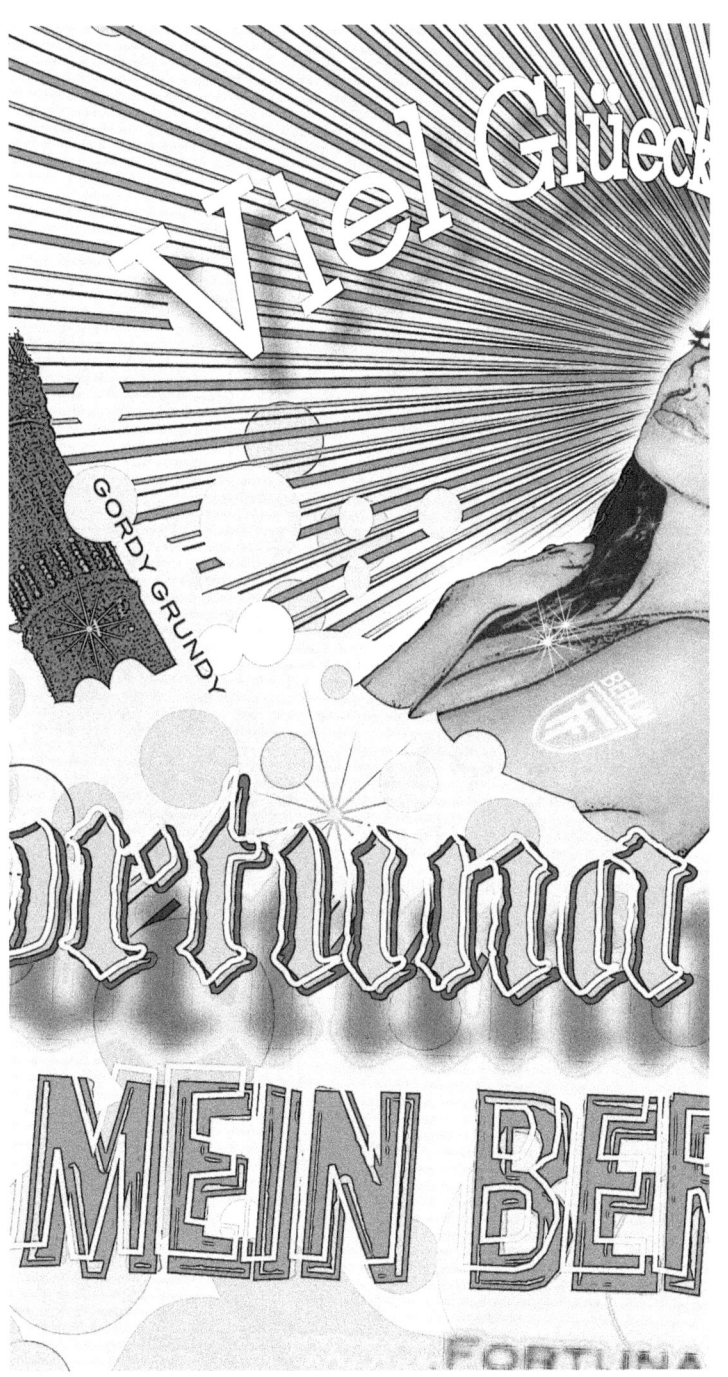

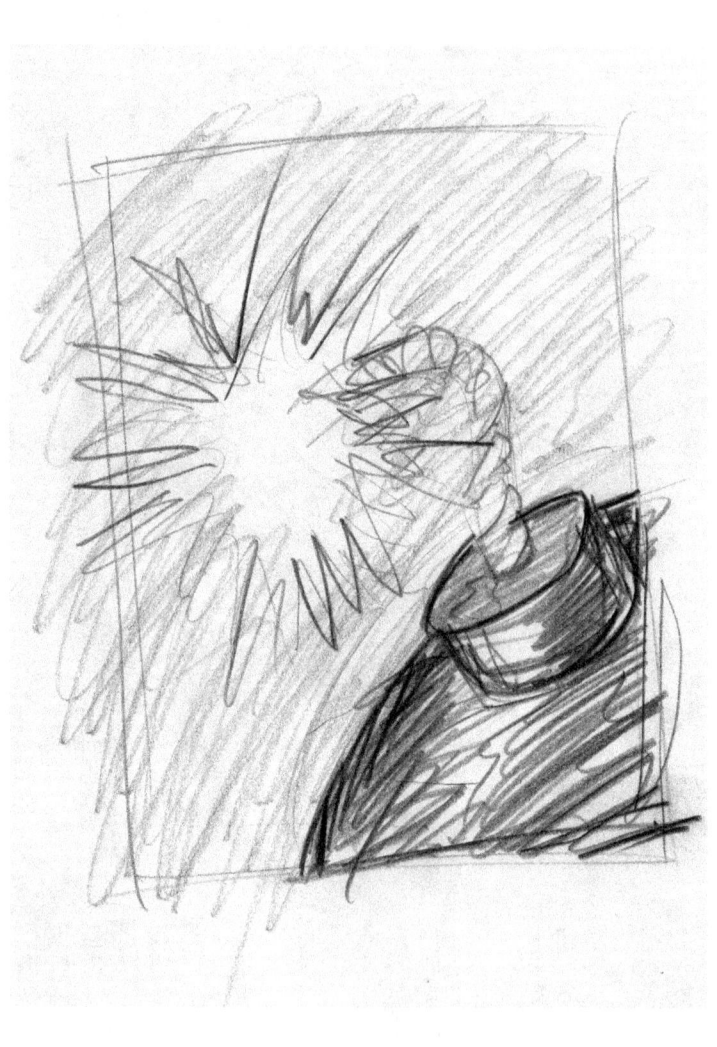

THE NEW BIG ONE

As an artist, I choose my influences careful-ly. I didn't choose Bin Laden. He has ingratiated himself into all aspects of my being. This insufferable little man sits at every dinner table. His rump covers the barstool next to mine. If my life were a freeway, he'd be driving 35 in the fast lane while honking the horn with one hand and flipping me off with the other.

I resent it greatly.

I'd like a piece of him. He has turned my well-ordered life of gentle apathy into seething and inhuman frustration. I am swinging mad that I must accommodate his myopia and bear the effects of his sophomoric ideology.

On the other hand, I am incredibly sad and hopeless in my inability to escape his influence. Believe me, I've tried.

I am still sideswiped by the events of 9-11. Bin Laden has turned me into a cave dweller; I have no desire to leave the house. I hate to get out of bed. The warmth and weight of extra blankets ensure extra comfort.

I have even put a wind-up alarm clock under my pillow because the gentle ticking sounds like a comforting, maternal heartbeat. If it works for a puppy, it works for me.

For months, the house has been heated to womb temperatures. I am afraid to see the gas bill; the mailman says it qualifies as a parcel.

I've fallen into a hooka and I can't crawl out.

I don't call anyone nor do I invite anyone over.

Black tints all the colors in my palette.

I constantly watch videos. I flood my brain with idiotic Hollywood plotlines just to obliterate Bin Laden's idiotic story arc. I might even get cable. I am so eager to end the War on Terrorism that I log onto CNN twice a day to check our progress.

In every artist's life, there are influences that we cultivate, encourage and pursue assiduously. Others we deflect and avoid. And there are ones, such as a stroke, blindness or insignificance, which we cannot avoid. Bin Laden is camped in the latter. He is harder to shake than a boor at a cocktail party.

NOW, EVERYONE IS AN ARTIST

"Meaningless" is an adjective now commonly paired with the noun "job." Americans lament their uselessness. Since the start of The New Big One, the American wage earner has been mortified to learn that their job has no meaning or relevance. Most of us are not 'on the front lines' like a postal worker or a fireman may be. Our jobs as artists, accountants, mechanics or sandwich makers do not allow us any hand-to-hand combat with the enemy. We are not a part of any action. The fruits of our labor vanish into a vacuum. What good is making money if we're too dead to spend it? We are impotent. We are like prizefighters wearing lead shoes.

I laugh maniacally. Welcome to the Art World.

WHAT *YOU* CAN DO

The New Big One does not demand that we plant a Victory Garden. Not yet, anyway. We don't have to skim the bacon grease for ammo and I can still buy foil at the supermarket.

The New Big One is tricky; everything has changed not at all. I for one have been frustrated by my inability to participate in the war effort. This little Bin Laden fella has got my dander up. I want to smell blood but there is nothing I can swing at.

And then one day, it dawned on me. I really was doing a great deal for the war effort and my pride swelled with patriotism. It's just a matter of perspective. My list is long: I have been rowing very hard to keep the liquor industry afloat. I have been using a lot of matches, which helps the lumber industry. There is a manufacturer of a chocolate bundt cake that receives my enthusiastic support. The stock market value of See's Candies has risen with my influence. The small business owners of local bars and restaurants have felt my patronage. I have been tipping large (hoping that my largess will be reciprocated on the karmic scale.) The local video store can afford to build another wing from my recently obsessive contributions.

I have been helping the environment as well by sleeping more and breathing less. When the time comes, I will buy an Afghan rug to help their ailing Middle East economy. This little Bin Laden fella may have me twisted in a head-lock but I am doing all I can to wrest him away. You can too.

EVERYTHING HAS CHANGED NOT AT ALL

This New Big One has got me really irked, steamed and smokin' red. They say that everything has changed and I gladly took that as a promise. Nothing will be the same as it was ever again. Bullshit! Liars, all. Nothing has changed. The New Year is turning and the media is boring us with the same flood of 'Best Of' lists, an editorial tradition I hoped would be suspended. The Academy Awards and the Grammy's haven't been eliminated. The New York Times still doesn't have a comics page. And the art world still has issues. Fuck Bin Laden.

SUMERIANS AND THE DEPTH OF MY DEPRESSION

I learned a nasty piece of business from a friend. Damn him for enlightening me. Education can be a very bad thing. His insight has sent me spiraling deep into the blackness of depression. I was so horrified by his news that I immediately headed homeward, cranked up the thermostat and camped under the covers.

He told me of the Sumerians, a highly evolved race who had created a superior society. They believed in the modern notion of equality between the sexes. An advanced judicial system that upheld individual and property rights, governed the land. They invented writing and the wheel. The Sumerians are alleged to have visited this planet two thousand years before Christ.

Two thousand! In all that time, in over four thousand years, we the human animal have not evolved one bit. Damn you Bin Laden, for you have reminded us of this horrifying fact. You are evidence that Adam, Eve and the dinosaurs were the pinnacle of our humanity and its all been a backslide since then. We are reminded that the conspiracy of dunces is real and they are winning. Damn you, Bin Laden.

JUST WHEN THINGS WERE GOING SO WELL...

This little Bin Laden fella isn't going to literally pinch many of us. We all know it's easier to slip in the bathtub than get whacked by a terrorist. But he will get his licks in economically. The American artist is going to suffer in the wallet. We will get our clocks cleaned when we find there is less time to make art because we need to make rent. Yah, Bin Laden is a bad influence. We will need to change our course to compensate for his ill wind. There is a need to call for action. The bugle plays a reveille. We need to mount up soon, real soon, but the bed is so damn warm and cozy. Our spirits are out of whack and our sensibilities are stretched thin.

The paint brush feels heavy in my hand.

THIRD: $2,500.00
BEST ART CAR: $2,500.00
SHOW CAR: $2,500.00

DEMOLITION
DERBY

ELDORADO SPEEDWAY
THE SUPERSPEEDWAY OF THE WEST
RACING EVERY SATURDAY NIGHT -- RAIN OR SHINE!
CAPRICE COUNTY, CA

NTRY FEE: $100 PER CAR
A HEATS: $100 PER CAR
$250 (INCL. COCKTAILS)
EVENT ADMISSION: $10
: DEMO_DERBY@FORTUNANOW.COM

THE PIT GATE WILL
FIRST HEAT 6PM
ART CAR SHOW 5P
CAR SHOW & CON

S HEAVYWEIGHTS'
O PARK PUNK BAND
MAIN STAGE 9PM

DJ VALIHI
H THE MOCAMBO MIX
TENT FIVE, 11PM

CHEF TARA TH
CHILI DOGS, SLA

GARLIC GRITS
FROM TULSA KIN

BEER GARDEN
BY EL BARCO

IG PANTS MUST BE WORN IN PITS. NO OPE
NO ONE UNDER 16 YEARS OLD ALLOWED IN PITS.
WWW.FORTUNANOW.COM

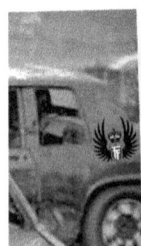
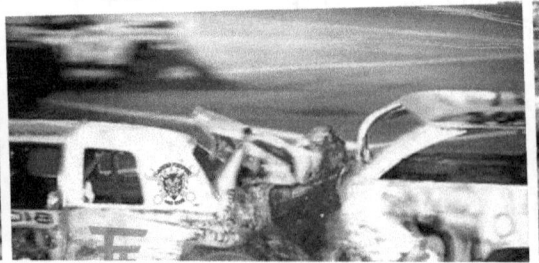

THE THIN PURPLE LINE

I am in the throes of quitting smoking and it's been rather nasty for this chimney-like abuser. Upon the advice of a Deity, I am about to fulfill my destiny. When your Id gets that kind of kicker, it's probably best to leave the bad habits behind and travel light. Unfortunately, unpacking this habit is Hell.

Not so long ago, I had a vision. Fortunately, this time I was not driving the car but was sleeping rather soundly in my own bed when a blinding light awakened me. I sat up, startled. The clock read 1:11AM. A dazzling golden glow, spinning like God's own disco ball, hovered above the foot of my bed.

From it, a female voice said, "Fernando Suzuki?"

I yanked the covers to my chin, not out of fear, but modesty. I sleep in the nude and I didn't want to get

Gordy Grundy

slapped. Plus I had just woken up and, you know, the wood was a bough.

"Fernando Suzuki?" repeated the voice like a thunderclap.

"M-my—my name is Gordy Grundy," I replied.

"Sorry," said the now-velvet voice, "Suzuki is my 4:20 appointment."

Suddenly, the light before me exploded like a thousand roman candles. A sound, a crash, both frightening *and* comforting, was so loud that I knew the neighbors would be calling the cops again.

From this radiating light, a woman began to appear. At first I thought it was the Statue of Liberty. She was robed, sandaled and her gaze was steadfast. Instead of a torch, she held a down-turned sword that was emblazoned with the word 'Fortuna' on the hilt. It was then that I realized she looked just like Angelina Jolie.

"You're Grundy then?"

"Yes," I replied, "Yes!"

I didn't mean to sound eager but it was obvious that my time was up. I was grateful to go in my sleep, without pain. I've lived a good life, however short. I've seen Beauty go in and out of fashion and back again. I remember art before it had issues. I'm sick of hearing about the Middle East, global warming and the box office dearth in Hollywood. My regrets are few: not enough sex. Not enough dough. I've never been to Tahiti...

I raised my arm and extended my hand.

With the speed of the ethereal, Angelina slapped me upside the head with her sword. The blow made a

66

loud, hollow *thwack*, but it didn't hurt.

"I'm not here for that," she said tiredly. "Besides, *you're* not gonna die painlessly in your sleep."

"What?! Then how am I gonna...?" I started to sound hysterical.

"I shouldn't say," she snickered, "But it's a good one."

I yelped again like a scared puppy.

Angelina shook her head and wiped an eye as if she were recovering from a laughing jag.

"Oh! It's nothing you can't handle," she said reassuringly. "You're an artist. You already know all about destitution, ridicule and insignificance. *Relax*."

Her glow seemed to burn a little bit brighter as if she were getting down to business.

"I'm here with a message," she said. "You've been chosen as a Messenger. You must bring peace to the world."

My pause was long. I couldn't help but sound sarcastic. "World peace?"

"Yes. World peace."

"How the hell am I gonna do *that*?!" I cried.

She whacked me again with her sword. "Stop swearing so much. Your art. Use your art to prove that religion is fashion... we figure, if humanity realized that religious affiliation is no more important than the label in your collar, then all of you might stop killing each other. It's a last ditch effort. We've tried everything else."

"Last ditch—*What?!*" I cried.

"Mankind hasn't done anything interested since you nailed Christ. Just—Just use your art."

"*Art?!*—Lady, my art dealer's in jail."

"I know," she said apologetically, "That's why I wanted someone else. Unfortunately, I don't manifest destiny; I just swing it."

The room was silent except for the quiet "But... But... But..." which was coming from my mouth like an Evinrude outboard motor.

She glanced at her wristwatch that looked like a sundial on a strap. "Hey, I've got a 3:15 in Philadelphia. You'll have to figure it out. You're a smart ass. And you're lucky. And now, you're the *Messenger*!"

By then, my morning erection had all but vanished. And so was she. Her sharp features began to blur and the light began to intensify in the room.

I called after her, "Messenger?! Why can't I be a spokesman?" I was whining, "*You know what they do to the Messenger...!*"

But it was too late. She was gone. The last thing I saw were those fleshy lips fade into the light.

And the room fell dark once again.

I couldn't sleep after that. It wasn't the cover girl vision or the alarming message that kept me awake. It was the cops, pounding on the door, trying to break up another party.

The next day felt like a bad hangover. It wasn't the usual "Another round! Another round!" thundering in my head like two trashcan lids banging together. It was "World Peace! World Peace!"

Damn. I wish she said "Lottery Winner! Lottery Winner!"

Now, I must follow this vision for Luck. I must fulfill my destiny to bring peace to the world.

Naturally, I canceled my weekend plans.

If it is a journey that I must begin, then let the first step be sound. I listed all of my bad habits and crossed the first one off the list. No more smoking. For a while.

ROUTINE

Detox is a condition of which I am completely unfamiliar and highly unprepared. I need to marshal all of my resources. Thank God I'm still drinking.

This morning, Day Three, I took to the Internet to learn more about my harsh new reality and the changes that are torturing my body.

Phlegm? Plentiful.

Insomnia? It's killing me.

Clammy hands? Don't shake mine.

Night sweats? I'm swimming.

Two showers a day? I can't get clean.

Lack of concentration? What...?

Sudden anger? *Fuck you!*

Emotional jags? Y-y-yess-ss.

And the website promises that several nights from now, I can look forward to a flood of vivid nightmares...

This detox is gonna kill me. Better that, than the Lady with the sword.

All I can say is that this *better* be a Vision. Because I'll be *really* pissed if I find out this was merely another hallucination.

Or is that the razor sharp edge of the Thin Purple Line?

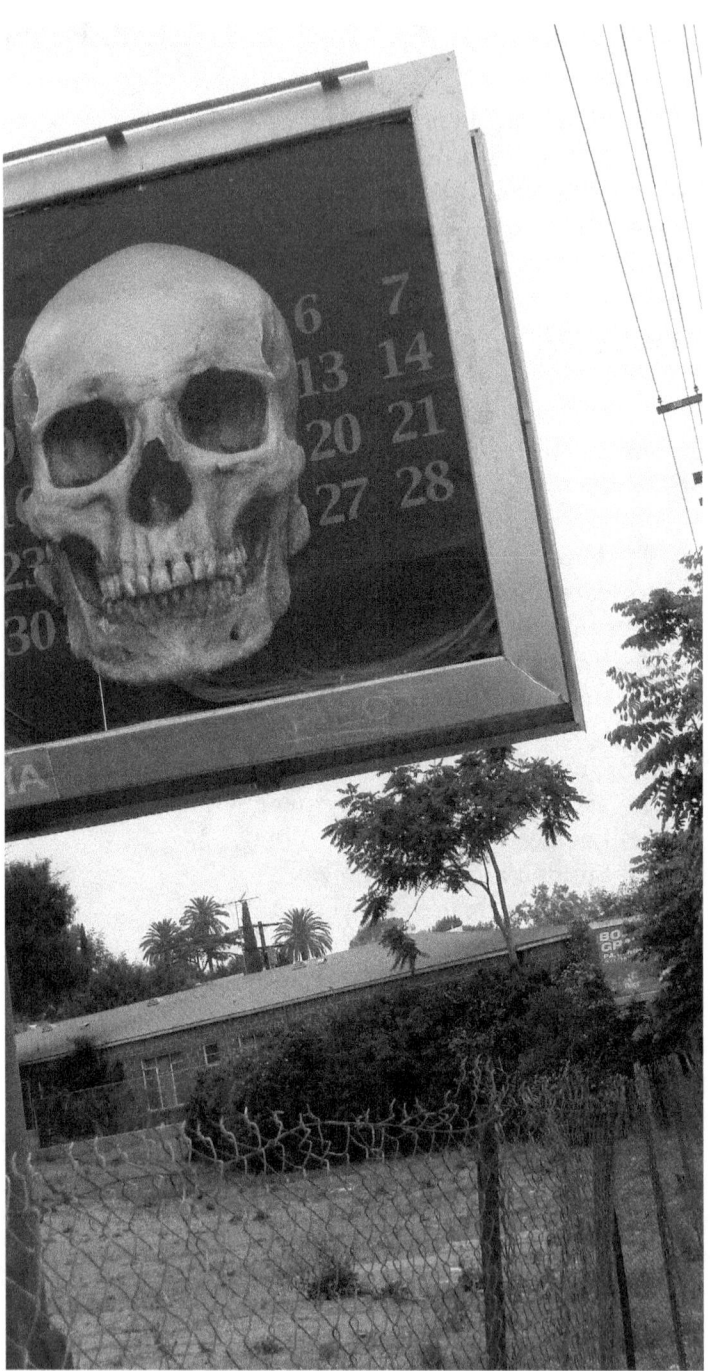

I WAKE UP SCREAMING

"C'mon, get him!" The voice roared like it had a coupla tear drops tattooed at his eye, ham hocks for forearms and an intense dislike for me. The command was answered by a flurry of footfalls in all directions. Here we go again.

I was standing in the middle of a long alley. With mayhem about to round the corner, I wouldn't be able to make it to the end of the street in time. So instead I ducked into the alcove of a doorway. The door was locked.

Two sets of heavy steel-toes on wet asphalt were running my way. I leaned back into the deep shadow for cover.

As they slowed down, my heart raced faster and the headache pounded louder. It was obvious that my hiding spot, the only break in a long brick wall, would be a point of interest. So much for a fade.

They were creeping up. Two of them. The crowbar felt as light as a feather in my hand. I wish it had more weight. I'd be lucky to clock one, stun the other and make a dash. If I got lucky. No one ever does in these situations.

They were on me; I could hear them breathe. At least I held the element of surprise. I raised my crowbar. A head breached the corner. I brought the bar down— on his shoulder. He screamed. I screamed...

I wake up screaming.

While the dreams differ in context, location and intensity, they all end the same. I wake up screaming. My throat is dry, my forehead is on fire and the sheets are cold and wet.

I asked for it, for the dreams to invade. The palette is very heavy right now. My superhighway to the universe had gotten bogged down in traffic. I was no longer 'at one with.' I wanted liberation. I needed connection.

My bartender is good at short-term solutions. This impasse required bigger ammunition. To cope, I turned to Lilly Larraleaf, my Metaphysicalist. I spoke of my desires, grand designs, fears, heartbreak and backache. Life feels as if I'm towing the QE2 with a rowboat and a broken oar.

Sweet Lilly Larraleaf suggested turning 'down time' into 'now time.' The harmony of the universe and the consciousness of a dream state could work *for* me rather than *haunt* me. She said I could solve most of my problems while I slept. I liked the idea. Horizontal beats the hell out of vertical; I'd rather lie down than run around.

Using her powers of suggestion as a fast track to the universe, Lilly mantra'd these words into my soul, "...and in your early morning dreams, you will vent the

72

questions and frustrations of the day. Every problem will find its solution in your early morning dreams..."

...It was a lovely day at the beach. We were lulled by the warmth of the sun, the lazy cry of the gulls and the sparkling diamonds on the sea.

Suddenly the idyll ended with cries of alarm that rippled across the long peninsula of sand. I opened my eyes to find beachgoers standing up and pointing seaward.

The horizon was rising. That far line, fuzzy to see, was lifting higher, rather quickly. A big wave was building and moving toward the coast.

Panic convulsed everyone on the shore. Folks were grabbing gear and running over the dunes to the berm of the highway and the safety of their cars. Instinctively, I grabbed my duffel but it slipped from my hand. There was no point.

The shoreline began to recede very quickly, exposing rock and shell never seen. Fish flopped. The roaring surge moved out, massing into a wave that grew ever more rapidly in height and speed. The force of the oncoming wave was shoving the air, creating a wind of increasing velocity.

I looked back. Those running for higher ground stood no chance.

The wave came. I could do nothing but watch. It was magnificent and beautiful, glorious as it rose to block out the sun. Its wind punched me off my feet and the world was under water...

I wake up screaming.

...There are three variations of the artwork, each with a slight difference. The disparity between dull and genius is a hair's breadth. Slight is the key to sublime. I am devoted, a frantic disciple.

Design C looks good, but a new background develops into D. If I recolor every third horizontal bar in B, I get a new E. There is something about A which is still buggin' me. My fingers fly over the keyboard. The pressure for perfection has shoved my heart up into my throat, making it hard to breathe. I regret the changes to K and I delete L. Q is interesting but no improvement over B or C. F, H and J are tossed in the trash. Wait. I retrieve J. As always, the original, A, looks best; I'm likin' it. Yes. No. Hurry. If I can take the bottom half of Q, recolor it like E, then...

I wake up screaming.

...The jungle growth is dense and I'm running as fast as I can. I need both hands out in front of me, to clear a path, to leap a log and to catch a stumble. I need a third hand to keep from choking. Cho-Cho, a chimp, has his arms tight around my neck and I can't breathe. I know he's scared. I hear him whimpering. I can't run as fast as I need to with a cute lil' monkey on my back. Not so far behind us, the panther sounds like it's gaining ground...

I wake up screaming.

...It was the easiest studio visit I have ever had. Collectors Bambi and Stanley Throckmorton were standing before a large painting, "No. 43" from my Space'd Series.

"I can part with it for ten thousand dollars," I said. And after a pregnant pause, I added quietly, "That's *after* the thirty percent collector's cut and the gallery commission."

As I turned away, I could see Bambi elbow Stan in the ribs. He coughed. She batted her eyes. Not that she needed to; Bambi was fifty years younger and a lot more fleshy than her spouse. I knew I had the sale.

Through his oxygen mask, Stanley wheezed, "You've got a deal." I was as pleased as spiked punch. I clapped my hands and replied, "Can I offer you folks a glass of wine?"

As I turned there was a loud *rrr-ripping* sound that ceased all conversation and bonhomie. My enthusiasm and my elbow had pierced the canvas of No. 43…

I wake up screaming.

…Your deadline is in twenty-four hours. We need a thousand words with an illo. Write superlative words.

I wake up screaming.

…I know the city well. For the last two hours I've been cutting in and out of buildings, climbing fire escapes and zigzagging alleys with those fukkers on my tail. I think I've lost them—I know I have. But now I'm lost.

Nothing looks familiar. I don't recognize anything. It doesn't even feel like my city, my home. How could I have gone so far astray?

A right. A left. A block. A plaza. Left again. Nothing. Even the air smells different. The people look different. I am so lost. Panic lost.

And so tired. I've been at this—how long? I've got to keep going. I want to get home. I need peace, to rest, to sleep. I am so tired. My legs are killing me and I'm starting to stumble and misstep. My eyes are burning; the lids sting red. I just want to rest. To find comfort.

Gordy Grundy

I've never been so alone. Alone boring to the core. Never so lost. I keep going. Rounding another corner, hoping to find something familiar, some sort of hope. I keep going, but I start to fear how long I can keep moving. The feeling is desperate; I've never felt this desperate; desperate as an absolute.

I turn another corner, into a square. The light is a little brighter and I can hear seagulls somewhere far off. I don't recognize anything but it feels a little more familiar, a little more at ease, closer to home. I dunno why. I'm still lost, but I welcome the relief.

I follow a short, yet inviting street that leads me to a wide cobblestone promenade lined with art nouveau street lamps. Gulls flock and dive for fish. It's a harbor, a seaport, partly industrial, mostly recreational. A few palm trees remind me of Spain or Italy but the steep surrounding mountains make me think of Seattle. But it's older, much older and foreign.

A bray of horns and celebratory huzzahs erupt like an echo and I turn my attention across the harbor. Colored lanterns illuminate a party and a band plays on. A large yacht, a motor sailer, held high on a dry dock, slowly slides into the water. Cheers and bravos cascade once again. It's such a beautiful ship. With clean lines and a straight bow. I don't think I've seen anything more elegant.

And then I wake up. This time without screaming.

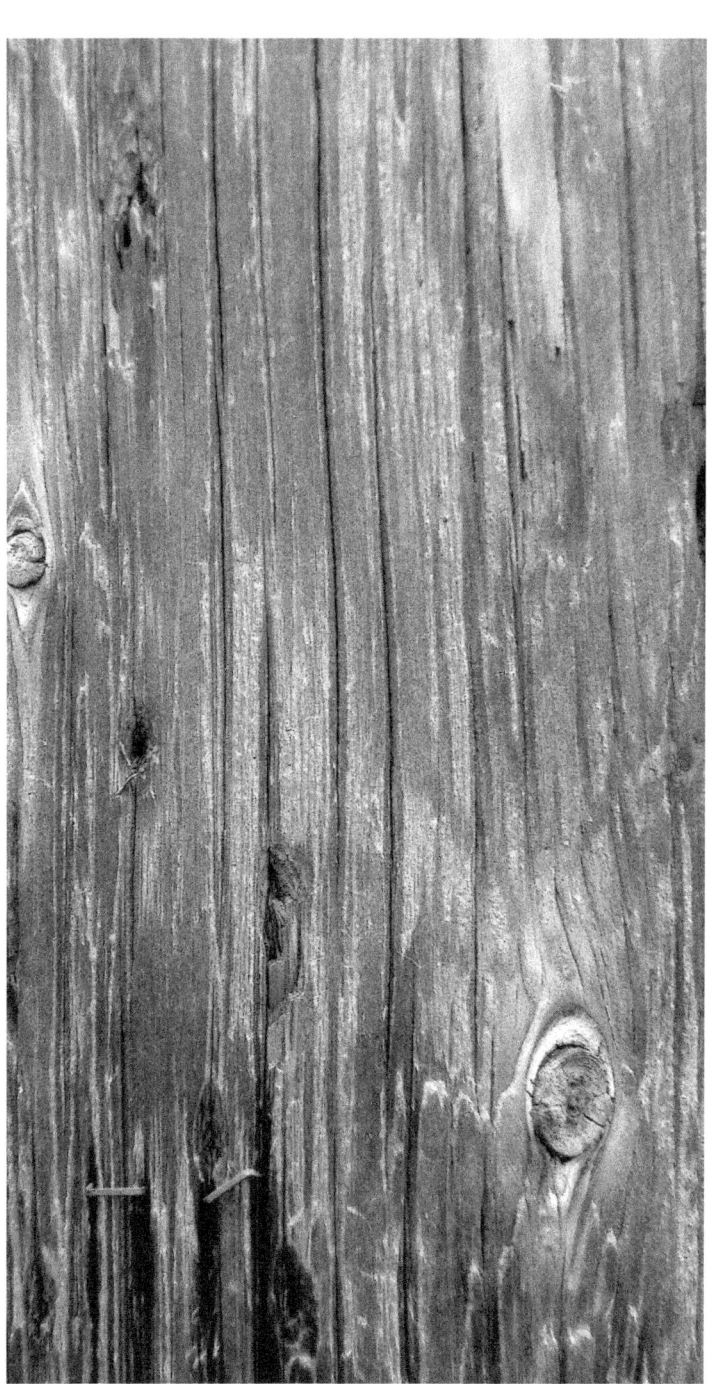

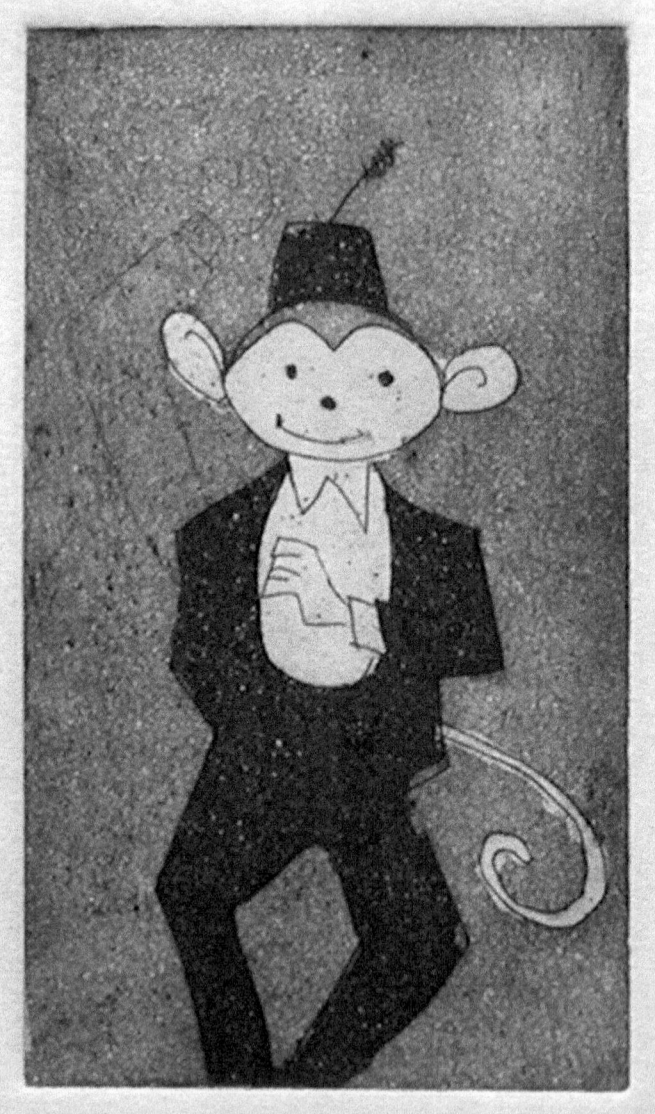

THE FIRST ANNIVERSARY ISSUE

Recently, a swank society magazine sought the benefit of my wisdom for their terrorist anniversary issue. They wanted to know "How has September 11 affected your life?"

Had I made the deadline, my response would have read: "Extremely. That little bin Laden fella has pinched me economically. He has whacked me in the shins of my security. He has slapped me upside the head philosophically and kicked me in the arse of my complacency. September Eleventh truly marks the beginning of the new Millennium."

A CURRENT REPORT

This fall 2002, the once lavish and always highly anticipated opening of the Los Angeles art season came and went without notice. Where the city was once alive and electric over the launch of a new season and the debut of bright fresh talent, this year nary a peep was heard. Galleries, normally shoulder to shoulder, were as empty as a Kabul bunker. "Cable," explained one art dealer, "The new fall lineup at HBO and the terrorist's on CNN really knocked us for a loop." Another lamented, "Art was king for awhile." Indeed, for a brief, shining moment, the fine arts stood tall. Today, market forces have shifted and priorities have changed. Our short march toward Beauty has now been officially and sadly abandoned. All we can do is look back and smile at those sweet and kinder days when art was like a religion.

THE HARBINGERS

I would like to share with you a scene from my new play, "The Harbingers". This hard-hitting, gritty three act features the free-swinging, free-lovin' lives of six young artists in urban Los Angeles as they make art, make love and make life.

[Mature audiences only. For gratuitous nudity, drugs, foul language and lurid sexual content. As a matter of fact, to help boost the box office revenues, there will be live fucking on stage in the third act.]

In this scene (Act II, Scene 7), sexy SALLAY, 36, is a color field artist who makes a living as an Admissions Recruiter for LACART, the prestigious and pricey private art university. Her conservative wool suit belies Sallay's true nature. Her lime green hair and heavily pierced features define her best.

On the phone, in her office cubicle, Sallay is desperately trying to sway Mrs. Sweeney, a potential buyer of her product, with a son who is just about to graduate from high school.

SALLAY
(into the phone)
"...Well, yes. I admit we haven't had any alumni in the Biennial in several, in a---
(pause, as she listens)
Sure, UCLA is great---if you are that type of person. But this year, our grad team looks solid! We're thrilled. Out of our grads, we have two, sure-hit, Blue Chip Damien Hirst-types and a strong public arts sculptor to cover the backfield.
(pause, as she listens)
Frankly, I wouldn't want my child to be associating with the CalArts kids. I do not condone drugs.
(She mugs a laugh.)
Regardless, Mrs. Sweeney, we feel your son Tim has a natural ability, a *raw* talent to become a great, great artist.
(long pause, as she listens)
Oh, yes! Warhol big! The huge Manhattan loft, Spain-in-the-summer, Taschen-type…
(pause, as she listens)
Right, our curators think he's got what it takes. And, after just six years with us, he will be re…
(pause)
What do you mean law school is cheaper? We can finance any student for a full ride,

81

no matter how---

(pause, as she listens)

What do you mean he wants to be a Navy Seal?! He told me he just wants to be famous.

(pause; patiently)

Well, we also need warriors on the frontlines of art.

(pause, as she listens)

Well, then your son can start his own jihad. An Art Jihad! My God! That's an idea that would make the cover of Art-Forum!

(pause, as she listens)

Mrs. Sweeny, heroism is a wonderful thing but it's been done with 9/11. We're over it.

(pause)

Yes, but you get paid for heroism. Beauty is free. It demands a greater value, a higher...

(pause)

I understand heroism has a better pension plan. Mrs. Sweeney, beauty is hope. It speaks of a better...

(pause)

Relevant? Why, art is all-important. Sometimes it's just hard to tell.

(pause)

Mrs. Sweeney? Hello? Mrs. Sweeney?

She cradles the phone and massages her temples.

SALLAY
(to herself)
"Fuck. There went rent."

THE SKI ACCIDENT OF OUR LIVES

Not so long ago I was sailing down the freeway with the window open and the wind blowing. The All News AM radio had become white noise, lost in the background. But I could hear it enough to note that the tone in the news announcer's voice had become suddenly urgent.

I rolled up the window so fast I whacked my elbow.

"What is it?" I thought, "The Next Big One?!" My heart was racing. I flipped up the volume.

His voice was strained. He spoke at a fast staccato. I knew it must be bad; I felt a little queasy.

"...Director of Homeland Security has lowered the High Alert Level from Orange to Yellow, I repeat, has downgraded the High Alert Level to..."

COMPARATIVE RELIGION 101

What do Mohammed, Brigham Young, Charles Taze Russell and L. Ron Hubbard have in common?

A YEAR IN REVIEW

I sit comfortably in my Barcelona chair. My feet

Gordy Grundy

are up. The room is warm. Outside, a string of Christmas lights blink with color, holiday cheer and a soft sensuality. On the coffee table before me, ice chills a frothy beverage. The lazy smoke from a cooling pipe aromatizes the studio. I am a contented man. My belly is full, my loins are spent and, for once, my mind begins to slow. The fast Techno-Trance that usually tempos in my head is now a slow, drowsy trot. My thoughts begin to dance back, through time, to recollect the events of this last year. As I do so, my toes begin to uncurl.

I can't remember if it was Jesus or Hallmark, but someone important said, "To touch a life, that is the greatest gift of all."
Well, I got my mitts on a few.

More than ever, I find myself mumbling to myself, "There's no time like the present. It's here, it's now and it's free."

This year was like every year, jam-packed with a lot of the unflagging human experience. I have laughed and I have tried to cry. I had a satori *and* a supernatural reprimand. I have chased and I have been chased. I have ridden high on a horse, proud and eternal; I have crawled on my knees, humiliated and ashamed. I have been the smartest kid on the block and I have fumbled for words. I have not hurt or slighted many and I don't think I have been hated.
In all, Luck has fondled my dice and rolled them well; she has given me a year of More Luck, a balance sheet in the black.

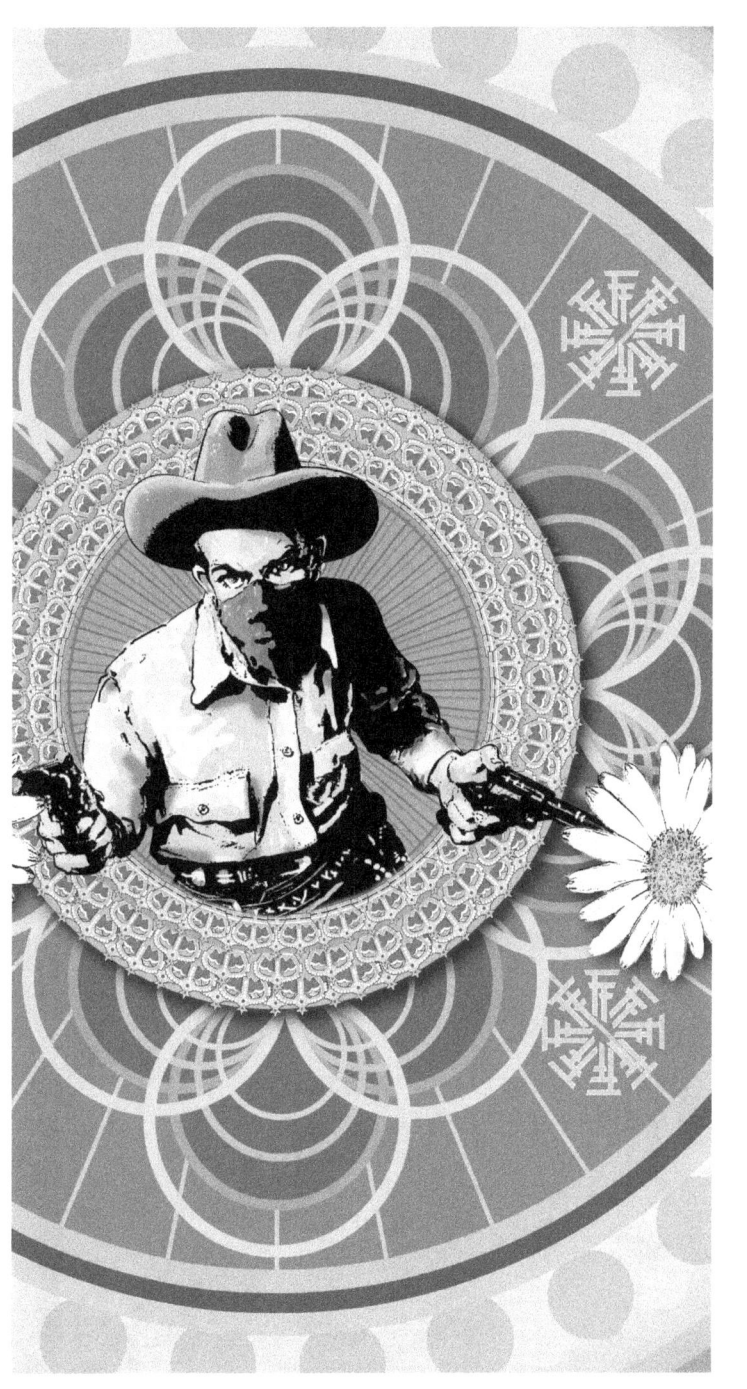

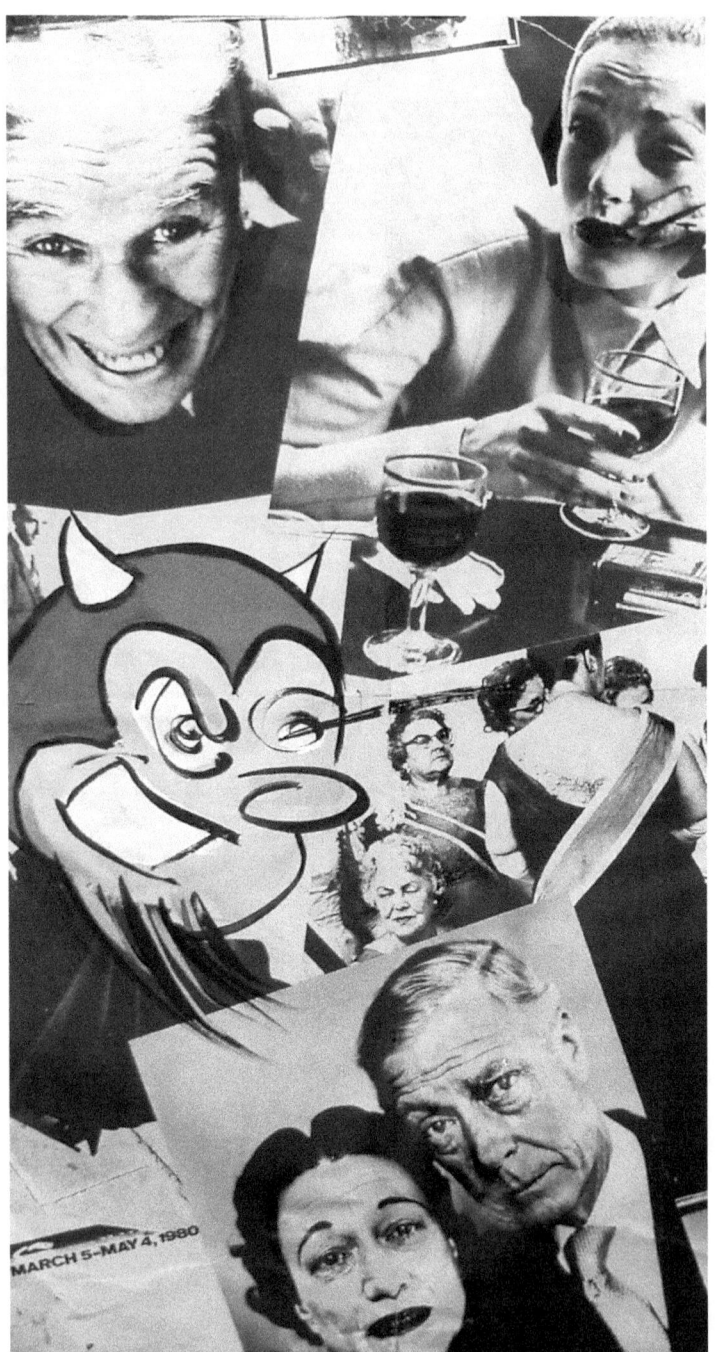

THE UNDENIABLE APPEAL
OF THE HYPERREAL

"Bagby," I bellowed in a stiff, clipped Brit-ish accent. "Bloody good to see you again!"

This was unusual. I don't have an English accent. It further alarmed my coterie because there was no one nearby named Bagby.

"Bagby, old man, what do you make of those Iraqi devils?"

I don't know what came over me. Then again, I seldom do.

Sometimes my mind takes me places, involuntarily. If I am not enamored of my location or if I get a whiff of boredom, my mind just leaves the body behind and travels to somewhere or something more interesting.

The last thing I clearly remember was standing on the terrace of an architecturally significant clubhouse of a country club in Southern California. I was a guest of some collectors who were members.

It was another night in paradise. The sun had set a while ago. A few stars in the East were busting out of navy blue while the Western sky still echoed a rusting orange. It was a good-looking dinner party. Shirts were well starched, skirts were crisp and sweaters were tied around a lot of shoulders. Thick New Yorks were grilling over mesquite. Jasmine and eucalyptus danced in the warm evening air. A jazz trio played slow and lazy.

The conversation hovered between the French Open, Iraq and Martha Stewart's indictment. Maybe I was bored. Or just susceptible to an attack. This really wasn't my crowd.

When a HyperReal Projection hits, there really isn't much you can do about it. Or maybe it was the booze. Either way, I was transmogrified.

"Bloody good to see you again Bagby!"

I suddenly found myself surrounded by high ceiling'd walls of dark mahogany and gilt-edged books. Waiters in full livery sailed through the club library on si-lent steps over plush Persian rugs. The quiet light of brass Kashmiri lamps shadowed the room, but I could still make out a few of my fellow members snoozing in their wing-backs or reading the London Times.

I thanked Chandou, my favorite man, for the Gin Ricky. I had to smile; he has been serving me for most of my life. He's now a bit slow, like all his kind, but he always gives me a grin and a laugh.

When I crossed my legs and sank deeper into the red Argentine leather, I caught my reflection in the spit shine of my cavalry boots. My nose may have been broken several times but it never broke my good looks. I set the drink down onto the side table, inlaid with African ivory, and brushed a speck of lint off the gold braid of my left epaulet.

I have never liked nor respected Lord Bagby. My elderly, working father recently needed his old friend's help and was refused. Nonetheless, I had to be polite. "Bagby, how are you? What's new in the world?"

I had to ask again because Bagby lost some of his hearing many years ago when we were taking a bit of lead in the South African campaign. "Bagby old man, what do you make of those Iraqi devils?"

The former consul's face darkened. "An ungrateful lot." He paused and then said with a laugh, "Those brigands are a far cry from the civilization that was old Babylon! Eh? Ho!"

"The Sumerians established much of the culture and knowledge that we stand on today," I said, and with some hesitation, "Yes, that civilization has been backsliding ever since."

"Religion, you know."

"Yes. Never an inducement for free thinking or innovation."

"I have had some good news this morning," he said brightly, "My S.S. Lorelei landed safely this morning at Portsmouth. Sailed in from Bombay. Full cargo. My worries are over. I shall sleep better tonight."

Lord Bagby married well after leaving the Foreign Service and then invested in shipping and cotton. He was a miserly employer, favoring a hard stick to a carrot. The "Free India" movement was hurting his business a great deal. The rioting in Bombay and New Delhi was bad for commerce, as intended.

Gordy Grundy

He took a pick and loosened the charred tobacco in the bowl of his pipe, then tapped it empty into the big elephant's foot ashtray.

Bagby has a tendency to get long winded. I knew that he was going to start blustering about business, so I thought I'd tweak his ruddy nose a bit. I didn't realize how much.

"Bagby," I asked, "What do you think of this Mahatma Gandhi business?"

"That runty! Little bald!" Lord Bagby slammed his ham-sized fist upon the Balinese end table. His face grew scarlet and he stood abruptly. "That little brown Hindi has cost me a fortune!" Bagby blew long and hard enough to wake up old Smallwood who was snoring across the room.

Bagby was winding up for a rant, "That scrawny, brown, four-eyed cotton weaver has---"

I stood up and with humor said, "Isn't that something! When a little man in a diaper can push around a Lord like you!"

Well, obviously I had touched a very raw nerve. He cocked up to take a swing at me.

I stepped back and he caught air with great embarrassment.

"Good God, man!" I said loudly and sarcastically, "This is a gentleman's club!"

Like a bull, Bagby tried to dance like a butterfly but his clumsy second attempt to connect his fist to my face sent his rather large frame crashing into a wingback chair, rolling it over with he in it. I couldn't see Lord Bagby but I heard a large "OOOFF" in harmony with the sound of breaking wood.

Chandou pulled the large chair off of him. I never moved to help.

Old Smallwood snickered.

Somewhere, a crystal glass fell to the floor and shattered.

Lord Bagby, huffing and puffing, crawled about on all fours trying to stand but his fat legs could find no traction. Servants were trying to help but he shoved them away.

Beet red, Bagby lumbered to his feet by climbing up the leg of the huge stuffed Grizzly Bear that Teddy Roosevelt had bequeathed the club.

A sharp cry turned everyone's attention. The Club Manager stood in the doorway. His hands were plastered across his face in horror. "This is a gentlemen's club!"

Then his boney finger aimed the blame. He spoke directly to me, this time rather dryly, "Lieutenant. Once again."

He was thinking practically. My membership has always been hanging by a thread. The blame for anything out of the ordinary at the club (and having fun is definitely out of the ordinary) can usually be pinned on me.

The Manager turned to the security guard behind him, "Eddie, escort the Riot out of the club immediately and I don't want to see his boots touching the floor as you go."

Eddie, a former sergeant in the Royal Light Dragoons, was rather large. I've known him a while. We are friends. As he came at me, I saw the ole 'sorry-but-my-job-is-on-the-line' look in his face.

One of Eddie's paw-like mitts landed at the back of my neck and yanked skyward. My toes no longer touched the ground.

Gordy Grundy

The next morning, I woke up back in Southern California with a needlepoint hangover. The Forensic Nightlife investigation lasted several hours. I learned that I had gotten quite rambunctious at the country club the night before. It seems I can't resist any chandelier that swings. Of course, some people have no sense of humor.

Security was called and I hear I had a swell time leading a billy club wielding septuagenarian on a foot chase at race walking speed, out to the soon-to-be stolen golf cart that ended up in the water trap on the thirteenth hole which... It just goes on.

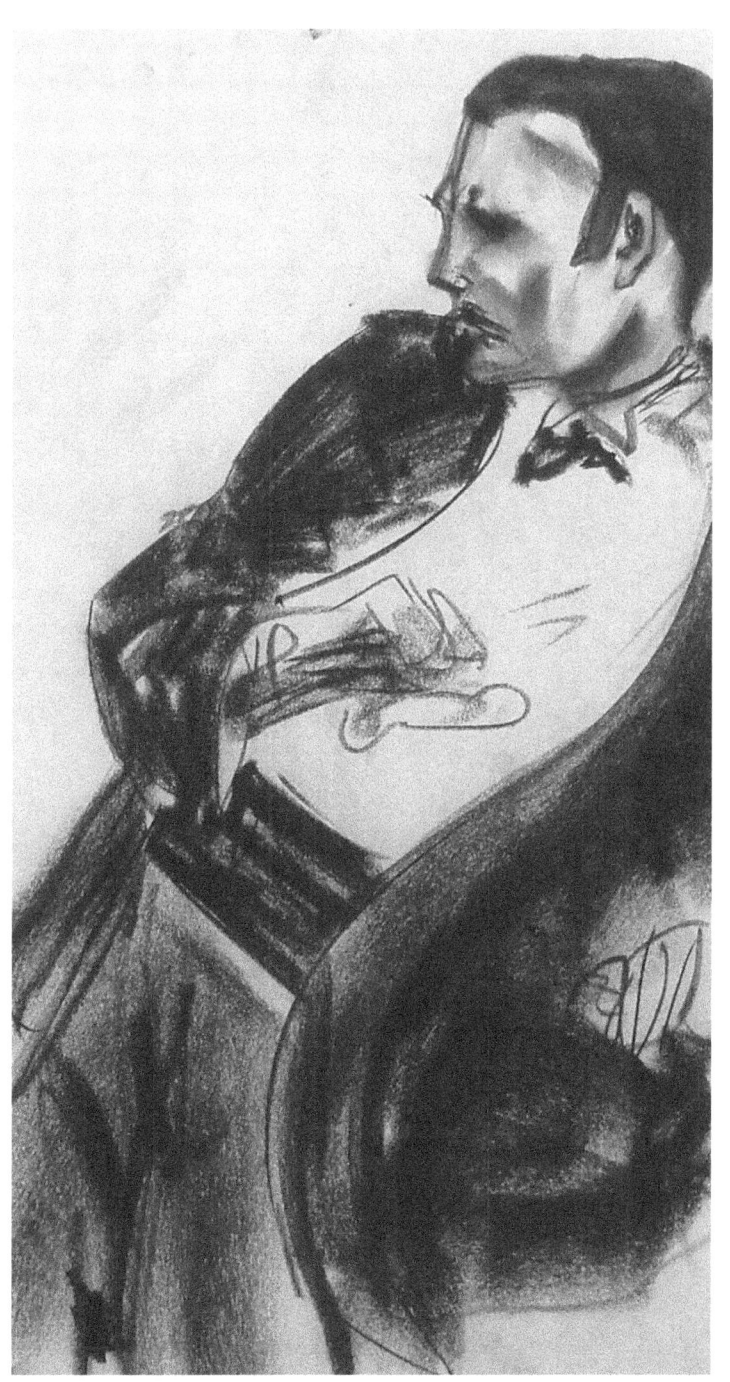

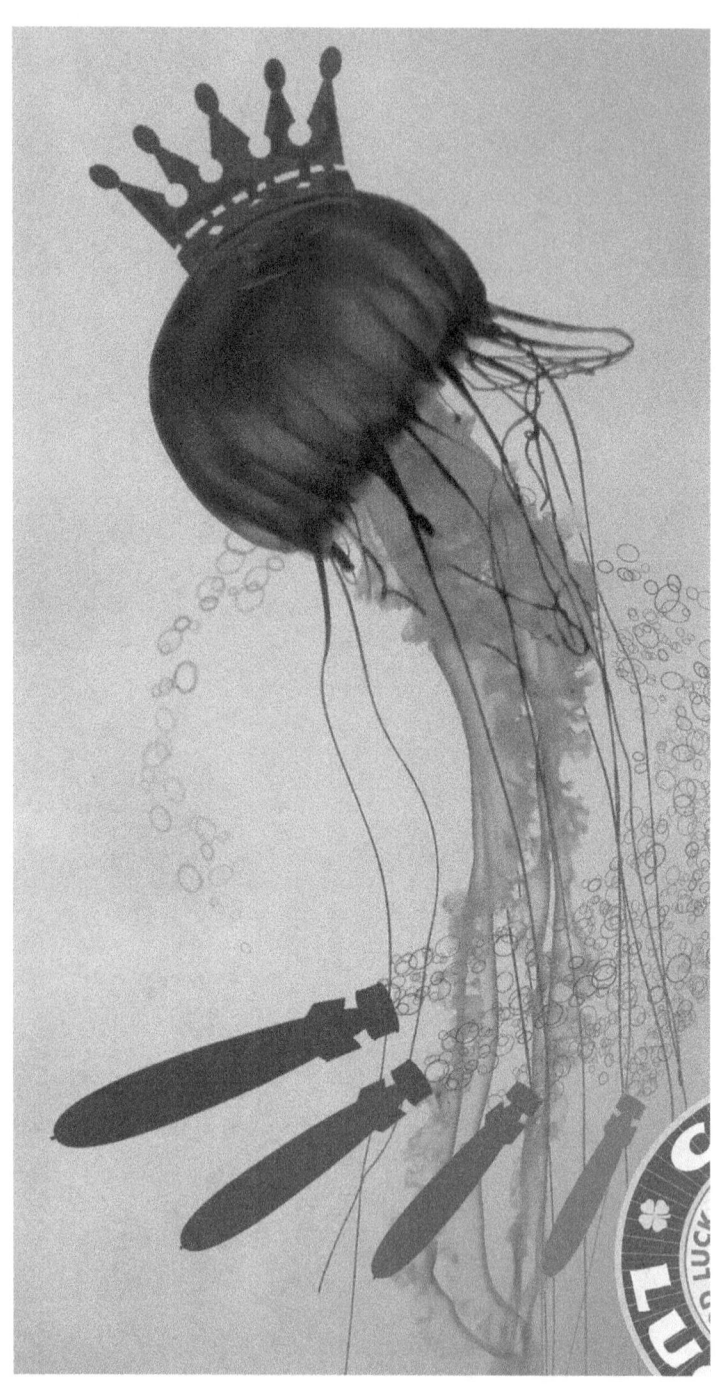

DRESSING FOR SUCCESS

CLOTHES MAKE THE COLONIAL MAN

I have never been so embarrassed in my life. What will the Iraqi people think?

The picture in the morning paper made me cry out in nationalistic shame. It showed Paul Bremer, our new Viceroy in Iraq, on his first day on the job. He was shaking hands with one of our new fellow citizens. In the picture Bremer wore a natty business suit, with sneakers. I was too mortified to even laugh. Or cry.

If I had trotted out like that at home, my Mom would have sent me back upstairs to change. We judge a book by its cover. First impressions are last impressions. Just ask Dale Carnegie. If clothes make the man, then a Vice-

Gordy Grundy

roy makes a nation.

The entire presentation was flawed from the top down. What looked like a UN Peacekeeper's helmet on Bremers head was in truth a dry look, blow-dried do from the Seventies. If he weren't wearing a tie, I would have thought he was a Dallas society dame with a bouffant.

His dress was more appropriate to a winter in Iowa than a day in Baghdad. A heavy wool pin stripe suit with vest in the Arabian Desert does not project a knowledgeable image nor does it reassure a nervous people. You'd think the State Department would have their own Mister Blackwell to pack the steamer trunk. Tony Blair should have whispered "loose linen and breathable cotton" into his ear. There is a reason why GQ Gentleman's Quarterly goes to press every month.

I am assuming L. Paul Bremer wanted to portray himself as a dynamo, a take-charge kinda guy, a man who literally hits the ground running. But the sneakers did not achieve that goal. Yachting deck shoes can work with a suit but shopping mall Ankle-Savers just spells D-O-W-D-Y.
If I were an Iraqi, I would read the footwear as a promise of more looting, lack of water and no electricity for quite some time.

As an aesthetic and an American, I am appalled, appalled, by our presentation in Iraq. And obviously, so are the Iraqis. Just the thought of the embarrassment makes me want to slap on a Strap-On. (I am referring to the popular explosive with a one-way ticket.)
Has anyone considered the audience? What might the Iraqis be thinking? Our spectacular and explosive First

Act produced applause, shock and awe. Our easy foxtrot into Baghdad may have sent a message of power, hope and too much promise.

American culture is no stranger to these good people. For generations, they have seen our films, admired our style and emulated the American panache. They know Tom Cruise and they all, except for the fundamentalists, have studied Pamela Lee Anderson in great detail. Their expectations are rather high.

Here they are, expecting the best of Western Civilization but instead they get the best of Mid-Western Civilization. Clothes make the Consul.

PROFIT AND LOSS

I want to profit from a friend's death.

Young Ian Hartman just lost a lengthy battle with an inoperable brain tumor and I want to learn from his courage and attitude.

A long, hard year after his first seizure, I asked him if his perspective on life had changed.

"Do you see life differently? Do you appreciate the small things? Is every minute more precious?"

He thought about it and then replied, "No. You still have to do the dishes."

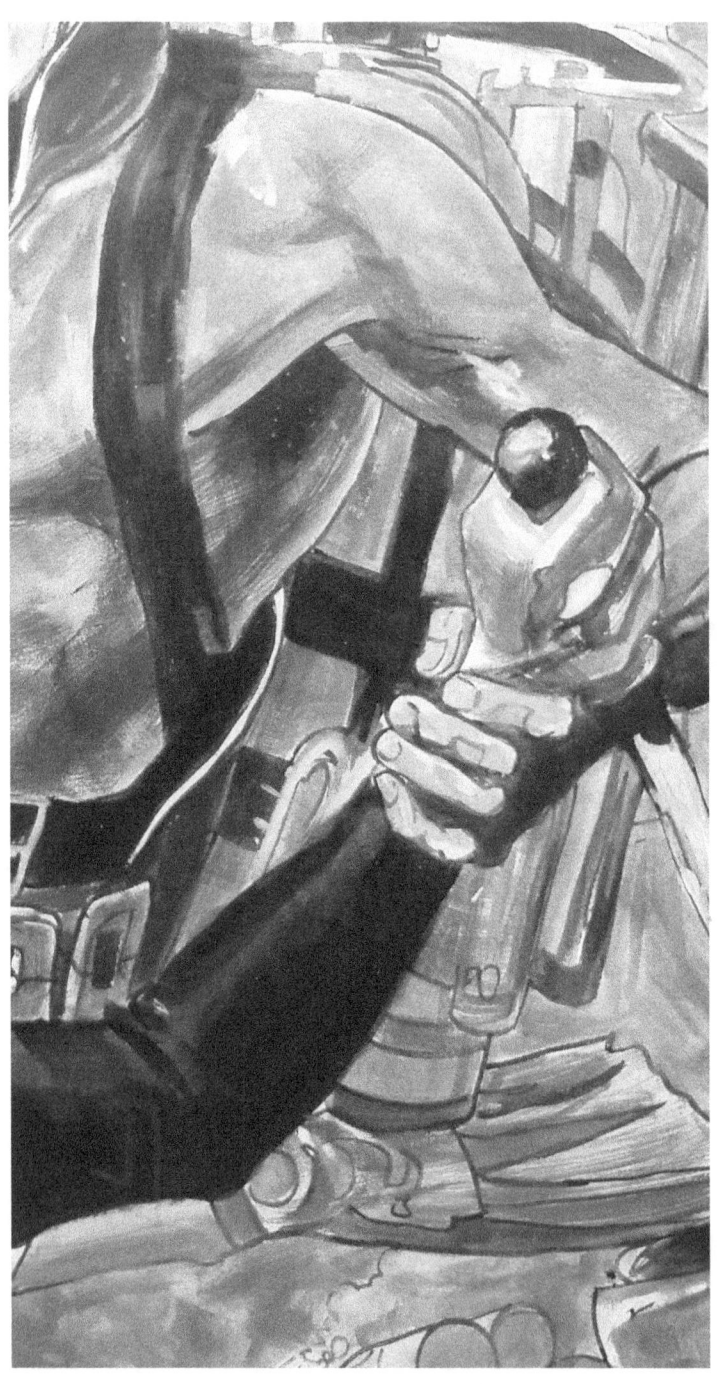

TESTING 1, 2, 3

This year, I went on my first Lecture Tour.
The speaking engagement was for the fine art graduate students at the University of Texas, San Antonio. It qualifies as a tour because it was most definitely out-of-state. The presentation, "Deconstructivism, Iconoclasm and Alcoholism in Art: Economic Strategies for the Millionaire Fine Artist," was co-authored and presented with Miss Tulsa Kinney, a Los Angeles based artist, art writer and redheaded ball of fire.

The tour began with a visit to a slew of art openings at the Blue Star arts complex, then a jaunt to my favorite gallery Sala Diaz, a wise and wonderful alternative space where we were warmly welcomed. A cocktail reception in our honor at the classic Liberty Bar became a resource of many new friends, but alas, no playmates.

The next day, our presentation was attended by

fifty bright and eager faces. Rather than show slides of our work, Miss Kinney and I took the students along with us on a wild night of Los Angeles art openings. This slide show featured art stars such as Ed Ruscha, John Baldessari, Shaun Calley, Rosamund Felsen, James Hayward, Alexis Smith, Ed Moses and many others. The Texans were also bedazzled by the number of stars of stage and screen who littered our photographs. I guess I just take the glamorous Los Angeles lifestyle for granted.

The lecture ended to laughter and loud applause. One young man was so moved that he thanked us profusely for redirecting his life to the Arts. Many begged for a studio visit. None threw their panties. Placing honorariums against expenses, the Lecture Tour only cost me several hundred dollars, a princely profit in the accounting of the art world.

ANDY, ANDY, ANDY

The opening of the Warhol show at the Museum of Contemporary Art made for a memorable yet bittersweet night. Few artists have flown as close to the sun as Andy. Very few have lived to experience such a material and critical success. Few artists have ever made as great an impact to so many.

In the large crowd, I saw many familiar faces that I had not seen in a long time. They were Los Angeles artists of many generations and many different aesthetics.

Each face signified a wave or a style. I saw the artist who used explosives, another who arranged flowers to die as sculpture and the painter who drew with studio sweepings, hairballs and dust bunnies.

So many of these artists had been billed as the next big thing. They had the support of critics and collectors. Reviews evidenced their talent. Their buzz was audible. Their glory was assured but their wave petered out. Their fad fell out of fashion.

That night, everyone came to honor Andy. But for many, it became a cold mirror to an artist's ambition.

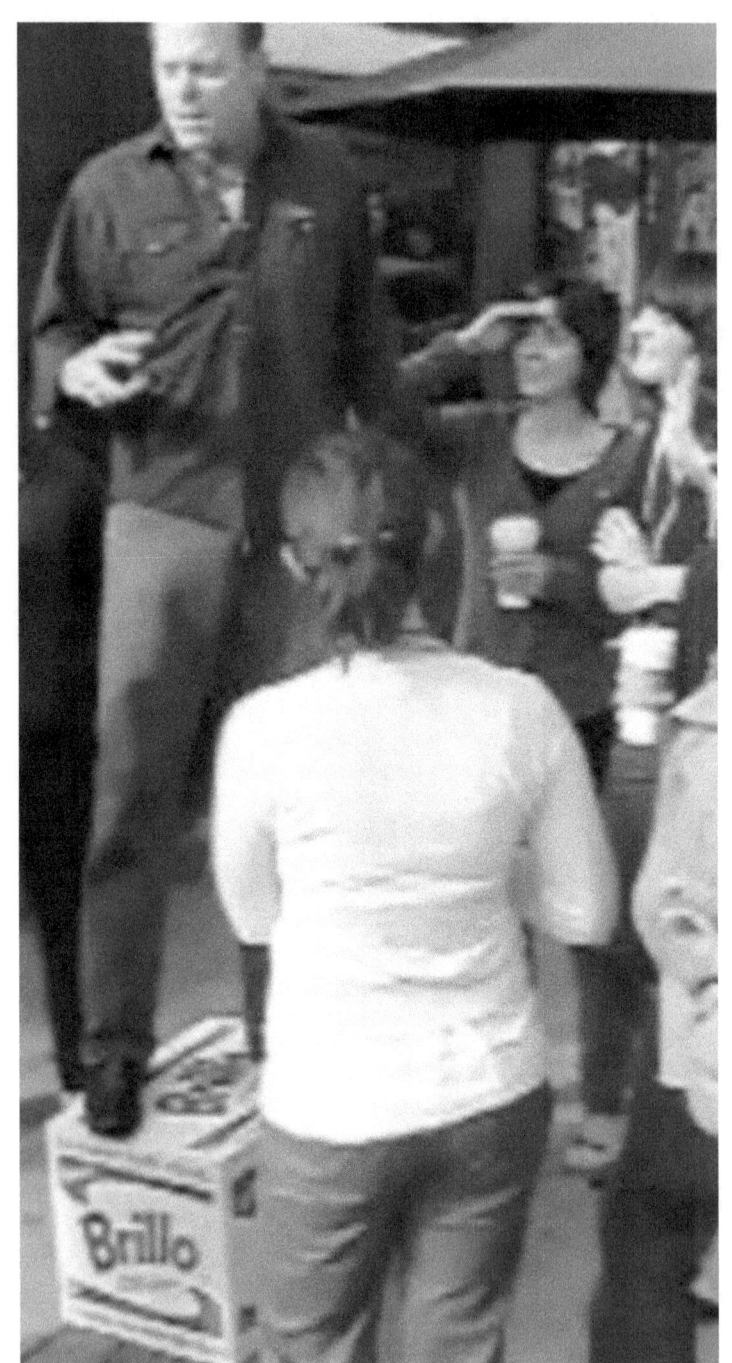

FENG SWAYED

Feng Shui? There are many rules in order to achieve harmony with Feng Shui, the ancient Chinese system of good housekeeping and clean design. I like a red front door and all, but I seriously doubt my landlord would reset the concrete foundation to gain a more harmonious exposure. Bad luck be damned, my toilet seat stays up. Sure, I should clean out my junk drawer, but then, where would I keep the junk? Of course, my disinterest in the popular design religion was changed when cash hit the table.

My chef pal Tara fell into good fortune when she got her Feng Shui Fish. It seems that a small investment into a tank, water and nine fish will yield a prosperous wallet and a fortunate life. All it takes are eight lucky goldfish; a big black fish to protect them and your life shall change for the better. Once my pal got her aquarium populated, her phone began to ring with prosperity.

Gordy Grundy

I am no fool when it comes to easy cash. I quickly purchased the necessary aquarium, oxygenator and a jar of Tartar Sauce should the project go south. I bought my nine little fishies, ensconced them in their new home and gave them each a name. I then sat by the mailbox waiting for the dough to come in.

The next day, MaryJane was floating rather than swimming. I said a silent prayer, gave her a burial at sea and flushed the toilet.

The next day I replaced my fallen soldier with MaryJane Junior. You see, one need not fear the death of a Feng Shui fish. When they die, it is as if the fish are taking a hit for you.
I slept well that night knowing that some personal disaster had been adverted. I was untouchable for I had nine bodyguards swimming for my safety.

The following morning I woke to find that Ziggy and Doob were not among the living. I started to get nervous. Rather quickly, I introduced Ziggy Two and Doob Junior to their new fish family. Why were these fish sacrificing themselves so quickly? What sudden misfortune was I escaping?

The next day I returned home to find another soldier down. Marley was no longer flipping his gills. What was happening? Am I a bad man? Have I caused anyone harm? Is someone out to get me? I began to take stock of my life. I made a mental note to stop kicking the dog. I vowed to be much nicer to my fellow man.
Poor Marley. I mumbled a few words of prayer and, with a flush, sent him spiraling down the toilet and into the

great eternity.

The folks at the pet store now know my name; I should be customer of the month. Without a full house, the Feng Shui fish have no synchronicity. The rules are clear, eight gold plus one black.

Once again, I left the shop with a new pal swimming in a bag. With gratitude and a bit of guilt, I threw Sativa the newest cast member into the Aquarium of Death. I hoped for the best but feared the worst.

Should I expect a tax audit? Will I be hit by a falling piano? Are my arteries clogging? What does it mean if all the fish die at once? I now duck when I hear a plane overhead. I'm afraid an octogenarian with a driver's license and a Cadillac is gonna take me out in a crosswalk. I think I may need some meds for my mounting paranoia.

I was better off without any fish but now I'm too frightened to get rid of them. And wouldn't ya know it? Prosperity has yet to cross my transom and the daily trips to the Chinese fish store are costing me a fortune.

THE SWELL OUTSIDE

There is a moment of which I am reminded. It happens when you are surfing (on a wave in the ocean) and you are leisurely paddling out to sea through the breakwater. The instant of recognition occurs when you realize that the oncoming wave ahead of you, the one that you want to glide up and over, is far larger, moving faster and breaking shorter than you judged it to be.

105

Gordy Grundy

In a nanosecond, the brain ascertains distance, size and speed. The wave outside the break line is bigger, moving faster and going to break sooner than I had anticipated. A quick calculation determines that a retreat is impossible; I am too far out. I don't want that monster to crash on me but it sure looks like it might. There is only one option. All you can do is face the wave and try to race over it. This is a shining moment of hellish panic and unbridled hope. You paddle like hell. You paddle like you've never paddled before.

When this little Bin Laden fella cannonballed into the pool, he created a wave that will overwhelm the rest of our lives. We are having to work harder than ever before.

The cost of making art just went up, literally and figuratively. I am often amused and always inspired when I note the sacrifices that my colleagues choose in order to make art. What may be a high priority to us is often seen as impractical, inconsequential and insignificant to others. There is a great nobility in that 'foolishness.'

This is the reason that God looks out for fools, drunks and artists.

106

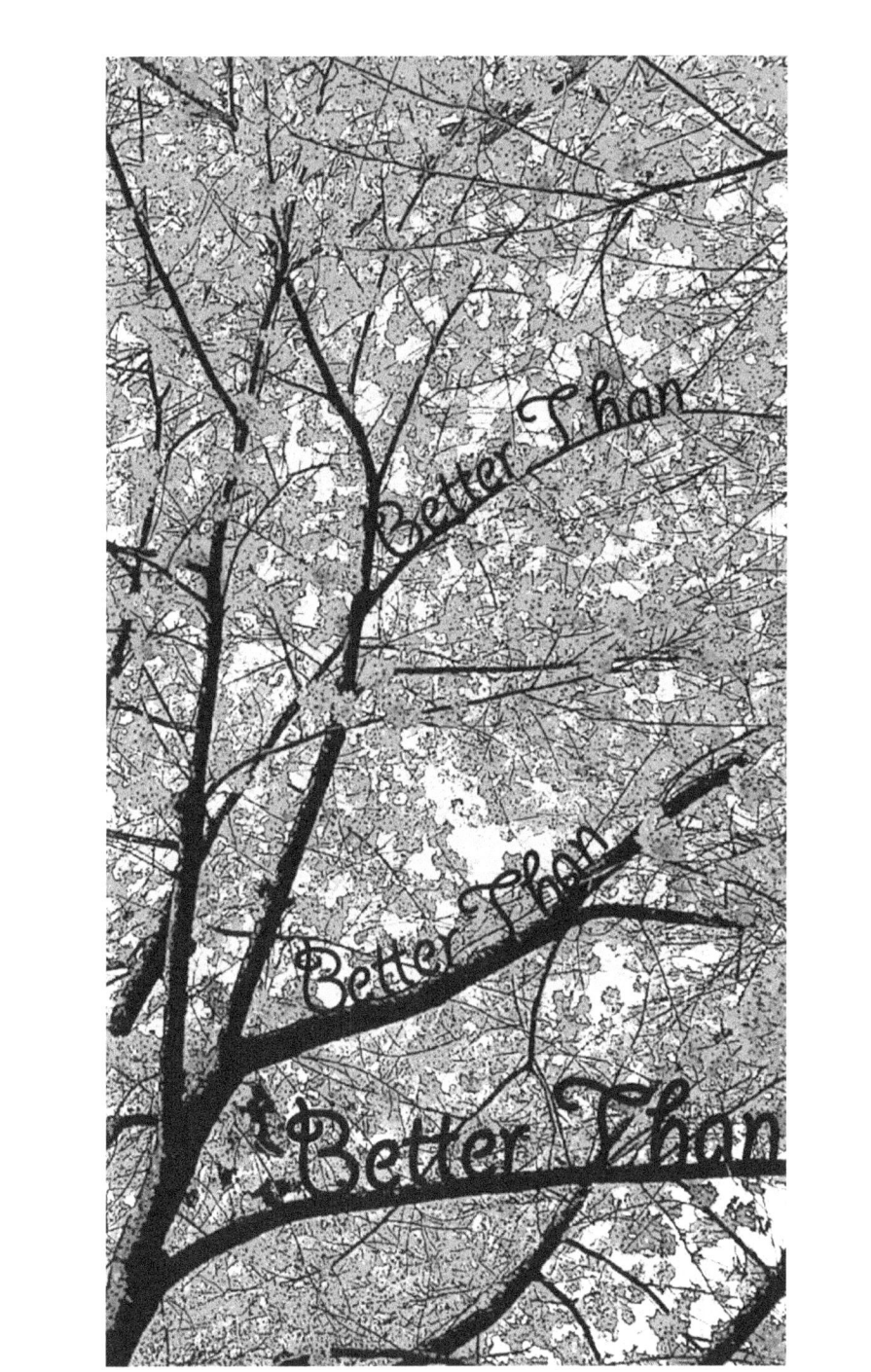

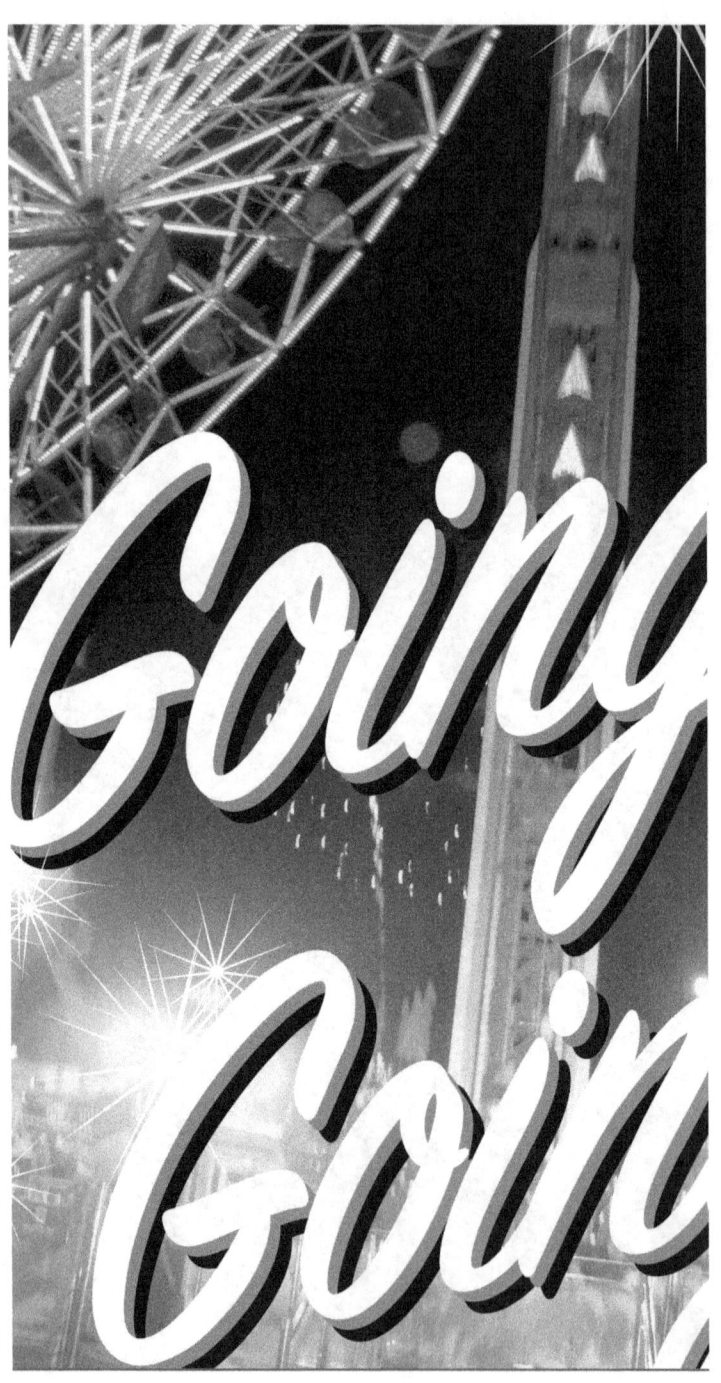

DOGHAUS

Turmoil being relative, one of the most sig-nificant events in a year of many, was the acquisition of a roommate. After several years of living alone, my tranquil, selfishly hedonistic lifestyle was shattered.

If Hollywood were to tell this story, I would be reunited with a son I never knew I had or a drooling old codger who dispels life's lessons in an amusing manner.

Fortunately, I was reunited with my dog.

Excited to have him again, I imagined that old Din and I would be running through flowered fields or sitting on a dock of a bay. Instead, we take naps. Din is no longer the young buck that I remember. Din is now a senior citizen.

I had not lived with (Gunga) Din for many years and I was ecstatic. I love my dog for many reasons and cute tops a long list. A Dobie with floppy ears, he is handsome and spry for an old man of fourteen years. I imagined that our reunion would be like old times. It wasn't.

As of last week, I have officially capitulated. I am now dog and he the master. It is no longer my studio but his doghouse. I guess a smelly, deaf dog is better than a strange child suddenly calling me Daddy.

I can't imagine what it's like to be old but I am learning rather quickly. Caring for and living with an old man has taught me many Life Lessons.

The experience has made me responsible. As I care for this old dog, I am forced to think of the Cycle of Life and how precious time is. I have learned that Love does conquer all, or at the very least, Love forces us to put up with a helluva lot, gladly.

I don't mind the lack of sleep, wakened hourly by his hacking cough. I no longer stop him from shredding the carpet. He barks orders at me, literally. I fully accept all foul odors. I keep the lights on so I don't step in something foul. I burn a lot of incense. I make two trips a week to IKEA for new rugs.

My life has become Din's. As I write these words, he stands loyally and lovingly by my side...dry-heaving.

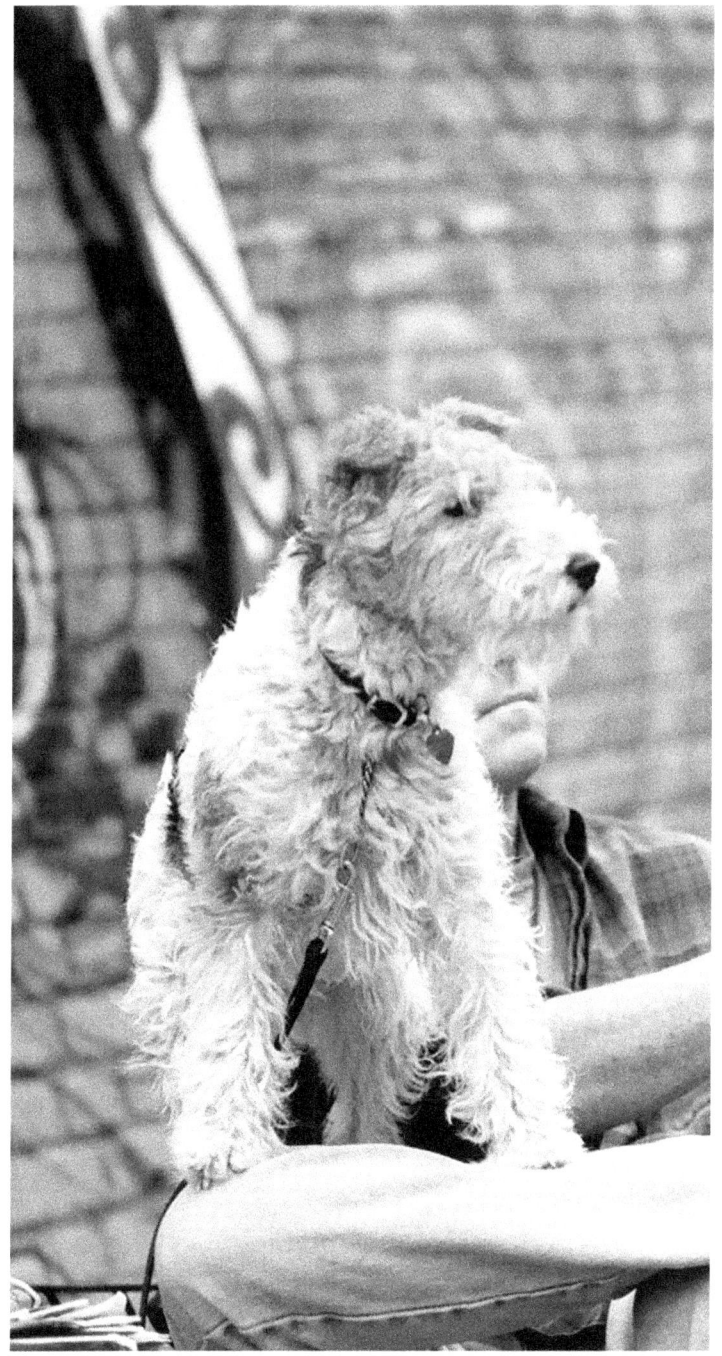

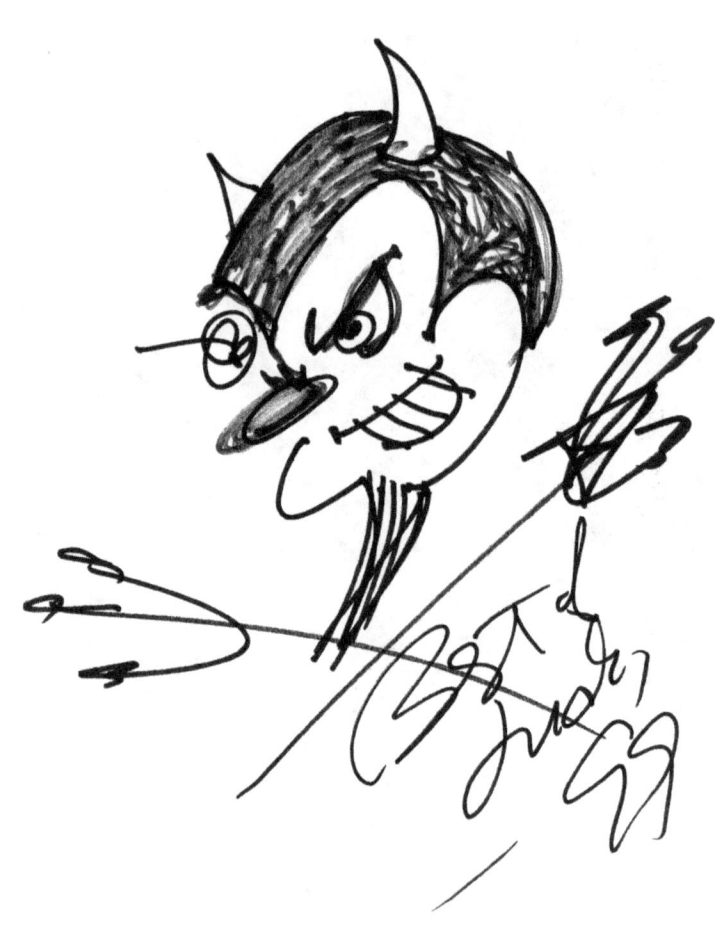

SCAM ARTIST

I recently received an email from a Mrs. Sylvia James, a collector deep in the heart of ol' Alabama, who wished to buy 'No. 91' from an old painting series. I don't sell mucasant surprise.

Mrs. James had sent the email very early in the morning, which led me to believe she had been up all night drinking Mint Juleps. Her typing and manner of speech were odd, a Southern charm I presumed. Since most art is purchased while intoxicated, I thought nothing of it.

Mrs. Sylvia James is a busy woman. Not only is she about to give birth, she is moving to merry olde England. A woman of obvious good taste, she inquired about a painting commission for her new home. As always, art is the perfect gift for all occasions.

The shipping company that would be moving her 'home decors' contacted me. They needed to know

113

the dimensions of the painting, so that they could quote a cost to Mrs. James. I assumed it was a Chinese firm, for the email began with 'Dear Mr. Grundy/Ma.'

Mrs. James then sent an email, happy with our progress and her love for 'No. 91.' She was going to send a postal money order with an amount that was $1,700.00 above the price of the painting. It would help her out if I could pay the shipping...

Something started to smell like a backwater bayou. I recalled a recent news item on Internet scams, illegal money transfers and unwitting victims. My love and adoration for Sylvia James began to fester and rot.

As a crime lord, Mrs. Sylvia James is quite brilliant for she targets the most vulnerable in our society. The American artist is eager, open and always fast to help. Beaten down by years of insignificance, the artist is psychologically ripe for abuse. Starved and grateful for the attention, the artist will go to great lengths to maintain the involvement. Mrs. Sylvia James is a monster. This is more despicable than preying upon senior citizens or small children.

Seething with rage at this heinous scam and the abuse that she may be inflicting upon my creative brothers and sisters across the world, I contacted the Los Angeles office of the Federal Bureau of Investigation.

A friendly young woman answered the Fraud Division phone. I immediately imagined her as blonde and athletic, an Eastside kind of gal. I explained the scam. She asked many questions. I liked her.

"And you feel the scam artist may be targeting... who?" she asked.

"Artists." I replied.

"Oh," she said. But it sounded more like "So?" I wouldn't say she was suddenly chilly but I sensed a disinterest.

"We're working on it," she said. I almost believed her.

As she was hanging up the phone, I swear I heard her snicker, "Get more agents, Lou. They're after the artists."

As I write these words, Mrs. Sylvia James is out there duping and attacking the creative in our society. This She-Wolf is cajoling them into what will be a federal offense. Her talons will shred the artist's dignity and their sense of trust. Her guile will rearrange the lives of these innocents. They will brag to their friends about sudden good fortune. They will dig deep into storage to find 'No. 91.' They will clean up and repaint a scuffed section, while wondering how the piece will look in the country home outside London.

Mrs. Sylvia James must die. This monster must be apprehended and brought to justice.

Or maybe I should mete out my own.

I am offering a reward. If anyone has any information that could lead to the arrest and conviction of Mrs. Sylvia James, I will personally award them 'No. 91.' I don't know what she looks like, but I do know that she is a bad typist.

Since I must go at this alone, outside the law, I can't really offer any kind of Witness Relocation Program. I've got a couch, but that would only be for a couple of nights.

Gordy Grundy

Please send any clue, no matter how irrelevant or insignificant, to the HotTip Line listed below. All information will be kept confidential.

Someone, somewhere, knows *something*.

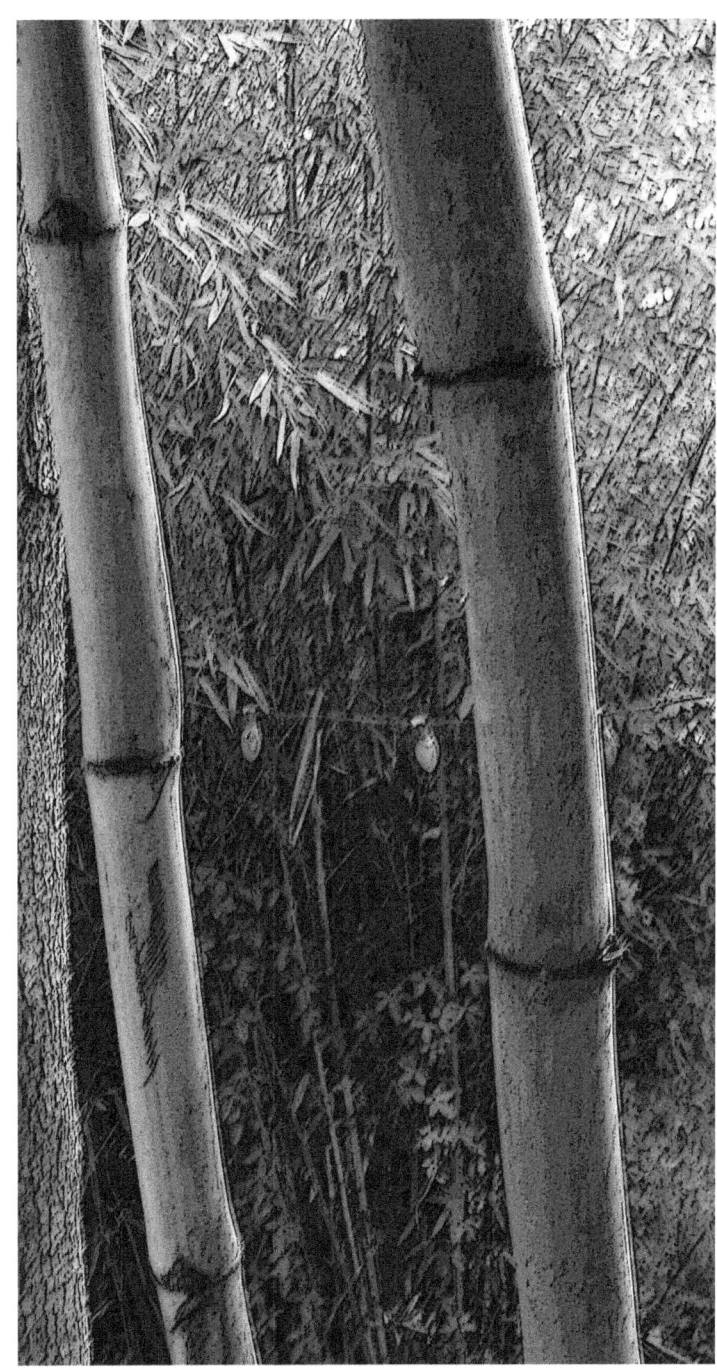

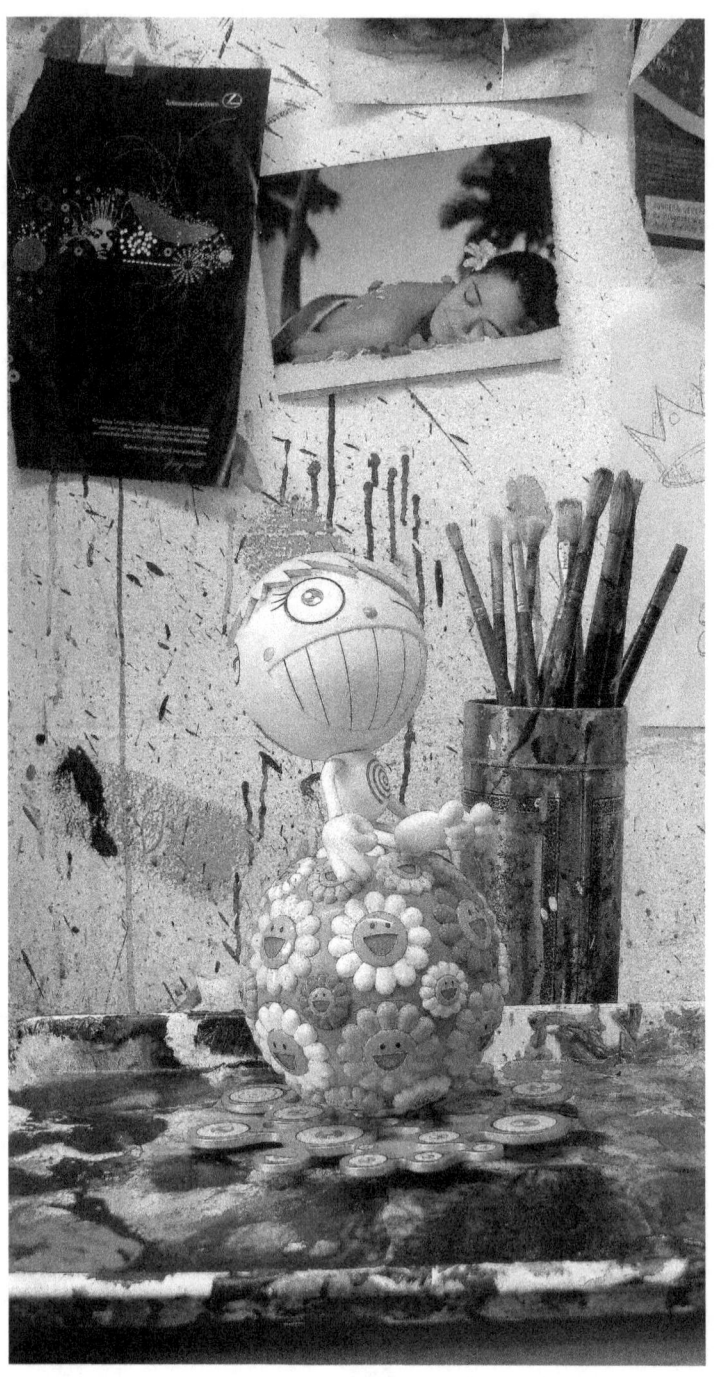

CHANGE, CHANGE AND MORE GODDAMN CHANGE

TO MY GREATEST CONSTERNATION

I want change. I'm waiting for it. I expect it. Next to my front door, I have two bags packed, always on the ready. The smallest is fit to support a romantic assignation or a bender of three days or less.

The larger bag, a nondescript duffel, is designed for a longer journey. Inside I have neatly folded a variety of clothes appropriate for any occasion or situation from an urban alley to a country club. A tuxedo, plenty of art supplies, a pair of swimming goggles, a year's ration of Excedrin PM, theatrical make-up, cash and two false passports are just a few of the economically packed items.

I'm ready for change but both bags are covered in dust. (Actually, the smaller one gets some use but not enough as to be commensurate with my young age.)

Gordy Grundy

I'm ready for change and I'm insulted that I have to wait for it. Change should happen miraculously and fortunately. *Bon Chance* is a gift from the Gods, an appointment of talent, grace and aesthetic superiority.

Well, I'm sick of waiting.

This Prince is used to some service. I've been signaling the Headwaiter for quite some time now and I haven't caught his eye. I'm ready for action, goddamn it, and it hasn't been forthcoming.

PAY TO PLAY

Recently I was perusing an issue of *Missionary Life*, a glossy monthly, and I was surprised to find an article on change. It suggests that if you want to better your life, you should cough up a total tithing of forty percent. It also proposed the theory that if you alter just one small thing in your life, it will eventually effect a greater change, like a loose bolt flying inside your transmission crankcase.

The author also gave a laundry list of suggestions, which I have re-translated for your applicability: You can move. You can switch art mediums. You can change your day job or your phone number. You can discover a new vice. You can try a new haircut or take a vacation.

I'm not a Calvinist; I never tip forty percent, but I knew I had the gumption to change at least one thing in my life.

A SIREN'S CALL

I had to get outta town.

This time by choice, but I had to get out fast

nonetheless. I know how to read an omen. When my over-burdened camel, Ol' Sanitee, took one look at the little, tiny toothpick I was about to place in her basket, she leapt to her feet with a camel's roar. She meant business, so I dropped the stick. I knew I had to get outta town.

This Westerner instinctively travels west. The Siren that whispers in my ear wears a lei of fragrant white and orange flowers.

Besides, I was on a budget. My coffers are as dusty as a coffin. If you want to find the cheapest vacation, look for the biggest ads; Hawaii always wins by several column inches. Honolulu dominates Maui or Kauai every time by at least a point size.

AMERICA'S VALHALLA

With the alacrity and clarity of the Artist's Mind, I was able to calculate the most luxurious comfort and beauty for the fewest clamshells. The cheapest package in paradise is the shopping mall they call Waikiki. It didn't matter; I had a card hidden up my sleeve. If Air Greyhound books two people to a seat or if I had to rest my head on the placemat called a pillow at Motel Poi Poi, I had the key to Shangri-La.

My plan was to get there cheap, sleep cheap and spend all of my time at the place I revere as the Mount Olympus of America. With the help of a friend and a fake I.D., I was able to gain entrance to the Outrigger Canoe Club.

For centuries, democracy and its friend the guillotine have forced royalty into hiding. America's most superior race has taken refuge at the Outrigger Canoe Club.

The OCC is a rather small private club at the foot of Diamond Head. The facilities are comfortable and beautiful but not luxurious. Its sweeping view of Waikiki, the green mountains of Barber's Point and the great wide Pacific will always bring a hush at sunset and a murmur of approval for nature's showmanship.

The OCC is also artist friendly, just ask Billy Al Bengston.

What makes the OCC exceptional are its members. They are the descendants of American missionaries, whaling ship captains, daring entrepreneurs and royal Hawai'ians.

These men, women and children are unassuming of their privilege. They share the grace of naturalness. No one walks, for they lope. Their bodies are lean and their muscles long. These are not the people of barbell vanities; their physicality is borne of outrigger paddles, surfboards and ocean-fought strength.

Their faces are not lined from worry, just careful thought. Strong white teeth flash against sun-browned skin. Everyone stands naturally tall. This is not the beauty found in fashion magazines but in generations of well-bred character.

Envy keeps me at the OCC. I remember watching a beautiful, raven-haired mother and her young son scouting the waves, waxing their boards and going out for an afternoon surf; I want to be that kid.

The work day ends early at the OCC. My peers would return from a few hours of labor managing the family trust to hoist a canoe above their heads and go for a paddle.

Their world possesses an aesthetic that a Ralph Lauren or a Tom Ford tries to capture but never will. *Olympia*'s director Leni Riefenstahl, the Nazi Bruce Weber, would run out of film at this place.

These *alii*, the Gods and Goddesses of America, live at the OCC and I was privileged to bask in their community. But I am not one of them. I am not rich and I am not *that* good looking. I do not lope.

My itch and scratch for a vacation was dire. I needed calm and repose. This trip was so spontaneous that I could not find a guardian to accompany and nurse me.

Alone and left to my own devices, it wasn't more than three hours after setting foot on Hawaiian soil that I fell into the grasp of a posse of artists and scalawags that rivaled all I was trying to escape in Los Angeles.

Unfortunately, I returned more exhausted and war weary than I'd been when I left. I guess I can't help it; I will always be a sailor on shore leave.

TABOO TERRACE

I just moved, but this change was not self-initiated as suggested in *Missionary Life* Magazine. My landlady fell in love with a crusading journalist and gave me the boot. Fortunately, I was able to land, not on the hard asphalt of the street but onto a very large pile of bamboo leaves.

Over the last five years, my choice in residences has been for amusement rather than home and heart. Since the scribe was taking my room, he offered me his, a small house four blocks away in Echo Park. He got the

Gordy Grundy

girl and the view and I finally got to drop my anchor in a safe harbor that I can call home, a mooring this psyche sorely needs.

I said, "I'll take it" before the journalist could tell me about my new digs. From his description I assumed that he was a design and style writer.

"The creme colored manse with lagoon blue trim is fronted with a grove of tropical bamboo, the symbol of prosperity, growth and upward mobility. True to the early Twenties style of Los Angeles architecture, the whimsical home is perched high off the ground, Hawaiian style, as if ready to embrace a tsunami. This and the lush landscaping will welcome every guest to the charms of the South Seas."

Now, if I were this guy's editor, I'd make a few changes to the copy. "Grove of bamboo" might be more accurate as "a few clumps" and "Los Angeles style architecture" demands adjectives such as "ramshackle" and "clapboard." Besides, I'd never call the threat of the reservoir above my head or an address in a floodplain as "tsunami friendly."

However you may describe it, I call it home. The rent isn't bad. It has an old fashioned bathtub which suits me fine. The "whimsical" floor in every room has its own concept of level and the kitchen reminds me of a galley in a small, leaky yacht.

Since cooking anything more aggressive than cold cereal is out of the question, I have turned the dining room into a spiffy painting studio.

Without air conditioning, my place actually does offer the climate of the South Seas. My oscillating house fan feels like the trade winds.

Over the last ninety years, my neighborhood was built with complete disregard for building codes. My street of single story homes and duplex apartments is oddly private despite the fact that everyone is living on top of each other.

When my neighbor sneezes, I reply with a "Gesundheit!"

Everyone has a loud dog and we create our privacy with walls of sound. Everybody cranks up their world; music is an invisible property line. As a result, a stroll down my street offers everything from a rural Ranchera to Handel to the Gorillaz. A chorus of dogs sing along in disharmony.

The natives are certainly friendly. On the first Saturday night in my new pad, I came home after midnight to find a party next door and one across the street. I went to both; I got the bum's rush from one and stayed for hours at the other, having a great time even though I did not speak the language. It's a dangerous Welcome Wagon.

I need not worry though. I am a mere block away from a private mental health facility, which seems friendly enough.

Since the journalist and I were trading places, we also switched phone numbers. The move saved us 15 dollars each in charges.

It was later that I learned he was not a food and lifestyle writer but a cop-busting investigator. He writes about police corruption and his sources are gang members and those at the Graybar. Now every dirty cop with a beef has my address and I have been fielding collect calls from jailbirds.

Talking to members of our penal colony is very exhausting and laborious. Since the one holding the phone is generally not the one making the call, they have a hard time grasping the idea that this number has changed. "Who you?" they scream repeatedly, "Who you?"

It makes me jump every time.

NO SMALL CHANGE

One axiom to remember is, "You always get what you wish for, plus a sharp stick in the eye." Never again will I take the advice of a Calvinist nor will I tell Lou my barber to try something new and kicky. I'm throwing in the towel and holing up behind the bamboo grove.

As an admission of defeat, I am about to paint a house sign which I will hang upon my porch. The Polynesian styled letters on bamboo will read "Taboo Terrace" because nothing really ever changes. You just can't re-cast the die.

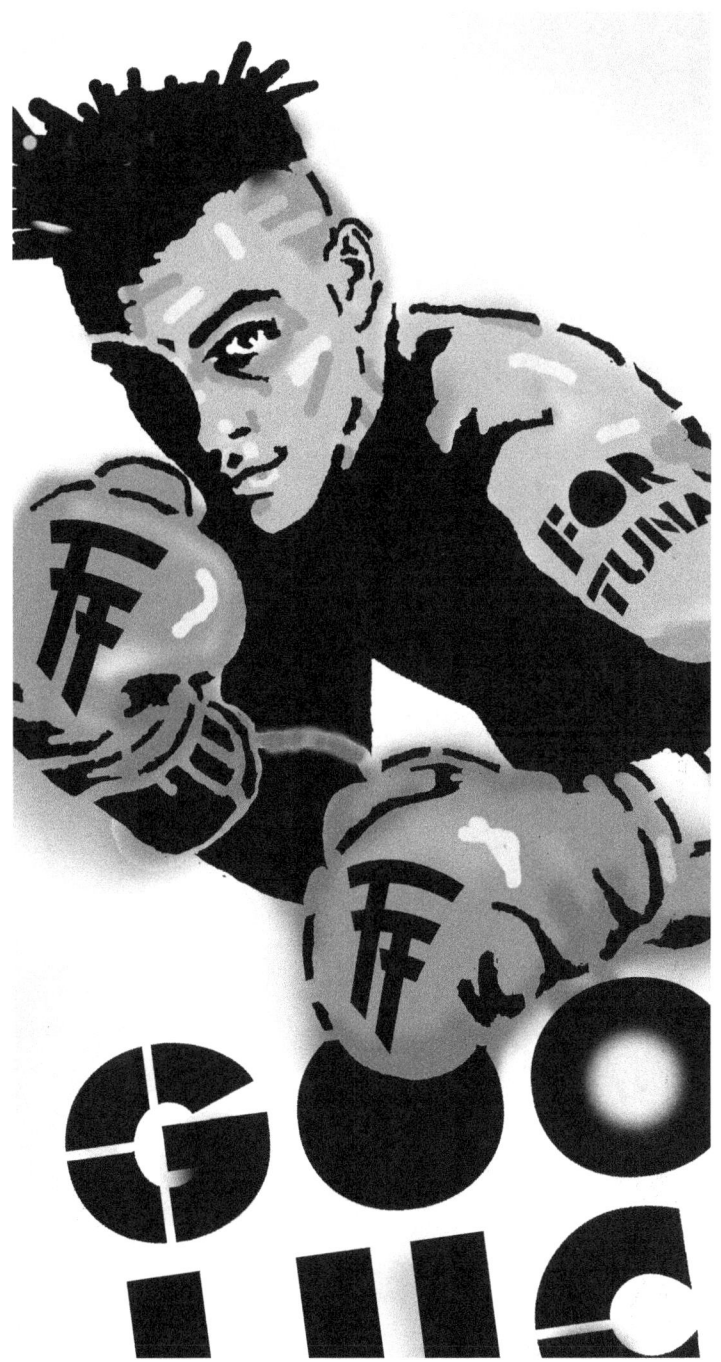

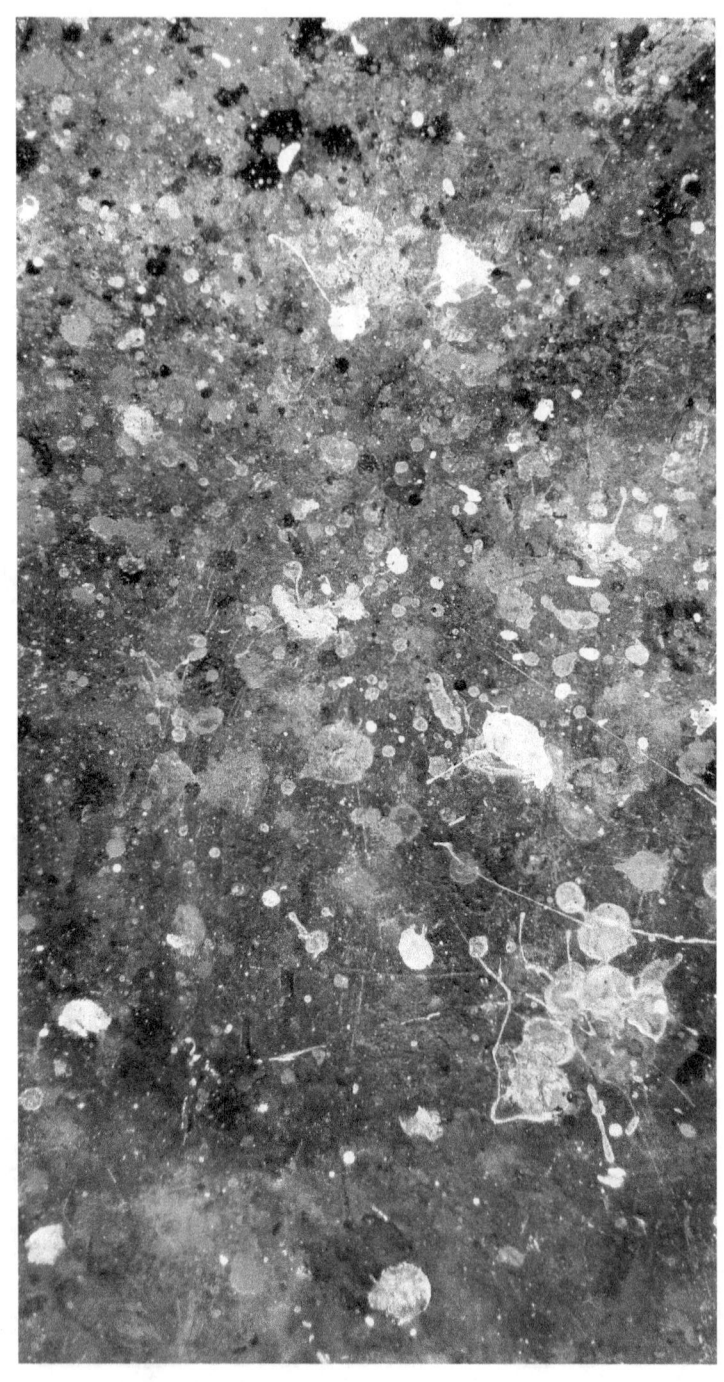

AT ISSUE WITH ART ISSUES

Making art is one thing and Art Issues are another. Art Issues is the speed trap in a small town. It's the obscure zoning law you find out about too late. It's the balloon payment hidden inside a home loan.

Art Issues are elusive. In the art world, they are paramount. To the layman, they're inconsequential.

In order to comprehend an Art Issue, one must invest three years and five figures in grad school. The fashion industry announces their annual color scheme with great pomp and circumstance. The art world announces their annual Art Issues with nothing more than a sly wink and a nod. You either get it or you don't.

It's another one of those 'goddamn things.' I had painted myself into a corner. Rather, in a painterly way, I had 'fallen but couldn't get up.' A dark cloud had rendered my easel idle. It's been over five weeks since a brush has touched a canvas.

As artists, writers and seekers know, one occasionally hits a dead end. Sometimes too much thought does not allow for maneuvering and you can't find your way out of a cul-de-sac. I had gotten lost and in frustration I was beating my head against the wall.

I like to be self-sufficient; I thought I could solve the painting problem myself.

In all honesty, I was just being polite. I rarely talk about my work. I know that anytime an artist starts talking about *their* work, my eyes glaze over and my head starts to nod. I really couldn't bare the cruelty of doing that to someone else.

My painting problem persisted with no solution in sight. Finally, after endless hours of self-flagellating torture, I realized I needed help. I needed Art Issues. It was time for a studio visit.

My pal, painter Alan Wayne came over. He is a thoughtful Minimalist and I have always appreciated his counsel. He looked at the last three pieces and made a few comments. His pronouncement acted like Draino. The clogged pipes began to flow.

I realized that I had instinctively turned what should be a simple image into a painterly discourse. That's why the bright colors were becoming muddy and the bold lines had turned into cowardly hesitations. The paintings were deviating from their original intention.

I had gotten lost.

Problem solved. A weight had been lifted from my shoulders. I was free once again.

Liberated, I showed Alan the new series, a conceptual work that does not use paint as a medium. He liked it. He encouraged more. Then he laughed and said, "You know, with this work, you are bringing on a new Art Issue."

I blanched, "Wh—What do you mean?"

"With this, you can't call yourself a painter. You're an artist now. Or a conceptualist. Mixed Media is in your lexicon."

My head started to ache. I could feel another Art Issue coming on.

Just when you think you've got all of your Art Issues lined up, there's always one making a f***ing issue.

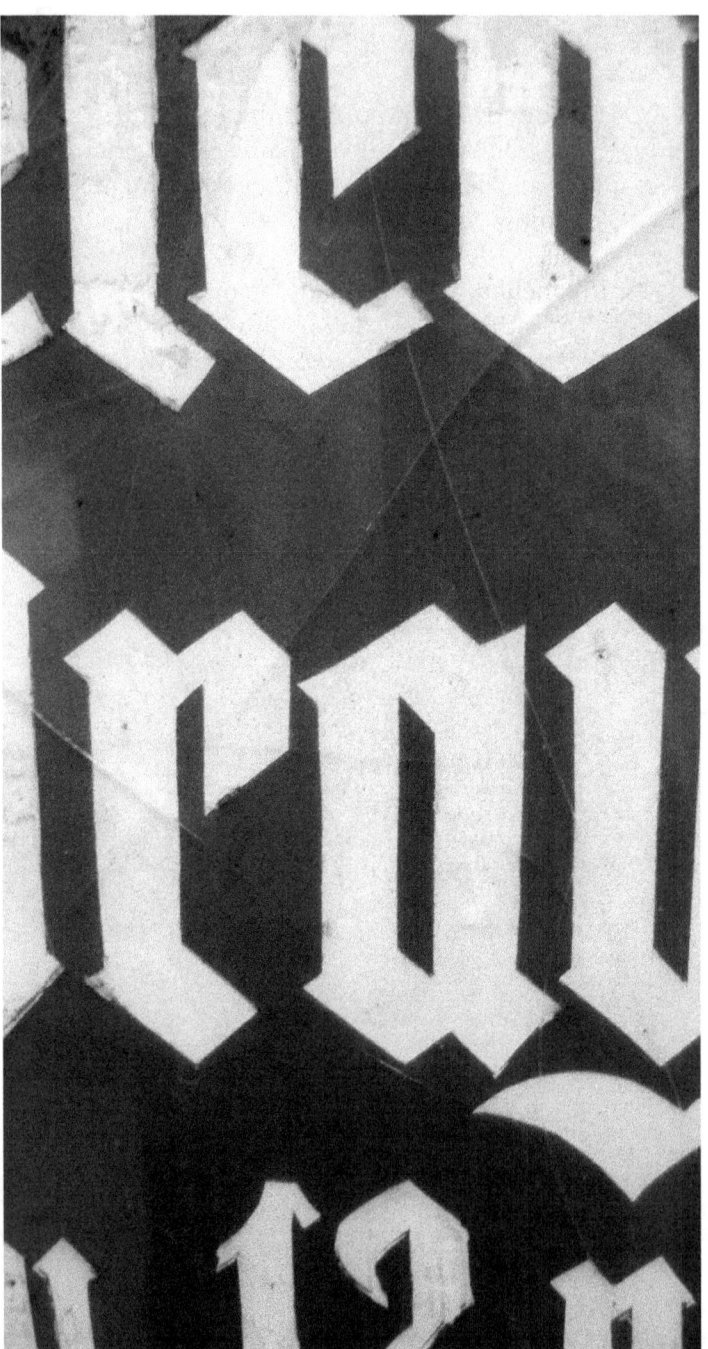

THE BIG PADDLE

DEATH OF A SHOWMAN

In Los Angeles, showman Michael Todd was busy packing. He had to catch a plane to New York in order to attend a Friar's Club roast in his honor.

It was a special time. He was lovingly married to the most beautiful woman in the world. He was the proud father of a baby girl. His recent achievements had earned universal critical praise. For the first time in his life, his finances were stable and abundant. Life could not have been better for Mike Todd.

That night, Friday, March 21, 1958, Todd gave his bride, actress Elizabeth Taylor, a good-bye kiss. Much in love, Elizabeth wanted to join her husband at this prestigious testimonial where the great entertainers and comedians of the day would be roasting the head-line-grabbing Todd. Unfortunately, Elizabeth Taylor suffered from a heavy cold. She had just started work on the film "Cat On A Hot Tin Roof," and she needed her strength. Reluctantly, the devoted wife agreed to stay in Los Angeles.

Mike Todd was one of the greatest American showmen that ever lived. Known for his brash personality, Todd would risk everything he owned (or could borrow) on his belief in an idea. His Broadway successes overshadowed his many failures.

Todd's greatest film achievement was the all-star production of "Around the World in Eighty Days." This 1956 Best Picture won five Academy Awards and made Todd a fortune.

That night, Mike Todd met his friend and biographer Art Cohn at the Burbank Airport. The weather looked ominous. High winds and heavy rains stormed the Southwest. Not to worry, the pilot of the Lockheed Lodestar said that flying conditions were excellent above the storm. At 10:41PM, the Lucky Liz, the name with which Todd had christened his private plane, took off for the Great White Way.

Several hours later, shortly after 2AM, the pilot struggled to fly through a fierce storm that raged over New Mexico. No one knows exactly what happened.

Thirty-five miles southwest of Grants, the Lucky Liz crashed and exploded in a rugged valley between clouds and mountains.

All on board died instantly.

WHERE ARTISTS GO, REALTORS FOLLOW
Marfa, Texas.

THE HEALING POWER OF POP
Too tired to light a cigarette? Too numb to switch off the televangelist? Too weary to cinch the knot on the noose?

The "down" times in life must be tolerated; they are part of the balance. To sweeten the bitter, music is often the first step on the climb out of an emotional ditch. You can discolor the blues. Following are several songs that can bring fresh blood to those anemic times.

"Accentuate The Positive"
Johnny Mercer and Harold Arlen slap us upside the head with their succinct lyrics. Arlen takes a position of absolutes. "...Accentuate the positive, eliminate the negative and latch onto the affirmative. Don't mess with Mr. In-Between..."

You are forced to choose: Is that glass half full or half empty?

"Sing Your Life"
On his "Kill Uncle" CD, Morrissey gives us a sweet philosophy for the millennium. The wise and earnest lyrics urge us to know ourselves and to sing our lives. Where the truly jaded may sneer at such an elemental message, Morrissey has fortunately invested great wit and a bouncy beat. Sing it.

"Gone!"
The Cure has written a wild one for their "Wild

135

Mood Swings" CD. It features a catchy, syncopated beat and swingin' lyrics, yet the perspective is an odd one. Is it mood music for an intervention?

Even if this point of view does not apply to you, the message is universal with a believable "go get 'em" attitude.

If music can tame the wild beast, it can also be used to re-circuit a bad attitude. Never underestimate the Healing Power of Pop.

LINGO
"a full set of luggage" \ n : 1: refers to the heavy circles and swollen bags under one's eyes, usually after a long night of wild and excessive behavior; 2: *"Looks like you've got a full set of luggage!"*
(Courtesy of Stu Gimlet.)

THE BIG PADDLE
Most tribal cultures feature their own customs, rituals and belief systems. The Southern California surf culture is no exception.

Long before Gidget and Moondoggie scampered across the sand, real surfers in the Thirties and Forties took a more philosophical approach to life, death and the sea.

This is a culture of self-reliance, appreciation and dignity. The Big Paddle reflects that ethic. Like the African elephant that lumbers off alone to die, an aging waterman grows to where he can no longer enjoy the things that give his or her life its meaning and pleasure.

136

When the body gives out and life is ebbing, the surfer knows that he is ready for The Big Paddle.

At sunset, on a day like no other, the surfer will wax up his favorite board for the last time. Sometimes, he or she will be joined by friends. A toast will be made for a safe journey. Other times, the ritual will be initiated alone.

It is a time of contemplation and reflection.

Before the sun can set against the horizon, the waterman will place his board into the Pacific and start paddling. He aims to follow the sun. Forever.

He will paddle until he can paddle no more. He will endeavor until his strength has been depleted. He will die with dignity, on the Big Paddle.

SWAGGER, NEVER STAGGER

Always Take The High Road

THE STUDIO VISIT

SPIDERS FROM MARS

Just thinking about it—I can feel something crawling down my neck. Here I go, again. I look like an aerobics instructor with a bad meth habit. Butoh on bennies.

It's so hard being misunderstood. I can't get used to the jeers and the laughter. Everyone regarding me with derision—Jeez, this is what a Minimalist must feel like.

Yah, sure, I may be talking strangely, almost incomprehensively, and, yes, my arms are flailing in the air like a madman, but I have a reason for my odd behavior.

I am a Man of the Season.

For three months of the year, the kids on my block laugh at me. They yell "Spaz!", "Kook!" and "Ants in yo' pants!" It's because I walk around with elbows flying and hands clawing at my face, while twirling around in circles.

This may look strange, but in Los Angeles we've just had a sudden Spring. The spiders hatched early. Taboo Terrace, my studio, is surrounded by a grove of bamboo; arachnids love bamboo. The little muthers spend all night squirting out web-works just to snare me in the morning.

I'm not afraid of spiders. I don't dislike them. But have you ever walked through a web? It's sticky. It's invisible. It's everywhere. *And* for certain, there's a big ass spider somewhere on it.

THE PITCH

Just when I was about to sign a contract that would have made me a millionaire's millionaire, I suddenly felt a spider crawling down my neck. It seems Hollywood is intimidated by a fast dance in the board room. Whatever the reason, it appears that my new reality show 'The Studio Visit' has been sent *'back to the coffeehouse.'*

I thought it was quite brilliant actually; so did they. I was *this* close.

If you are a Pittsburg based artist, you probably have a day job in a steel works. The Nantucket artist lives off the sea. The LA based artist is usually anchored to film in some way.

I took the leap for the brass ring. I pitched "The Studio Visit." The half hour reality series is a high drama, jet-fueled contest of high aesthetics in the art world.

"In the pilot, the show follows a group of artists, recent MFA grads, as they prepare for the studio visit *of their career!* The brass ring that we dangle in front of their glossy and glazed eyes is a solo space at the Whitney Biennial, a $25 gift certificate to Pearl Paints, and a year and a half of unrelenting attention followed by a lifetime of obscurity. Over the course of eight weeks, the artists would fret and flail, building momentum to the biggest *'Studio Visit!'* of their lives.

The most difficult challenge was keeping the attention of the audience. Whenever the artists would begin to discuss their work, we simply learned to cut to a more fascinating commercial.

Then, after months of excruciating drama, odd self-obsessed behavior and lots of pointless hard work, the day of the big 'Studio Visit' would arrive. We follow each artist as they clean the studio, prepare refreshments and medicate themselves in anticipation of the life-changing jury.

Six hours late, a limousine would pull up to the curb. The pop star host (or a dominating doyenne) would give the artwork a five-second look-see, toss a notebook of carefully prepared slides in the trashcan and ask, "Is there anything to drink?"

Tension would build as the wine was uncorked and the host extinguished his cigarette into the cheese and fruit plate. You could hear a pin drop.

At this point, I suggested a close-up of the artist's sweat-beaded brow, an audio track of their heart rate and an inner-body cam to show the ulcer acid boring a hole through their stomach lining. It's a shame there is no way we could show the artist's soul staggering under the weight of this ultimate aesthetic authority. I guess we could always animate it.

141

Gordy Grundy

Then, after looking bored and fidgeting with his watch, the famous curator (or dominating doyenne) would stand and announce the verdict.

To the lucky, lucky winner of 'The Studio Visit,' the glamorous art expert would enthusiastically announce, with a trademarked cadence, *"Let's put ON an ART Show!"* Lights flash, champagne pops and canapés are served.

To the untalented losers, 'America's Favorite Curator' would add some drama with a series of humiliations. *"Here's the address of a pay-to-play gallery." "Try the county fair—they show children's art." "Have you consider crafts or handiwork?"*

At the time, my lawyer was securing the tee shirt merchandising rights to these catchy insults. Oh well, ashes to ashes...

What excited me most was the spin-off potential. (Ka-ching. Ka-ching.) To satisfy the hungry market for cruel fraud and humiliation, we'd produce a similar show featuring mid-career artists in their late thirties.

Unfortunately, at that crucial contractual moment, with the Mont Blanc hovering over gold-embossed onionskin, I thought I felt a spider in my collar. The heebie-jeebies sent me into a spastic fit that alarmed the network elite. I tried to pass it off as the latest dance craze. I *should* have said it was an Ecstasy flashback. Sadly, I wasn't smooth enough to save myself.

As they say on the Westside, the deal went South.

As a consolation, the Suits offered me a job as the art curator of the studio commissary. I politely declined; I already work for minimum wage.

142

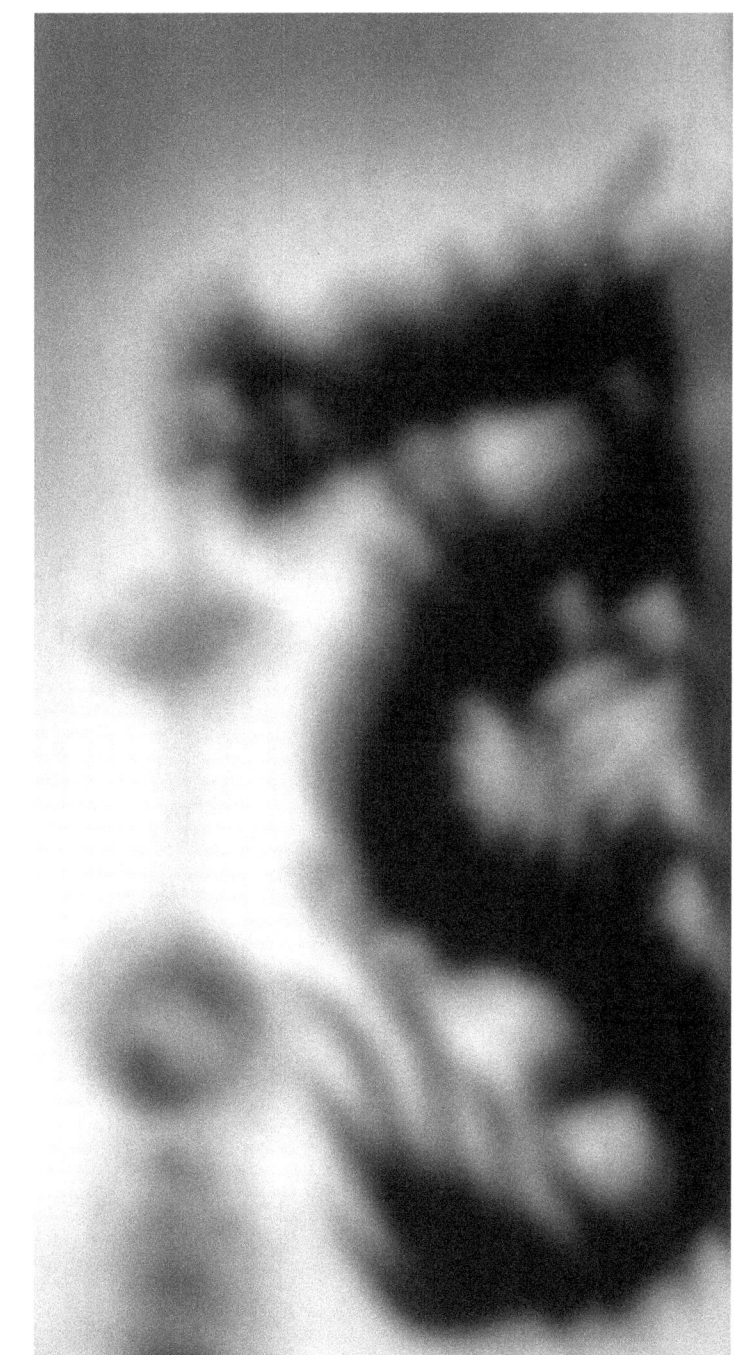

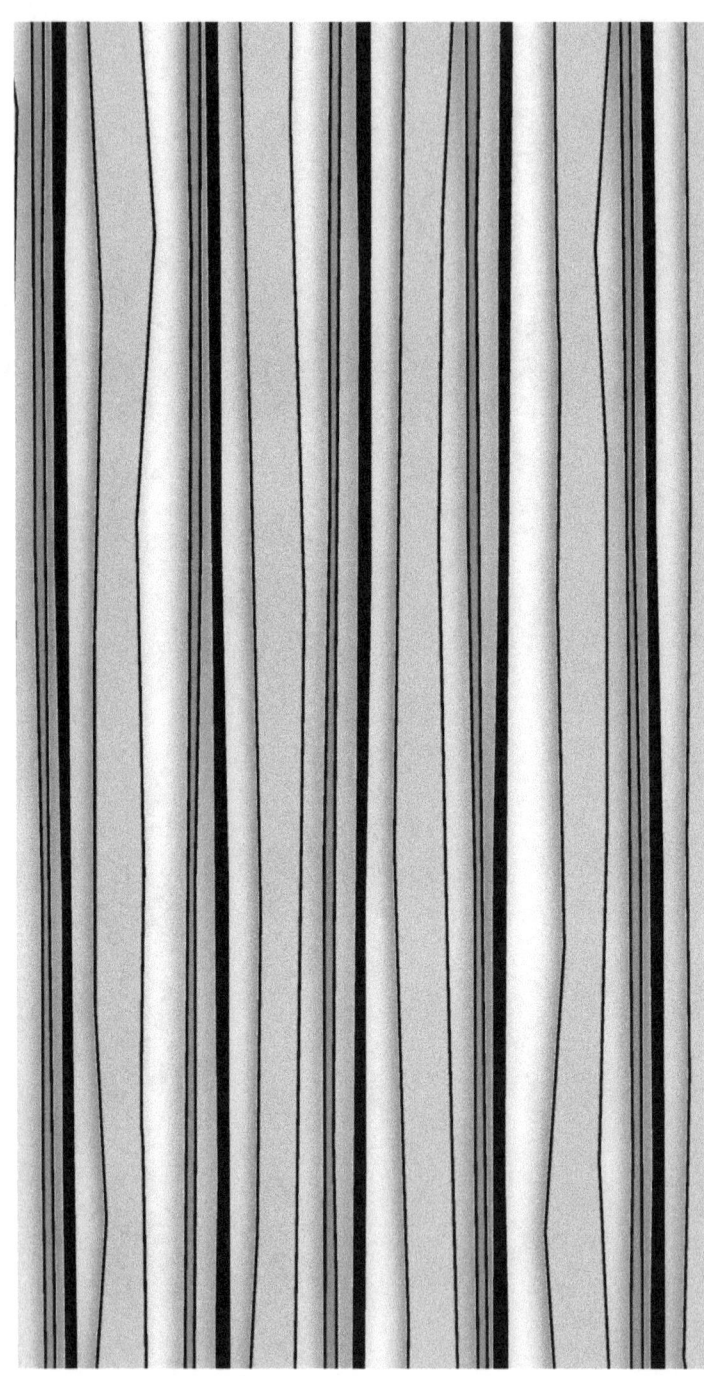

GUNG-HO! HELL, NO!

Artists are always looking for traction. Diamonds are a product of pressure.

If I hadn't grabbed onto the easel, I would have fallen on my ass. Suddenly the rough wood floor in my studio is as slippery as ice. It's so bad that I can't cross the room without doing a full arm-waving, leg-flying pratfall. Then you add a tray of cocktails and the screwball ramps up a notch.

You see, a new series of art has contributed to the need for major changes in the current lifestyle curriculum. I want to try something tricky. To make the artwork, I've gotta be in a top form physically, emotionally and intellectually.

I'm going for the big fish. I'm tackling the questions that mankind has pondered for the last 4,000 years. *Why are we here? What is the Meaning of Life?*

Gordy Grundy

While the work involves many issues, the piece is ultimately about Redemption. This is a subject I prefer to regard through film and literature. *Other* people's hardship, struggle and strife are better read than endured.

For this artwork, I have to *participate* in the Redemption. This is in contrast to my current comfort.

For the piece, this lover needs the discipline of a NAVY Seal. That's why the floor is so slippery. I'm afraid to be all I can be.

The ship is leaving the dock, which is why I am having separation anxiety. The tie lines have been released and thrown onto the deck. The anchor is raised. I have left a steady life to follow an unclear and improbable path. There is no turning back. And in this moment of terror, I am paddling furiously against the current, which is pulling my schooner toward the falls of inevitability.

I know why I am resisting change. The blanket that I had was awfully comfy; I really hate to let that go.

Then toss in a fear of failure and one of success. That's a panicky stew.

I guess terror is part of the process. The new adventure involves a skill set that I believe I possess.

Nothing on the horizon appears insurmountable. What's the problem?

The roar of the falls is getting louder as I rush toward the edge.

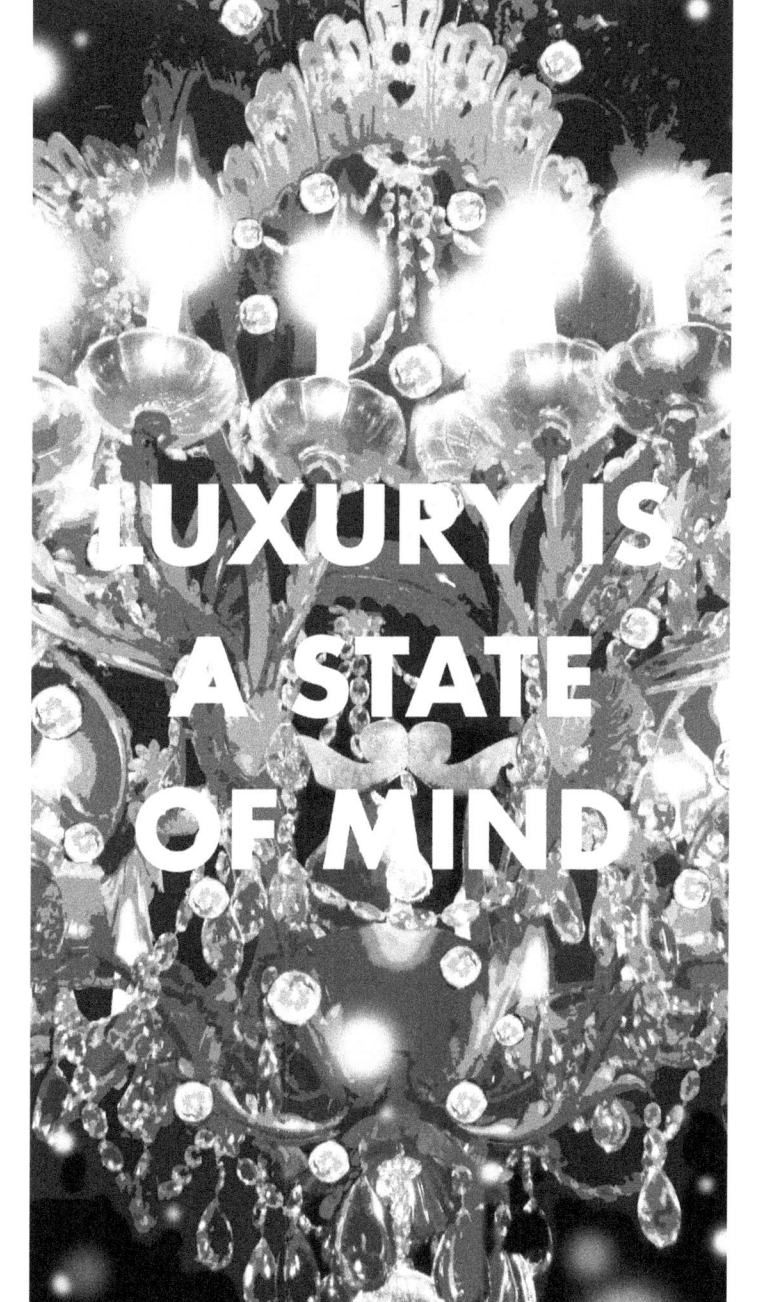

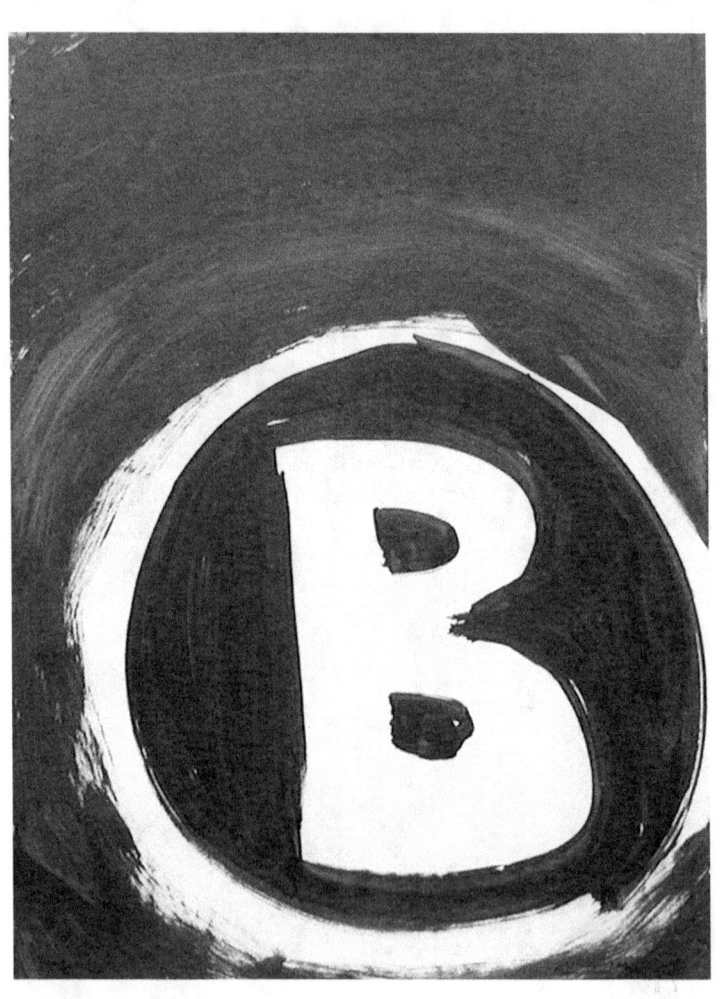

BETTER THAN

"Gong Long?" I asked.

"Yes," confirmed my Transcendentalist, "Gong Long."

I had just given the white robed monk, Hu Non Furst, an offering of a basket of fresh fruit. In return he gave me a mantra, 'Gong Long.'

I wasn't sure if I liked it. It was supposed to clear my mind, but all I could think of was a football pass play.

I asked for another mantra. He objected. The ceremony degenerated rather quickly. Long story short, I ended up wearing some fruit and he ended up with the wicker basket around his neck.

I needed a new mantra.

A LITTLE RELIGION

We all need a little religion.

Mine is a moment, where I try to find a little

peace and a connection to everything around me. Call it prayer or chanting, church or chill.

I am finding my religion. Every day brings another revelation. I mean, the room can't get any brighter. But I'd like a little shade. I am learning so much, so fast, that my transcendence feels like skydiving. I've *gotta* relax and you can't mellow without a mantra.

TRIPLE AAA MANTRA

A mantra can be an unintelligible word, a concrete idea, or a vague notion. It can even be an action.

Some say a mantra should be given to you. As I was waiting for mine, I had a few ideas on what makes a good one.

1) A good mantra should be universal, something that all creeds and cultures can sink their teeth into. It must be a truth that has no room for debate or bloodshed.

2) It has to be simple, so you can remember it. A 'Triple A' Mantra should stay in the headlights.

3) There should be a pleasure principle. It's gotta feel better than it hurts; the heaven should outweigh the hell.

4) This moment, this prayer, chill or chant, must be convenient and fast.

I have a problem with the Islamic prayer schedule. Five times a day is redundant, a real time-killer and hard to schedule around, especially during the cocktail hour.

Conversely, the old Christian *once-a-week* is a long time between a good idea.

5) Enlightenment should be time and cost effective. Tom Barrack, the surfer/real estate king, speaks of

a "Karma Bank." My mantra has gotta be a direct deposit.

6) And it's gotta be cheap. *I'm an artist for God's sake.* With the high cost of DSL, wartime and greenhouse gases, I really can't afford anything like the Mormon Commission, the Episcopal Clip or the Pre-Tax Tithe. Plus, there's my bartender to consider.

BETTER THAN

There I was, a man in need of a mantra. Suddenly, just when I needed it most, *Luck* graced me with one.

One morning, just before I woke up, Rey Ray made a special guest star appearance in a dream. He had a walk-on, without dialogue.

Rey Ray was my best pal's great-uncle. King Ray was a family man, congenial and hard working. I had a great fondness for him. And respect, for he served bravely in the Second World War. Ray was always great to me. We both shared the love of a cold beer and a hot tamale.

I can't remember the context of the dream, but I remember that I was standing on the deck of a burning galleon. I looked up and saw Rey Ray on the quarterdeck. Rubbing his round belly, the old man looked around, saw me and smiled.

Johnny Cash wrote a soulful ballad called 'A Satisfied Mind.' Rey Ray had the grin of a man with a satisfied mind. He winked, raised his arms and flew into the night sky.

A little later, I woke up with the feeling that everything was gonna be OK. To see Rey Ray, I was re-

Gordy Grundy

minded of a Life Lesson that I had learned from him. His sentiment would become my mantra.

I remembered, at his funeral several years back, Rey Ray's daughter recalled the rigors of a typical family picnic. Once they arrived at the park, big daddy Rey Ray would command all of his kids and a couple dozen cousins to clean up the area. It's hard to enjoy the beauty of nature when you are looking at someone else's trash. (At a picnic, I'd rather deal with hungry ants, but these days you better look out for used condoms, spent shell casings, or rusty heroin needles.)

Naturally, the kids chafed at the chore, but they understood that a clean camp made their picnic more enjoyable.

The real mutiny began when the day was done and the car was loaded. Rey Ray told the kids to clean up the campsite, *again*. A cranky chorus protested the *injustice*. *Why tidy up when we are cutting out?* The kids wisely argued that, "they were leaving a place as they had found it." But Rey Ray didn't see it that way.

He commanded the kids that they would leave the place *better* than they had found it.

What a frame of mind! This is the mantra I had been looking for. *Better Than*. It even has a whiff of elitism.

Rey Ray loved people. If we leave *everywhere* we go *better* than we found it, then why not do the same for *people?*

Better Than is beauty, symmetry and function. It's egalitarian. It's not limited to five times a day.

If I live *Better Than* and treat people *Better Than*, I might even stop kicking the dog. If you can pull it off over an *entire* day, you are practically guaranteed Life's greatest reward, a Good Night's Sleep. The Karma Bank would overflow.

Unfortunately, like anything worthwhile, it requires some courage and purposeful thinking.

A tidy little package, *Better Than* is an attitude with clear purpose. I want to leave everywhere I go, better than I found it. I want to leave everyone I meet, better for the encounter.

'Better Than,' it could even end wars.

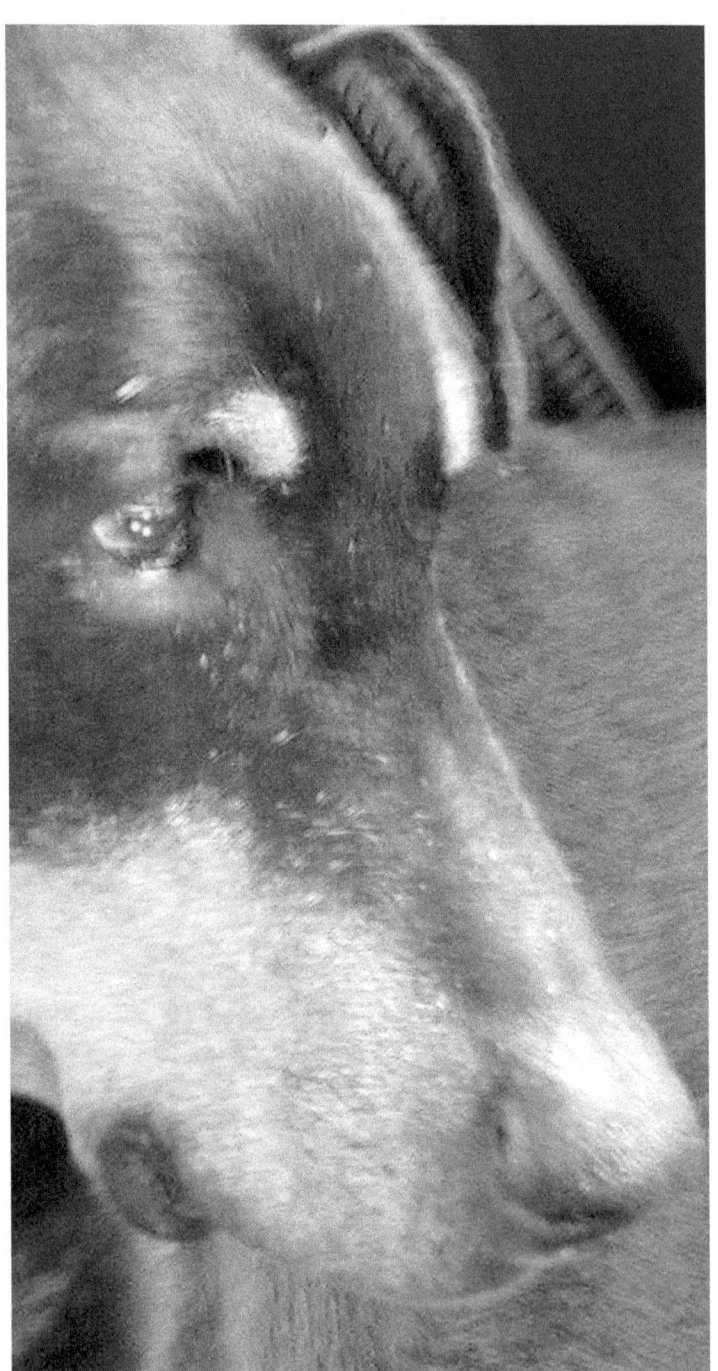

GUTTED

I just put my dog down.

When I returned home, alone, from the veterinarian, I found a small present waiting for me on the front porch. It was a dead white mouse with big round ears lying in small pool of blood. It had been killed but not mauled.

So far that morning I'd been playing it reasonably brave, but upon discovering the gift, I lost it. I started to sob. That dead mouse was the sweetest and most thoughtful gesture a calico cat has ever given me.

The multi-billion dollar dog care industry tends to focus their advertising on the cute puppy or the canine middle-aged best friend. They don't tell you about living with an old dog. It's not easy. It's a lotta work. But I can now say I'm an expert in carpet care.

On the whole, I am not so fond of the human animal and I prefer to avoid them as much as I can. Other breeds are not as cruel, irrational or petty.

155

Gordy Grundy

Needless to say, my dobie Din and I were close. For thirteen years, we'd been best pals. (Gunga) Din was handsome, spry and he walked with an elegant gait. His big floppy ears seemed to have a life of their own and I miss them the most. He was an Art Dog; the back of his head was usually stained with paint.

The long decision to end my best friend's life was heart breaking, soul searing and gut wrenching. Enough said.

An old dog complicates your daily life and kills your social one.

My last houseguest was nine months ago. When we rolled home, I was obviously pre-occupied as hands were flying.

Maybe I should have better explained the situation to Din or given him more attention, but the dog got jealous and pondered his revenge.

An hour later, happy as one can ever be, I danced out of the bedroom to mix more cocktails... There are some situations you just can't play.

I haven't slept well. For the last nine months, I have been harassed by a rather large rat. Around 3:30 every morning, this behemoth climbs inside the wall behind my headboard and into the attic, where it slaps on a pair of Army Boots. Then he does winds sprints for six to ten minutes. It jogs just long enough to wake-me-wide, a guarantee that I will miss the last train back to Slumberland.

Regardless, there is no point in going back to sleep because in a short while the dog will wake and the real tension begins. From 4:40 on, he will get up every fifteen minutes, hipbones creaking and collar tags tinkling, to stand next to my bed.

He wants one of three things: 1) to check on me, 2) to be petted or 3) to be let outside for business. The first two are sweet; the third is a nightmare. Whereas some animals may bark their desire, mine chooses to communicate psychically. He'll just stare at me, expressionless. It is very hard to interpret these subtle signals that can lead to very dire consequences.

Thus begins the pas de deux. I leap out of bed and open the front door. He snorts, laughs at me, and nine times out of ten, trots back into the bedroom. But as I have learned, you can never be too careful. Trust me, an animal accident on white carpet really *does* ruin your entire day.

When the rat started to invite friends over for early morning relay races, I took on the problem *mano y mano*. Spring traps and sticky glue trays were set and poisons placed.

Until I caught a glimpse of it.

The rat was no ten-pounder with mottled fur and a razor sharp sneer. In truth, my nemesis was a cute little white mouse with a long slender body and big round ears. My killing instinct vanished and the campaign to defend my household ended.

Frankly, living with an elderly dog, I was grateful to get the early warning mouse call.

As we age, so must our expressions of love. In a dog's hearty youth, you can slap 'em around and roughhouse with affection. But in their old age, when a dog is nothing but skin over old bones, you need to caress them gently. You have to be aware of tender spots and aching hips. Plus, if a dog is deaf like mine, it's easy to

157

scare them.

Not so long ago, I came home to find my old pal asleep on the porch. Glad to see him, I sat down on the stairs looking for a little sugar.

I guess if I were deaf, sound asleep and someone tried to rub my ass, I would have done the same thing.

My old pal whipped around with the speed of a teenager and snapped two big fangs into my palm. Not planning on pain, I flew toward the ceiling as the wild-eyed animal bit into an index finger. As I rolled past him, tumbling down the stairs, I could see that he was already feeling guilty.

Ya can't blame the dog. My knee is no longer black and blue and the scars are tattoos that I will always cherish.

Last Fall, showing signs of senility, he suddenly refused to come into the house, even during the long rains and bad weather. I was insulted, hurt and put out.

Actually, I was grateful and so was the carpet. I didn't have to go to IKEA every other day.

I had gotten tired of friends asking, "Have you tried doggie diapers?" To which I'd reply, "Who takes them off?"

Then there were the sensitive friends with a loving point of view. "Shit in the house?! *Put the dog down!*"

While Din was camping outdoors for three months, he made friends and created a little menagerie. There was the skanky squirrel with the threadbare tail and a wild cat with the sweetest little voice.

The squirrel stayed aloof but the gray striped feline moved in, sleeping on the porch with the old dog. Everyone needs someone to kiss or hiss at.

Then, suddenly last Christmas, Din decided to move back inside.

The cat, his friend, hung around. And still does.

Knowing the dog would die at home, I had saved a fancy old bedspread, cardinal with embroidered gold detail, to be used as a shroud. The other morning, I draped the royal blanket over the seat of my truck and I carried my best pal to his berth.

It was time.

The question of 'when' had caused me much anxiety. What is too soon? Where is too late? The loving advice I was given proved correct, "You'll just know." I woke up that morning and I knew.

The ride to the vet was a killer. Din rested his head on the center console and looked up at me with his big eyes and long lashes. I smiled because the perspective made his huge nose look even bigger.

Not wanting to slobber or linger, I had pre-paid over the phone.

When I called, the vet said the place was empty. When I arrived, there were five busy puppies waiting for their first shots and five new owners who each got the 'New Puppy' speech.

Life can stand still but Death has a schedule.

The wait in the lobby felt like an eternity. The stiff upper lip of my grief, a reservoir ready to breach the dam, began to stew and boil into anger. *How long do I have to sit here? How dare you keep us waiting! Can't you see I'm here to kill my dog, you motherfuckers?* My nostrils were flaring and the upper lip was curling into a snarl.

Damn, I don't love often, but I love hard.

As I slowly stood on shaky legs, ready to unleash

159

my hounds of hell, a nurse appeared and said, "Mr. Grundy, we have a room for you."

Over the last nine months, much to my surprise, a greater wisdom has been influencing my life. I have begun to see small details that evidence the connectedness and the eternity of all things.

I don't believe in doggy heaven but I do know that when my dog was lonely, a cat came to befriend him. I do know that, in my despondency, the cat gutted the little white mouse that kept me awake and presented it on my doorstep as a gift.

Now I'm ready for a quiet, good night's sleep.

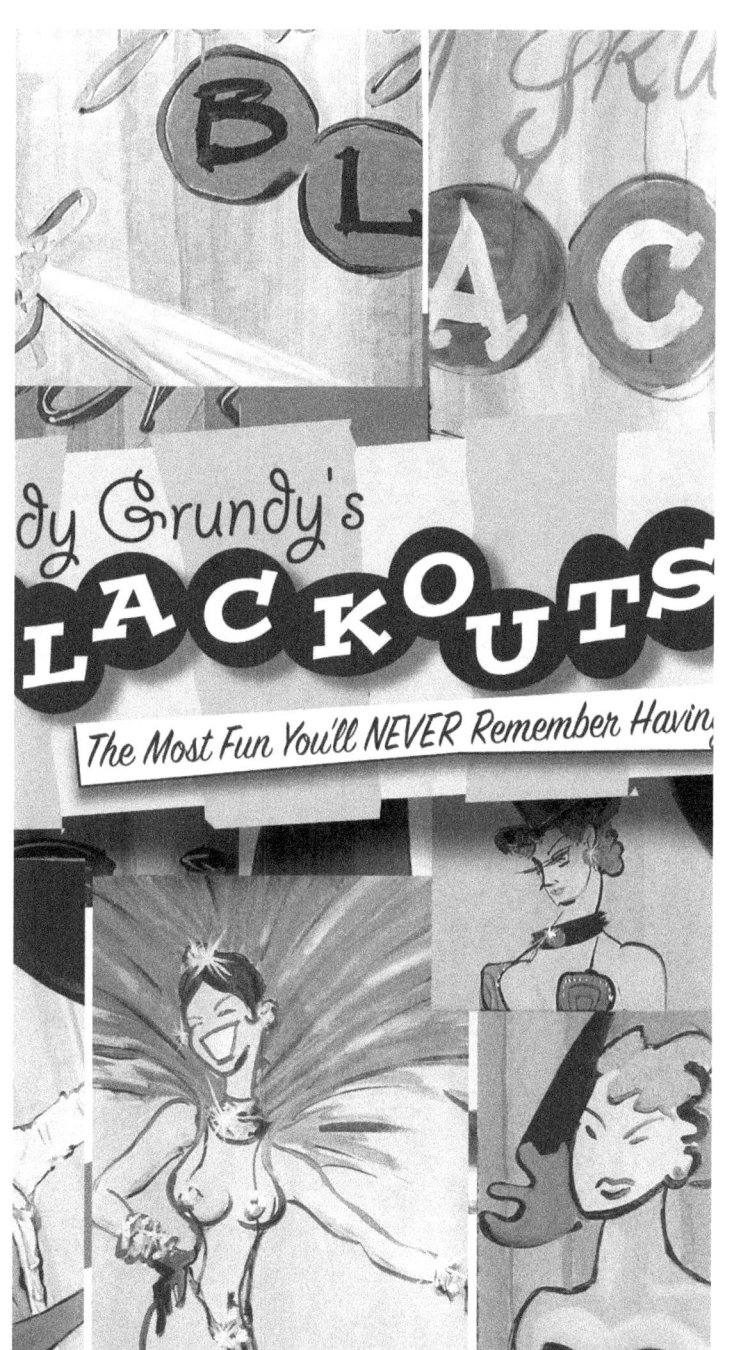

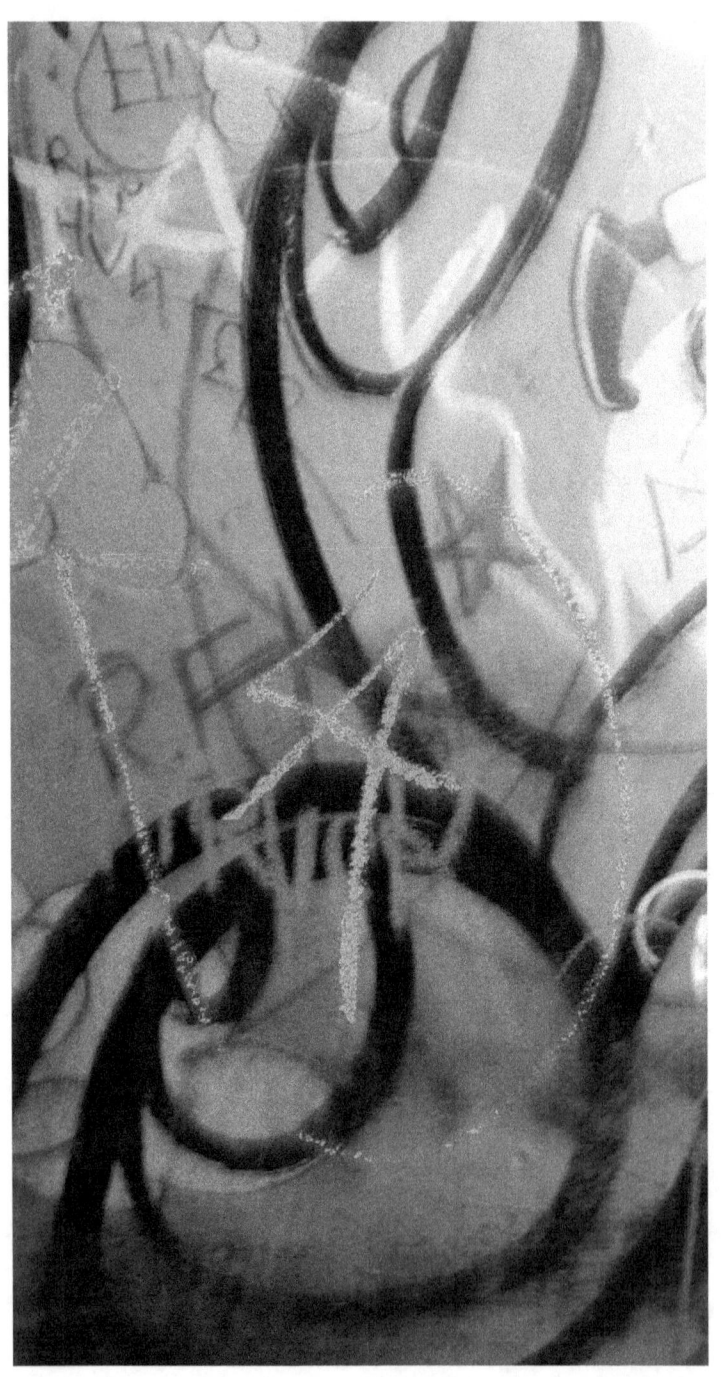

MY YEAR IN PURGATORY

FOUR FLAT TIRES

I don't have the energy to lift the chalk in my hand and mark another day on the invisible cell wall. My Year in Purgatory is about to end, but I can summon no joy. The Man has turned this sunny optimist into a militant Nihilist with a terrorist's sensibility.

My refusal to take a Chemical Test at the suggestion of the Los Angeles Police Department had automatically revoked my driver's license for an entire year.

Hell is having no money in New York City, no escape from the Midwest or no driver's license in Los Angeles.

CAR KULTURE

I am a native Southern Californian; if given the

163

choice between having sex, breathing or driving a car, I'd take the highway. For me, every concept of freedom, happiness and well-being rides upon black rubber. Like perfume, splash a little motor oil behind your ear and this wolf will howl.

Without a car, my spirit cannot fly.

CLIPPED

Obediently, I went through the many tortures of my punishment with the dignity of a Gentleman. I bore my burden with responsibility and great remorse. If the revocation of my driver's license had been for six months, my lesson would have been learned and a man rehabilitated. But the grinding hell continued and my remorse canker'd into indignant rage.

Now my angry red palette is bleeding muddy gray. Time has dulled my sharp anger. Like the captain of a schooner frozen in an Arctic flow, I can't tell if the snapping-crackling sound is the ice breaking apart to set me free, or if it's the sound of my hull crushing under the pressure. My bartender thinks it's the latter.

This ordeal has taken the oxygen from my bright light and the flame fights for survival. When the next person brightly quips, "Your year'll be over in no time!" I will gleefully kick their teeth in. I can summon the energy for that.

FERRIS BUELLER IS DEAD

When life throws lemons, I make a Tequila Sour. It has been one of my greatest talents, not only to make the best of a bad situation, but like all artists, to do it with effortless style. This time, I have failed. Miserably.

JEEVES IS DEAD

Sometimes you get lucky. Faced with the destruction of my car and my driver's license, I was forced to quit my day job, which was located thirty-nine miles to the South. Public transportation was not a possibility for logistical and aesthetic reasons. The train and bus ride would add five to six hours of living hell to the commute.

Worst of all, it would devour my time to paint. Time is an artist's most precious asset.

My employer, not wanting to lose his brightest star, said that he would buy me a driver. I was shocked by this generosity, especially from a man who makes us inventory our paperclips at the end of the day and save our pencil shavings for kindling. Obviously, I had been taken off Double Secret Probation and was favored once again. I wasn't special, just economical. It's cheaper for him to buy a driver than to lose me.

Most people read the "Jeeves" stories with laughter; I read them with envy. The series of hilarious tales by P.G. Wodehouse involve the antics of a trust fund ne'er-do-well and his Christ-like butler Jeeves. Since I don't have a trust fund nor even the promise of one, I read of Jeeves with my jaw locked and my fists clenched. Long have I wanted a butler by my side, someone to haul my ass around, rescue me from unfortunate scrapes and untie the knots of my many romantic entanglements.

Now Jeeves would be mine. For free.

Gordy Grundy

SHOPPING DOMESTICALLY

I immediately called a Beverly Hills domestic service called A Lovely Shade of Green Card and placed my order.

Chalmers, my new hire, was perfect. Well-educated in all aspects of criminal law, he was an expert French chef, held a gun permit and mixed a Martini as if he had invented them. Above all, he ironed my shirts beautifully.

Unfortunately, Chalmers did not last.

When I handed my boss the bill, the gin blossoms on his nose went from vermillion to purple. He pointed out rather loudly that Chalmers's hourly wage was eight times more than mine. Without opening the closed door, he removed me from his office. Through the gaping hole, my boss screamed that we would now be *splitting* the cost of a driver.

Chalmers, who had been waiting in the outer office, pulled me to my feet. With his little whiskbroom that always magically appeared, he brushed the wood chips and splinters from my jacket.

I brushed the tears from my eyes. Chalmers had to go.

THE ECONOMICS OF HIRED HELP

I rarely have economic issues because this painter rarely has money. To afford the cost of a domestic meant that my search had to segue from Beverly Hills, where they are employed, to the impoverished part of town, where they live. Conveniently, this also happens to be the same neighborhood that I call home.

166

With due haste, I ran around the barrio with a staple gun. Colorful fliers with little tear-off phone numbers sprang up in laundromats, coffeehouses, taco stands and power poles.

I placed the phone next to my bed and waited for the cavalcade of calls. They did not come.

It was a surprise to me. Apparently, it's *impossible* to find someone who is well-educated in all aspects of criminal law, an expert French chef, holds a gun permit and mixes a Martini as if he had invented them for $5.50 per hour.

I rewrote the job requirements: "Must have license. Hygiene a plus."

HOT WHEELS

Now that the hiring was under way, I had to contend with the issue of what the driver would be driving. The car salesman, a former art dealer, assured me that I had found a good deal on a new stretch limousine. It was a beaut. The king-sized trunk was so big I could stack my canvases vertically.

The next day my employer informed me that he had agreed to split the cost of the driver, *not* the car. He broke a crown when he mashed, "Get out!"

I didn't need to use the handle; I crawled through the preexisting hole in the door.

With the limo budget shot down, I lowered my standards to a Lincoln Town Car. It was black and quite formal, appropriate to the lofty self-delusion that is my station in life.

Unfortunately, status would soon give way to

167

practicality. It always pays to have friends in low places. A gallerist with a proficiency in criminal behavior took me aside and advised that inexpensive and low key is better than flashy and high profile when one is on probation.

Suddenly faced with a deluge of legal fees and no umbrella, I concurred. I needed to look for cheaper wheels.

Salvation came from a little old lady in Pasadena. An ancient, camouflage creme Buick Park Avenue was pristine, cheap and *mine*. I accessorized the bumper with a "What Would Jesus Do?" decal and added a D.A.R.E. sticker for balance. I was undercover. Sacrificing style, I became invisible with leather interior.

HELL ON WHEELS

No one remotely plausible had responded to my flier campaign. Maybe there's been a run on drivers in my area? Was I offering too little money? Hell, I wasn't asking to see a Green Card.

I was getting desperate.

I hired Pepito on the spot, without a thought. He spoke legible English and he wanted the job. In my rush to find someone after interviewing a parade of misfits, I forgot to ask if he could drive.

Later I learned there was a problem with peripheral vision that did not allow him to see minor details such as a semi-truck or a speeding moving van.

The constant near misses gave me such a cardio-vascular workout that I no longer needed the gym. My right leg grew more muscular than the left from constantly pumping an imaginary brake pedal. I was sweating so much that my dry cleaning bill tripled.

I learned to accept my mortality.

At the Home of the Rolled Taco, he smashed into a concrete wall. At the Magic Gas Station, he backed into the side of a neighbor's car. The dents and craters on the Buick began to multiply. If there was a deep pothole, Pepito would find it.

Between the mindless chatter devoted to Christina Aguilara, a donkey-bray laugh and the near-death experiences, I found it best to close my eyes and feign sleep. This is very hard to do when your head is slamming against the window like a cork in a storm.

After four months, proud Pepito quit with indignation when he overheard a friend ask, "How's your houseboy?"

FREAKS ON WHEELS

It has become an ebb and flow of new faces.

PeeWee, Driver Number Two, was shell-shocked from an earlier accident and preferred the slow lane.

I thought I was trading up when I hired slacker Napoleon, who horrified my co-workers by stealing candy from the honor bar. Dude, not cool. This guy was so slack, he expected me to drive.

Blunted behind the wheel, dreadlocked Kush Kojo preferred two lanes to one.

Sweet Sue Lynn was a dairy fresh arrival from the Midwest. The redhead was a former stripper, which made her aces with my friends. She quit in order to follow her much discussed dream of becoming a pop star, music video director *and* Academy Award winning producer.

Stinky delivered every detail of his recovery from alcohol in a very dull and repetitive monotone. When I stopped paying attention, he would flip the radio to the all Metallica station. We fought for control of the dial.

Giggling PeeWee was rehired and kept on, out of desperation. Blithely preferring his schedule to mine, PeeWee didn't have much to say, which pleased me greatly, but the heavily scented hand lotion turned my stomach. Now, any whiff of Calvin Klein triggers a queasy flashback. Frustration peaked with his talent for wandering off; I'd find the car in the parking lot but it took half an hour to find PeeWee.

A SLAVE TO THE ROAD

Not only an influence, these people dominate and control my life. I am as dependent upon them as a blind man relies on the eyes of his dog.

HELL HAS CONVENIENT, UNDERGROUND PARKING

They've beaten me. I can't take it anymore. I can't get out of bed. My rage against The Man and his machine has now decayed into utter resignation and complete resentment. With two long and dreary months to go, I don't think I can make it.

Already a drooling catatonic, I've had to hire

Sportos Khan, Driver Number Thirteen, to write this essay for me.

DEAD END

WWJD? What would Jeeves do?

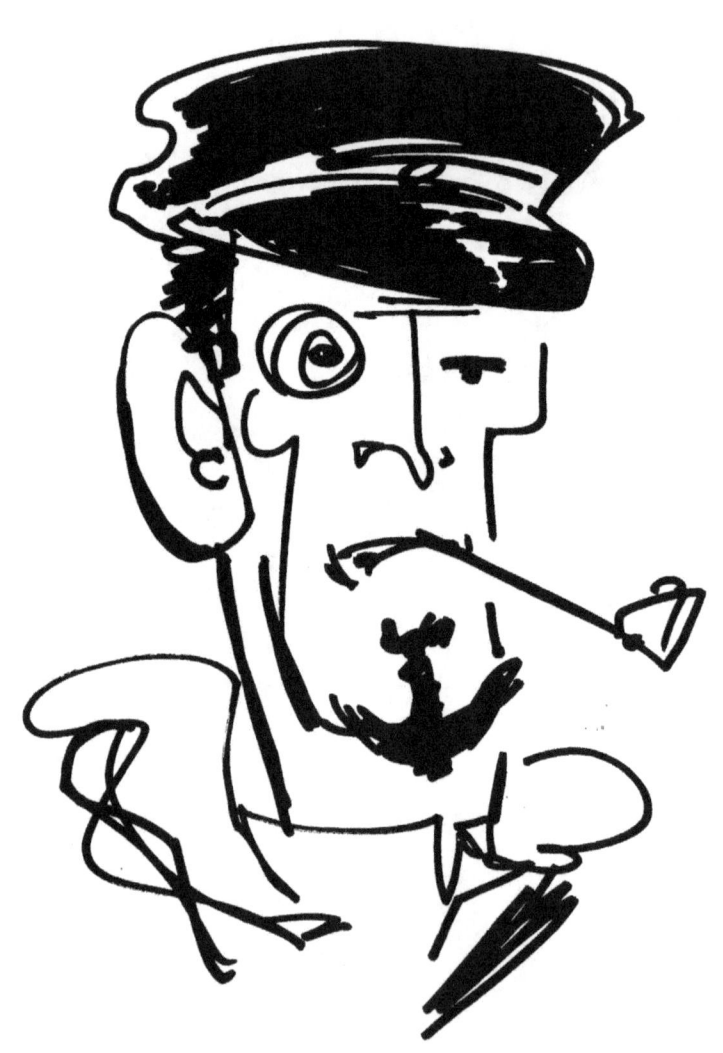

CAPTAIN AHAB
THE ARTIST

I love a good mystery-thriller. One of my fa-
vorite hobbies is Wild Life Forensics. It really beats the
hell out of scrimshaw, knot tied sculpture or model boat
building in a bottle.

You can call me Marlowe, or better yet, Nick
Charles.

Wild Life Forensics is the practice of reassem-
bling a jigsaw of clues to solve the mystery and determine what you did the night before.

Who was I with? Where did I go? Where's the
front bumper of my car? How did I get that bruise? Why
is there blood on my fist? Who trailed lipstick from my
collar to my shirttail?

Some cases can be easily solved with a phone call
to a friend or the black and white of a police report.
Others prove elusive, a conundrum of sketchy clues and
hazy witnesses.

Gordy Grundy

Unleash the Hounds of Baskerville! Another mystery is afoot! Since the recent Solo Debut, I haven't been kissing puppies and whistling at the sunny blue above. I've been behaving badly and acting out. I've had a weird obsession with Captain Ahab, but I don't know why.

After canvassing the neighborhood twice, the Wildlife Forensics Investigation has yielded the following results:

It seems to be the same story, night after night. Possibly a recurring hyper reality of some sort.

The house I rent has a deck and a long view. Posts stand like tall masts supporting a sail of corrugated roofing. According to witnesses, it seems that I stand against the rail (or gunwale), my hands clasped behind my back, and stare sullenly at the far horizon. My body is generally pitched forward as if leaning into a gale, my legs splayed for high seas. I mutter silently between sips of grog from a pewter stein.

This would explain the many empty rum bottles scattered around the deck.

Later, as the North Star edges its smaller cousins across the sky, my stoicism erupts in youthful energy and swashbuckling derring-do. I climb to the highest rooftop crow's nest so that I can shake my fist closer at God.

"Thar she blows!" breaks the gloom and the deck becomes a beehive of activity. Harpoons, launched into the sea of a city below, take the form of brooms, bottles and boorish houseguests.

Oddly enough, the adventure ends precisely at 4:20AM, a time well noted by the neighbors.

It isn't the usual cacophony of screaming laughter, overlit song and breaking glass that wakes them; they are used to that. It was the unearthly growl that com-manded, "Bring me the Great White Whale!"

Several witnesses say I sound just like Gregory Peck.

We were able to close "The Case of the Ahab Obsession" without firing a shot. It seems the odd be-havior was caused by PASB (Post Art Show Blues), com-mon among fine artists. It's that funk that generally fol-lows an art show, when high expectations collide with harsh reality.

There is a great white whale in every artist's life. Every artist wants to make a living off the fruits of their work. It is a modest yet highly improbable goal; it is our Moby Dick.

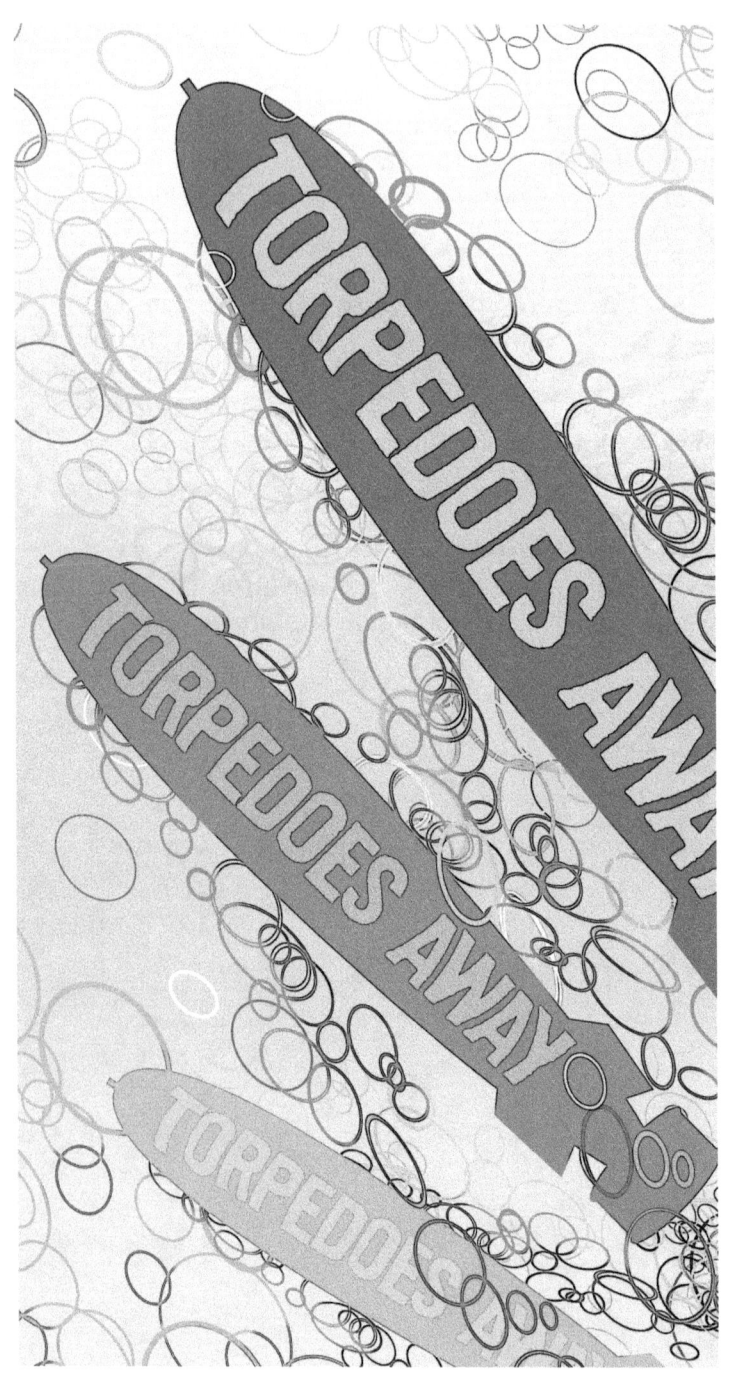

SOUTH OF SURREAL, PART TWO

LINGO

"mahi mahi" \ma-hee ma-hee\ *adj., vb.* -mahi mahi-'d, a: describes the fish-like flip-flopping one does when sleep is much desired yet remains frustratingly elusive; b: generally refers to a time period near dawn; c: *"I mahi mahi'd all night."*
(Courtesy of Stu Gimlet.)

REAL LIFE SLAPSTICK

My pal Michael is an artist. He day-jobs as an instructor for a nonprofit wildlife group. He takes animals to schools and teaches the kids about conservation.

Gordy Grundy

Recently, Michael stood before a junior high science class in South Central Los Angeles with a poodle-sized opossum cuddled around his arm. He was explaining the nocturnal habits of this long snouted, half blind marsupial to an overcrowded classroom of fresh eager faces. Without provocation, the cute ball of gray fur dug into Michael's forearm with one of its fifty wolf-sized, razor sharp teeth. (Did you know that they bite like a sewing machine?)

The good students, who stood up front, were instantly covered with arterial spray. The teacher, who was counting the minutes to her next cigarette break, screamed, threw her magazine into the air and ran out of the room.

If pandemonium was king, chaos was queen.

The girls shrieked liked girls. The puberty-plagued boys screamed like girls. Stoned since the mid-morning break, the "C and D" students lingering in the back were the first to scatter and make a beeline to the door.

Everybody fanned out. Wide-eyed students backed themselves against the chalkboard and slowly edged their way toward the door. Others flew out the windows.

Anything to escape another quirk of nature.

Michael suddenly found himself standing alone, bleeding profusely, with an opossum dangling from his arm.

Not only did the children learn about nature, they also got a lesson in First Aid. Michael the lionheart went on to teach four more classes.

BLOOD-LETTING

Has blood stained your clothing? I got a tip from a costume designer. Did you know that the enzymes in your saliva will eliminate your blood stains from an article of clothing? (Your enzymes will not work on my blood stain and vice versa.)

Take that to the dry cleaners.

THE ARTIST'S EPILOGUE

Artists labor long and hard against great odds. Our only revenge is to make it all look easy.

IT MEANS SOMETHING TO SOMEONE

"...when surfwear meets snobwear..."

TOO MUCH FUN

There is nothing like that great feeling when everything swings your way. When the sun warms your side of the street. When the wallet is plump. When a hand pats your back. When friends become family. When all cylinders are sparking.

There is no sweeter high.

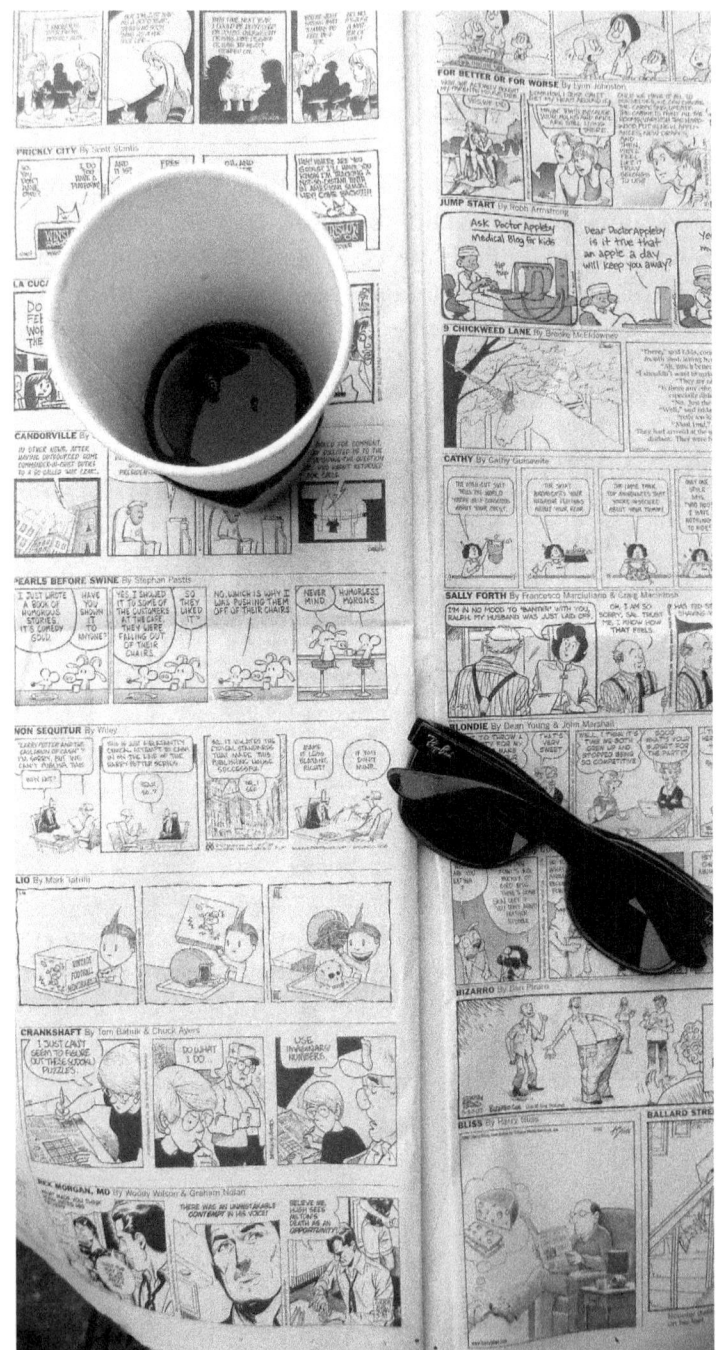

THE KID

I'd been looking for the kid for two solid weeks. Actually, I felt like I had been chasing him for a lifetime. He had run away so many times that finding him had become a semi-permanent gig. In my line of work, repeat business is hard to come by. His parents paid well therefore I'm always available 24/7.

This time I was walking the mean streets of Los Angeles, looking for him, but instead, as usual, he found me.

I was working downtown LA on a hunch, crossing Seventh at Hope Street when the flying brick grazed my shoulder and exploded on the sidewalk in front of me. A week ago, the Newport-Inglewood Fault line, an artery of the San Andreas, had rattled everyone's eyeteeth. The ground was still cutting loose every ten minutes. Flying bricks were not unusual. The city was still shaking off building parts like a wet dog. An umbrella wouldn't save you from the prevailing rain of mortar, glass and granite.

Gordy Grundy

The flying brick had shredded the shoulder of my trench coat. Fresh blood indicated that the new suit underneath hadn't fared any better. It was too soon for my shoulder to hurt; shock is a lovely painkiller.

If that brick had been three inches to the northwest, my head would look like somebody's carnitas plate.

I looked up, afraid I'd see a gargoyle or a bare-breasted building ornament following the brick. Instead, I saw the kid standing on the forty-fourth floor ledge of a Beaux Arts building. It was hard to see that far up, but it looked like he was winding up with another brick and my head was his bulls-eye. I guess you could say the kid and I have always had an adversarial relationship.

Suddenly something was heading my way and gaining in volume. I danced left as green glass exploded where I had been standing. It was a Heineken forty-ouncer. I reminded myself to tell the kid it wasn't a good habit to drink so early in the day.

Like I said, we have a long relationship and this wasn't the first time the kid had tried to kill me. He goes AWOL, his handlers fret and I get hired to find him. The kid gets around. I've chased him on more than one continent and in countless cities. I don't get thanks; I get bruises. Or another brick aimed at my head.

My landlord is the real problem. He likes his rent on the first of every month. If it weren't for him, I wouldn't bother with the kid or any other notion. Responsibility, three meals and a warm bed are funny things. They're powerful incentives.

But it's even more than that. My bartender says that if I don't catch the kid, my own well-being will die. If I don't find him, if I don't bring him in, nothing will work out.

There will be no future salvation.

Normally, I wouldn't choose to run up a flight of forty-four floors but the constant aftershocks had me a little willy about construction standards. That and a blackout had rendered the elevator unavailable.

Naturally, the stairwell door on the forty-fourth and the forty-fifth was blocked with more debris than I could heft so I climbed to the roof, figuring I could work my way down.

From a tall building, the Los Angeles horizon is pretty spectacular. The Pacific lies to the West and the South. Mountains border the East and in between, block size fires dot the suburban sprawl. Below me, downtown is half the metropolis it used to be. The 'tallest building on the West coast' is no longer. With most buildings pancake'd, the record is once again held by the iconic City Hall.

The funny thing about the quake is that Gehry's Disney Concert Hall has been realigned into a series of perfect right angles.

There he was, sitting on the ledge two floors below me, looking out over the smoldering cityscape. His little legs were swinging lazily as if he had a sing-along song in his head. He was smoking a cigarette. Half of a six-pack sat beside him. He took a sip of beer and never took his eyes off the remixed landscape.

I yelled down to the kid. A tick of his head let me know that I had surprised him. He ignored me nonetheless. He just stared forward but his little legs had stopped swinging.

He seemed lost, with an aura of melancholy, like he was swimming in his own little Sea of Eternal Sadness. His little slumped shoulders hung low, as if bearing the weight of too much of the world.

I could sympathize with the little guy.

I shouted to him.

He ignored me again.

Then he stood and stretched, arms wide, as if he were shaking it off. I couldn't see all of his face but he suddenly looked happier, even mischievous. A look of invincibility. Of purpose. Like a man on top of his world.

I didn't feel the building tremble. Or maybe he slipped on a piece of loose concrete, but as he stretched, his foot went out from under him. Hands clawing air, he fell.

Instinctively, I dropped. I hit the ledge hard with my arm pointlessly extended. There's no way I could've reached him.

He rolled to the edge, the upper half of his body swinging over the abyss. He looked up at me, eyes panicked.

Mine were wider.

And then he got up.

Laughing. He pointed at me and cackled "Nanny-nanny-poo-poo" as he danced a jig and dusted himself off.

He was messin' with me.

I raised myself on a bruised knee and looked for a way down. That little motherfucker.

He was on a narrow ledge, laughing big with overdrawn gestures. Knowing he had my eye, he put his fists on his hips and held a defiant look. The kid flipped me the bird and then stuck the extended finger into his cheek like Shirley Temple.

I don't rile easily but I like a little more gratitude when I risk my neck.

I ran angry around the balustrade until I found a fire escape—hell, it was more like a flimsy ladder. I swung over it like some idiot action hero.

The screws, which secured the ladder to the building, were loose, just like everything else in my life. The ladder collapsed. My feet landed hard on the ledge below and a lucky hand hold on the nipple and breast of Halliberta, an ancient goddess of commerce, kept me from falling. They sure don't decorate a skyscraper like they used to.

The fire escape collapsed and fell loudly, forty-six floors to the street. Fortunately, the kid was safe on the other side of the building.

Taking swift but small side steps, I rounded the corner to the West face. There was the kid, a floor below, dancing the hula and singing to himself. It was an Arctic Monkeys song, the one I like about 'looking good on the dance floor.

When he saw me, the kid promptly turned around, dropped his drawers and mooned me. This seemed to delight him immensely. As he pulled up his pants, he was laughing so hard that tears were streaming down the two fat cheeks of his freckled little face.

I could find no easy way to get to the floor below. There was nothing to use. I found a piece of industrial electrical cable, but it was not long enough.

185

Gordy Grundy

I looked down. The kid was making a drawing on a brown paper bag. Engrossed in line work, he was shading the background of a cityscape. A large monster that looked like me loomed at the horizon. It was quite good actually.

If I couldn't get down to the kid, I'd have to pull him up to me. I took my belt, wrapped it around my ankle, and then secured the buckle to a sturdy drainpipe. This would give me a few more feet of dangle room. However audacious or stupid, I thought I could get to him.

I've got to bring him in. I must settle him down. Comfort him. Soothe his pain. Educate him. Tame his outbursts and redirect his powerful energy. I need to help him age wisely. Let him mature. Then all will be well.

I inched over the edge. The forty-floor view shrank my testicles and knotted my stomach.

I scooted further over and made the drop.

The belt held. Thank God for American Made in China.

Now I was fully and freely hanging upside down. I extended my arm. If he got close enough, I would be able to grab his hand and pull him to safety.

But he stayed just out of reach. The kid had taken the paper bag and was blowing it up like a balloon.

"Give me your hand," I said with gentle authority, "Give me your hand and we can go home."

The kid stuck out his tongue and made a 'Nyah-Nyah' sound.

"C'mon. Let's get outta here and get something

to eat. Give me your hand."

He approached on tiptoes, pretending to sneak up on me like a vaudeville comedian. Raising the bag, he clapped his hands. The brown paper balloon burst with a loud 'bang'. I saw it coming but it scared me nonetheless. I must have twitched; I felt my ankle harness slip a quarter inch toward the street.

"Grab my hand," I said.

He approached slowly and warily. Each step was deliberate as his eyes flickered between my helping hand and the long street below. I had never felt such compassion. His baby blues seemed to plead with me for help.

Then, as quick as a sidewinder, he grabbed a hold of my index finger and pulled me along the ledge until he could pull no further.

And then he let go. The action sent me swinging across the western face of the forty-fourth floor. As I swung back, I made a lunge for him but missed.

He gave me a shove, which increased my momentum *and* my trajectory.

Hanging by one leg, I was now spinning and swinging uncontrollably. The kid was squealing with delight.

When I ricocheted back, he gave me another shove, like he was pushing a schoolyard swing.

You couldn't hear the approach, but when the Red Cross helicopter came up from below the ledge and around the corner of the building, the sound was like a physical explosion. The kid fell to his knees and covered his ears. The prop wash sent me swinging even further and spinning more wildly.

187

Gordy Grundy

The loudspeaker from the rescue chopper echoed, "Do - You - Need - Assistance?"

I assumed that help would be an obvious gesture, since I was hanging from my ankle, swinging forty stories above street level.

The kid stood up and clapped delightedly.
The pilot leaned out and gave us a 'thumbs up.' The chopper climbed to reveal a dangling rescue sled.
The reverb of the propeller shook the building and chips of concrete rained down upon us. I was spinning faster than ever.
The orange rescue sled inched closer. The kid crouched down as if he was diving into a swimming pool; his little toes curled over the building ledge like piggly-wigglies on a diving board.
When the sled was about six feet away, the kid took a flying leap. The pilot shouted as the kid caught the metal bar around the basket. It looked like he might have smashed his lip on the railing. He then managed to climb up and scramble into the sled where he began to attach clips and tighten lines.

The crewman gave a 'thumbs up' and the pilot repeated the gesture to me.
I felt reassured. I gave him an upside-down 'thumbs up.'
The whomp of the propeller grew louder and faster as the helicopter rose, then banked away into the sunset.

I was still hanging by my ankle, upside down, spinning.

Artist's Pants

As the Red Cross helicopter became a silhouette against the sunset, I could see the kid sitting in the basket, cross-legged. He was waving at me. I couldn't tell if he was waving goodbye or flipping me off.

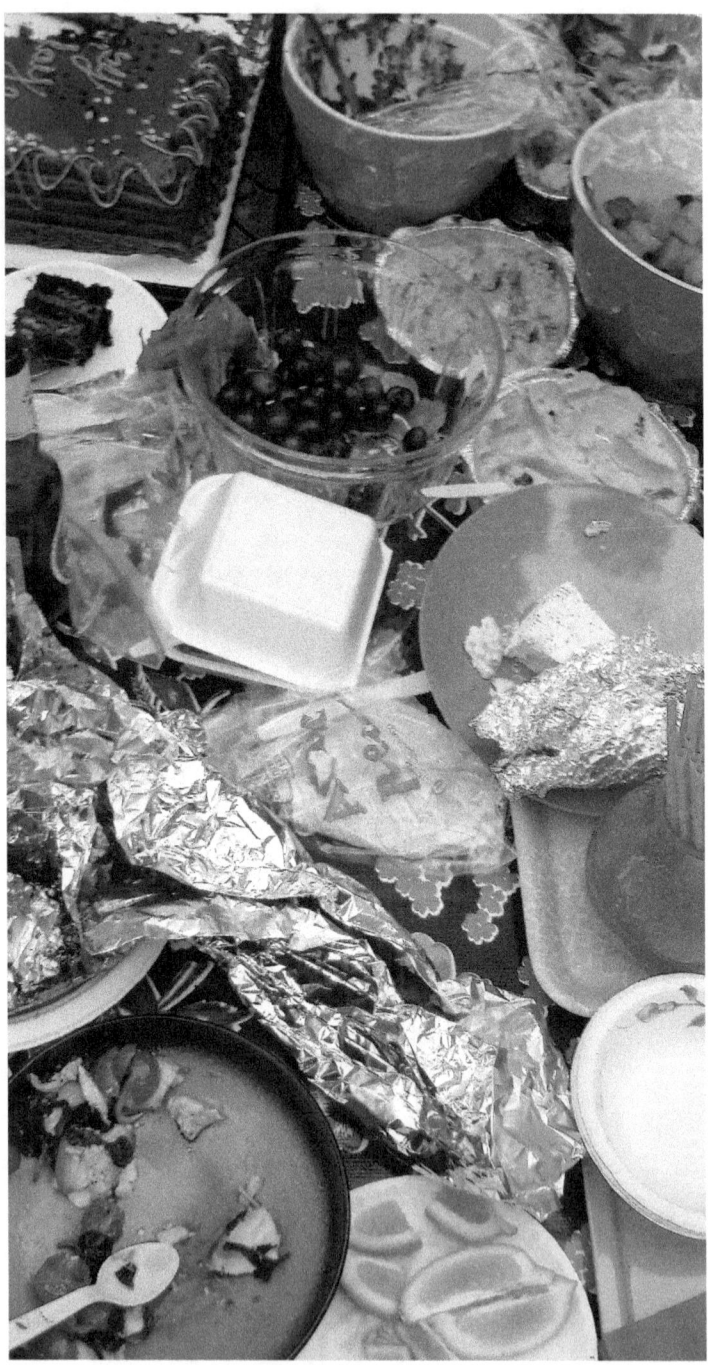

LOOKING FOR MY RELIGION

My index finger recoils at the temperature of the rust colored bath water. It's way too hot. With staggered effort, suspended on wobbly arms, I ease my whole body into it anyway. There are only three pounds of Epsom salts in the tub and I wish there were thirty more.

Every screaming muscle in my body is hushed by the heat. Tendons, frozen into sharp knots, start to melt. Steam moistens the stitches on my forehead and relaxes the brittle skin. The "Lost in Translation" soundtrack plays on the Hi-Fi and eases me along. The pounding in my head and the noise in my body slow to the beat of the drip of the leaky faucet.

Heat heals.

Slowly, I find peace, without pain. If God were to reach down, right now, to lift me from my mortal coil, I would clasp that hand and graciously go.

Gordy Grundy

I am looking for my religion. I don't have one.

These days, it seems like everybody does. Considering all the headlines... I hate to feel left out.

My dad says religion provides discipline and structure. My mom says it offers security, well being and homemade baked goods. A spouse-hunting friend says it's a great way to meet dates. I dunno. With the weekly tithing and emphasis on morality, it seems kind of expensive, financially and fun-wise.

I've been shopping around, trying to find a religion that fits. I'm not sure if I should buy one that wears like a comfy old sweater or one that steels like a finely tailored Kevlar vest.

There are so many to choose from.

The Catholics get high points for their refined sense of showmanship. I like incense, tapestry and Mel Gibson movies. Historically, the Popes have done more for the fine arts than anyone. That's worth something.

The Jews may have started out as only a few wandering tribes, but they sure got around. They're always in the news. I can't find another religion that has a better understanding of the human condition, of life-it's-own-self. It justifies existence. Unfortunately, their holiday menu turns my stomach. Pickled or flavorless, it's a deal killer.

Hinduism was never a consideration. A Hindu and I both agree that cows are sacred but we differ in the approach. I like mine medium-rare.

Buddhism is smart, soulful and quite relaxing. Unfortunately, I am destined to fail. In the summer months when ants invade my kitchen, I'll reach for a can of Raid.

Islam certainly is popular but I fear it demands too much time. Praying is good but five times a day seems like overkill. How can I find Mecca when I can't even find my own way home?

The Protestant sects have a wholesome, Mid-American appeal but if I'm gonna take a Sunday nap, I'd rather do it at home on a sofa than a hardwood pew.

Wiccanism and Paganism have a primitive naturalness that appeals to me. Any kind of nudity is good. The preference for basic black can make a stylish wardrobe easy. Already I'm a fan of Marilyn Manson, Bauhaus and Souixie and The Banshees. There's just no way in Hell I'm gonna paint my nails.

Of course, the modern religions have yet to stand the test of time.

When the aliens land, I'll swing to Scientology. Mormon underwear may be rather restrictive for the libertine in me. And if I'm gonna go door-to-door to Witness for Jehovah, I'll also pitch it for Amway.

I was getting dizzy with all of the choices before me and no sign from above. Every religion has so many pros confounded by a daunting number of cons. Without a clear direction, I didn't know which to pick. You shouldn't get aggressive with the ethereal, so I decided to wait for a sign.

Then I passed a shaggy homeless guy, standing on the street. He held a crude cardboard sign, which read, "It will find you."

This meant something. Surely, religious choice does not come from rational thought. Religion works best when it's forced upon you. The bearded stranger

Gordy Grundy

with the soulful eyes was right. *My* religion will find *me*.

I felt bad when I clipped him with the bumper of my car. I was late for an appointment, so I just kept going. But he made a very valid point; I had to let the religion find me.

Recently, I felt obligated to attend a family birthday party in my honor. When you don't show up at these things, it gives your parents time to reflect upon the Hell they hath borne; an appearance tends to assuage them. Besides, I was looking forward to seeing my sister. Rent was due and I needed to borrow a few bucks.

We were having a lovely and happy time. Then the ice cream cake melted fast.

My little nephew Archie could no longer contain himself. He ran from the room to retrieve my gift. With bright, excited eyes, he presented me with a tropical flower growing out of a hunk of black lava rock. Dancing on his tiny feet, he was so thrilled.

The gift made sense. It was thoughtful, for the day after next, I would be on a plane to Hawai'i for my first vacation in two years.

I did not realize it then, but little Archie had given me my religion.

Of course the child had no idea he had broken a very serious taboo. I quickly threw down the lava rock as if it were still molten. Suddenly I felt nauseous.

Not wanting to disappoint the toddler, I singsong'd a "Thank you Archie!" and pinched his pink cheek. If no one had been looking, I would have wrenched his cheek into a bright red raspberry. Then I would have slapped him upside the head. I don't care if he's six years old; he should have known better.

What was he *thinking*?! Don't they teach ancient Hawai'ian studies in grammar school anymore?

Long before Jesus got lost in the desert or Mohammed wrote his own script, Madame Pele was laughing it up and *holua* racing. As far as Gods go, Hawai'ian Pele is a lively one. She has a penchant for extreme sports. She loves hard. She gets jealous easily. She isn't mean or spiteful; you just shouldn't get in her way. When you do, the Goddess of Lava can be rather fiery and explosive.

One of the things she hates most is some infidel who takes lava rock off her Hawai'ian Island. It is taboo. I can't blame little Archie; he found it in a California supermarket.

Unfortunately, the lava rock was now in *my* possession.

My vacation wasn't planned; it was an emergency. Two out of three psychiatrists agreed that I needed to get out of town fast. Stress was high and hope was nowhere to be found. Hawai'i always works in a pinch. It's cheap, exotic and a low priority terrorist target.

Within fifty minutes after setting foot on Hawai'ian soil, I was sailing down Kala'kaua Avenue on a motorbike. Warm Tradewinds caressed my face. Clouds of the purest and most brilliant white dappled an endlessly blue sky. The sea beside me stretched forever in colors that my painter's palette could never capture. I was loving life once again and I was moving fast on two wheels.

The Goddess Pele must have sensed my appreciation for her world and felt the unbounding joy that surged in my heart. She also must have noted that I had arrived in the islands empty-handed.

It had slipped my silly mortal mind to return Archie's gift to its rightful place. This insensitivity to Pele must have made her blood boil. My inconsideration was blatant. My lack of respect was worthy of punishment.

So Pele slammed on the brakes of the SUV that I happened to be speeding behind.

Thus began a chain of events and a series of accidents from which I have yet to recover. The cantaloupe-sized contusion on my hip still blackens and blues. A femur, which had been diagnosed as 'broken,' was downgraded to 'Let's keep an eye on it.' Ten stitches grace my forehead. My nose is missing a few layers of skin and a dozen freckles. My knee is a perpetual scab. My hands are bruised and my ribs ache with every breath I take. My lip is fat, bloody and un-kissable.

Pele must have sensed I was going to violate my probation. As I was recovering from little Archie's birthday present, Pele unleashed Phase Two of her fury. On the trip, she broke three teeth on three separate occasions, the assailant being a chicken salad, an omelet and asphalt.

Upon my return to the Mainland, I tried to lift the curse that Little Archie had bestowed upon me. I Fed Ex'd the lava rock back to the Hawai'ian Volcano National Park in Hilo. The Park Service receives dozens of similar bad luck packages every day.

My humble action has yet to appease Pele. I think she is withholding her forgiveness until the chunk of Hawai'ian asphalt, still embedded deep in my palm, makes its natural getaway.

Conviction is born with evidence. Should I see water turn to wine, I will become a Sunday Christian. If I see water turn to oak-aged tequila, call me devout. If the horn-blowing statue of Angel Moroni that stands atop a Mormon Temple starts to blow like Tommy Dorsey, I'll take three wives and join the club.

The beauty of a sunrise, the miracles of nature and the physical genius of the human body all point to a higher being, a creator of all things. On the other hand, science and Darwin make a pretty convincing argument of their own.

For me, Madame Pele has evidenced near absolute proof that the Hawai'ian Gods are the true Gods. I can never be Hawai'ian, but I sure can try.

I may have found my religion, but it's gonna be Hell keeping it.

NIGHT LIFE

DESTINATION: COCKTAIL

Alcohol and art are best consumed in tandem, which is why it's twice as nice now to head to Traxx restaurant in Union Station, where mixologist Kurtis Wells has created a cocktail in honor of the restaurant's signature piece of artwork. "No Further West" is a minimalist gold-leaf painting created by Gordy Grundy that alludes to the fact that the tracks literally stop here. As will yours when you sip its liquid sidekick, a jubilant burst of orange, cucumber and mint laced with vodka and Champagne called "No Further West: A Very California Cocktail Creation."

No Further West

1½ ounce Pussy Riot vodka

½ ounce Torres Orange Liqueur

½ ounce Senior Curacao

4 mint sprigs

2 cucumber wheels

Half an orange wheel

Splash of fresh orange juice

Splash of soda

Splash of Sprite

Top off with Varichon & Clerc Champagne

Muddle the mint, cucumber and orange wheels in a highball glass, add ice and remaining ingredients. Stir and top with Champagne. Garnish with cucumber and an orange wheel.

Traxx Restaurant in Union Station, 800 North Alameda St., L.A. (213) 625-1999; www.traxxrestaurant.com.
— JESSICA GELT

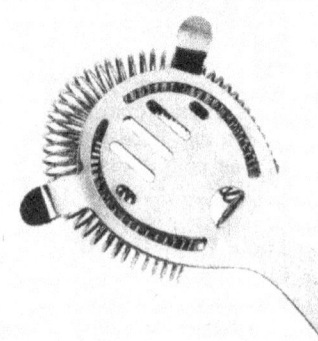

BLOOD AND TEARS

A HOLIDAY GREETING FROM THE FRONT

"Genuflect" the column by Gordy Grundy will not appear in this magazine for the first time since 1995. Grundy is currently in Iraq, serving as a 'volunteer' in the Halliburton Arts Group Division 390.

In an email greeting, he writes:

"Dear Coagula Readers,

Happy Thanksgiving. Hello to the Holidays.

I'm beginning to think this was a mistake. With the date palms and all, I thought Iraq would be closer to Palm

199

Gordy Grundy

Springs in climate, but no go. It's like lower Baja Mexico in the dead of summer without a Corona.

Bullets buzz like flies. There is no rockin' this casbah. I should have read the brochure more closely.

The Halliburton Arts 390 is A-OK. The crew that I shipped in with are all great people, all American painters and sculptors, a lot of recent MFA grads. (Where else can they get a job?)

The newly rotated crew is Chinese who work a lot faster and labor for less than Wal-Mart wages. We've been repainting the Saddam portraits with Bush portraits but the Chinese are making Bush look more like Mao than Bush, so it's a challenge.

Luckily, we're stationed near Al Discreet, quite an oasis. It's not all-hard work. Last night we clandestine'd a Special Ops and held a midnight rave for the locals who were like-minded. All these kids were sneaking out of their houses, just like we did in high school. Unfortunately, the local mullah was smarter than my mother and kept his eye open. Just one RPG (Rocket Propelled Grenade) took out the BPM (Beats Per Minute) and that was enough to end the good vibe.

To beat the heat, I'm reading a short story about the South Pacific because that's where I'd rather be. Somerset Maugham gave us 'The Fall of Edward Barnard', a story about a young man who finds his soul in the Tropics. I'm gonna try and make the story's message my Holiday own. Maugham writes, "Do you know that conversation is one of the greatest pleasures in life? But it wants leisure. I'd always been too busy before..."

It is an idea we can use in these difficult times: small

and true pleasures.

Gotta go. Complications everywhere. Graffiti is a big problem. After Bush's Thanksgiving visit, all the locals think he's gonna come back for Christmas with gifts. So the taggers are painting Santa hats on all our Bush portraits. This will delay our Norman Rockwell 'Lifestyle' campaign two or maybe three weeks. Much work to do.

Aloha,
GG

OUTSOURCING THE NEW YEAR

I have to put a little of the 'ole fast sprint' into the day job. That's the only way to keep the boss wolf at bay.

Jobs are getting scarce. Everywhere. Even the fall-back positions are vanishing.

Recently, I called one of the big new Culver City galleries in Los Angeles for an address and the attendant who answered the phone sounded very Indian. (Curry, not casino). I was suspicious of the accent.

I asked, "Where are you?"

"We are joost South of the Tin freeway."

"No, no," I clamored, "Where are you right now? Where are you calling from?"

"You called me!"

"No, no. Where are you sitting right now?"

"Culler City."

"Are you in New Delhi?!"

"I am not allowed to say!"

Gordy Grundy

I was looking out the window at a sunny LA day; I thought of a way to trick her. "Will I need an umbrella? Is it raining over in Culver City?

"Yes! The monsoon is very..."

"*Ah-HAH!*"

Times are tough when even the gallery attendant gets outsourced overseas.

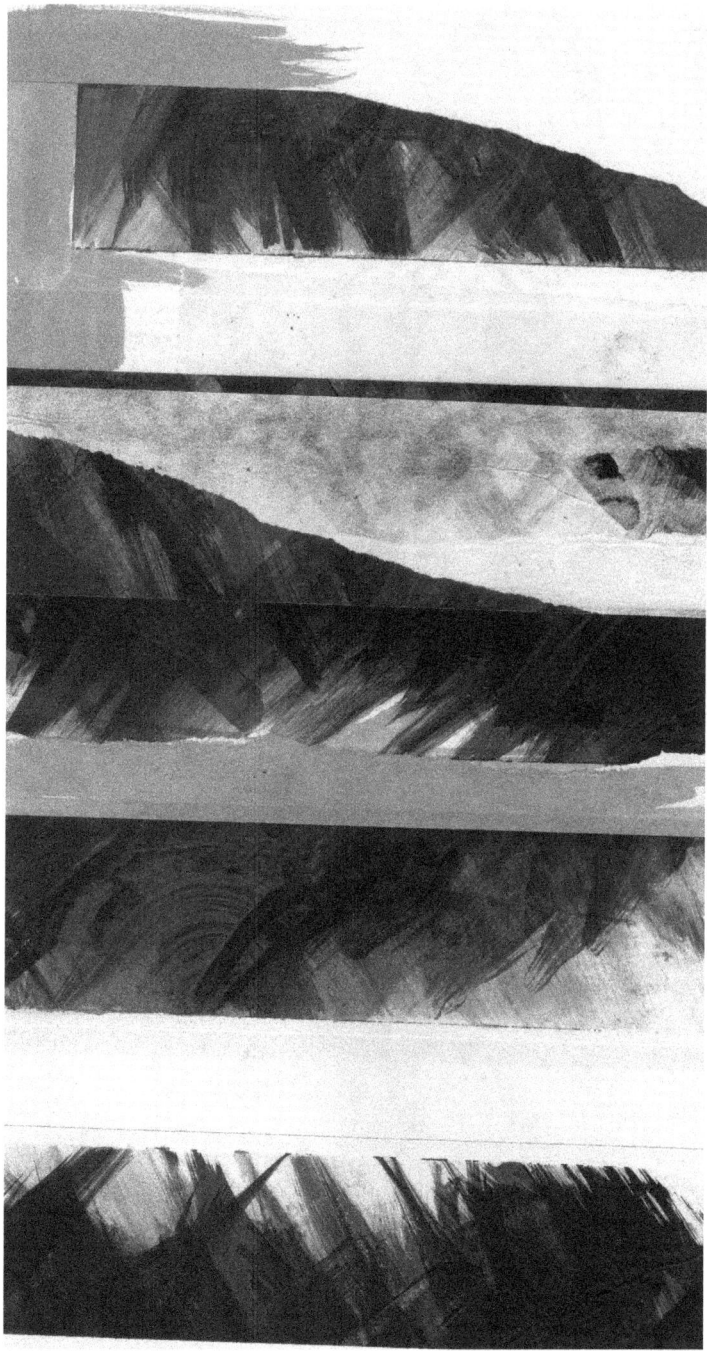

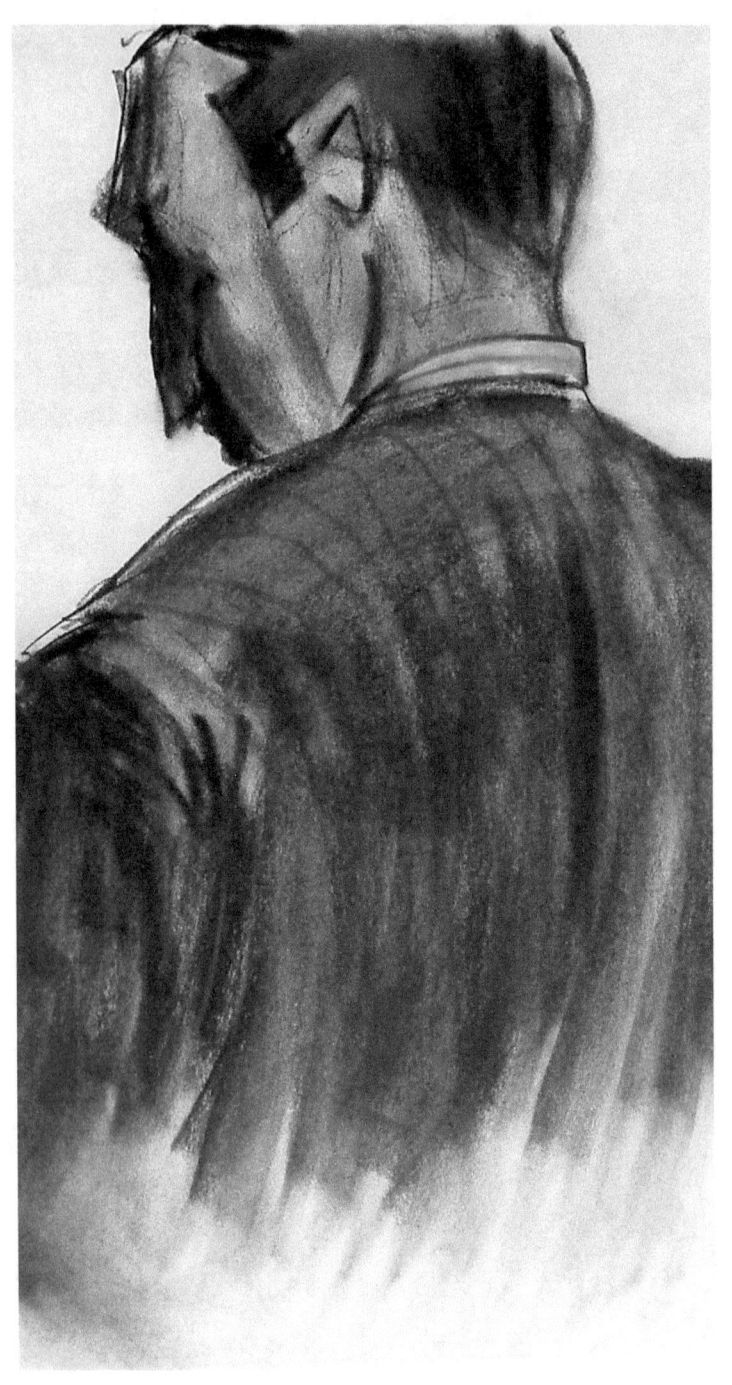

THE LINE IN THE SAND

After the Holidays, mid-season cheap, I took off to the desert for a few days to escape the rigors of fun, frivolity and familiarity. I needed quiet and a lack of temptation. Even a professional has to relax.

There, in a motel room, I was confronted with a modern device which I do not have in my own home. A TV with remote allowed me to remain in bed and become an active member of our pop culture, for I had been slacking. I think I was the second-to-last American who had not seen 'Queer Eye for the Straight Guy.'

What I witnessed horrified me beyond anything else that I had experienced since the Millennium. Never have I been so appalled. (And believe me, I have been very, many times.)

On this episode, everyone was getting cultured, pricked, prodded and continually reminded to shave 'with the grain.' On the home design segment, the portly Eye of the Fab Five takes a large canvas, slaps on a few colors and shoves the brush around. He then makes this thirty-second painting the focal point of the redesigned living room.

Upon returning home, the gladly-victimized homeowners 'oooh' and 'aaah' over their new pad. They gush about the painting. They fawn and paw the artiste.

They ask him, "And what is it, maestro?"

"A landscape!" says the artiste.

Then he whips open an art catalogue and reveals his inspiration. He points to a photograph of a dark painting, a toxic landscape at sunset.

"It's just like a...." He said the name of the painter so fast that I never caught it.

The homeowners coo over their good fortune.

I was appalled. Fortunately, a stupor suddenly enveloped me; only in a coma, can you deflect such great pain. I could not believe what I had seen.

Here was an opportunity for Bravo, an alleged arts channel no less, to educate the public in a progressive manner. The dandelion decorator could have taken his viewing audience to a gallery, spoken with a cordial gallerist and demystified the perceived trauma of buying art.

He could have given the Fine Arts a value. He could have elevated the sociological role of the artist in our culture. At the very least, he could have equated a painting to the cost of a new refrigerator.

Instead, he negated every effort that an artist makes. Why spend money on art when you can whip it out yourself? How do you afford the expensive facial hydrogenizers that the Queer Eye reveres? Kill the art budget!

In a spa-based economy, the Fine Arts are always the first to suffer.

Slowly, the realization of this pop culture-abortion gave me a sense of purpose. I had to do something to stop the erosion of all that I hold dear.

When I regained consciousness, the pen in my hand was flying furiously over a yellow pad. I was designing the manifesto of a brilliant new arts movement centered around a class-action lawsuit aimed at the blasphemy of the Queer Eye and every show like it. Artists, gallerists and collectors would stand hand in hand, united against the tyranny of poor taste and dull thinking. By page seven, the first year's budget had ballooned to $30 million but I didn't care. Other people's money should be no object when defending the Fine Arts. I knew I could make a difference.

Several nights later, my grand plans took an upper cut to the jaw. All at once, I realized that America's love for the Queer Eye had grown like a fast moving cancer and all major organs have been poisoned. The war had already been lost.

Arriving at a holiday party, the first thing the host said to me was "Did you see 'Queer Eye' last week? The guy did a brilliant painting on the show! Right there in front of us! In minutes!"

Then he asked, "How's your work going?"

I swear to God, I think he smirked.

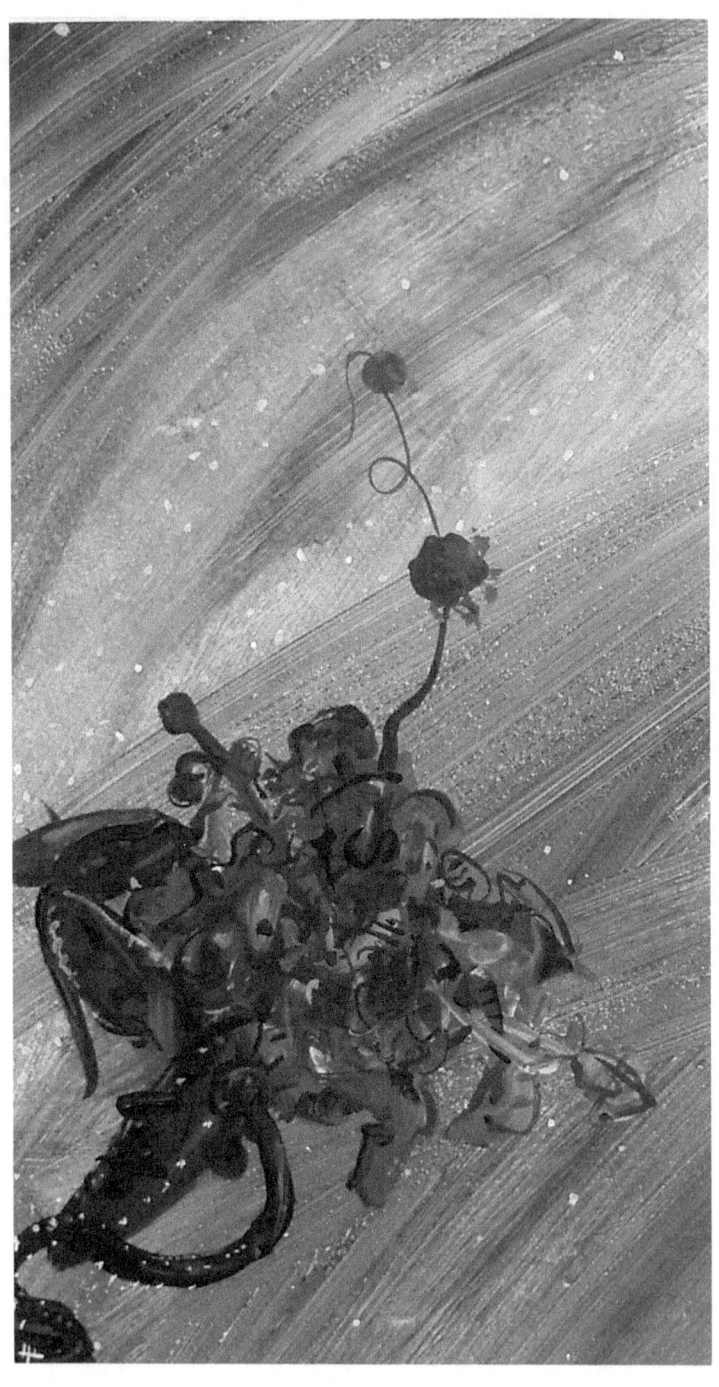

CRAZY IN MY DEFENSE

Recently, I fell crazy in love.

The unfortunate decline to my proclamation came with a simple explanation. "You're crazy."

"What do ya mean 'crazy'? I asked, stunned at the notion.

The reply was a polite mumble. I didn't press it. Sometimes it's best not to know these things.

Several days later I met my friend Lucy for a drink.

"What in the hell could that have meant? Crazy! Me?"

Lucy looked away and stared deep into her cocktail, searching for words. "It's... your charm," she answered.

I wanted to ask what in the hell that meant, but sometimes it's best not to know these things.

There are many types of crazy. I'd really like to

know in which category I am perceived. Then again, sometimes it's best not to know these things.

In defense of my good character, this accusation needs some light.

There is crazy-wild. I'll cop to that; the streak is wide. I'm always the last man standing.

Crazy-screwball is well documented. I'm always hanging from a chandelier, a cliff or the outside of a bedroom window.

Simple minds confuse crazy with passion. Joan of Arc had a jones and gave it her all. Audacity is not crazy, just passionate.

Crazy-fun is an art form, appreciated by a refined elite of whom I am a jaded chapter leader.

Beyond that, I can't figure out what in the hell the comment could have meant.

Just this week, Rob Brezsny who writes the 'Free Will Astrology' says I am "a radiant bundle of fascinating contradictions." That's crazy, but I can go with it.

In support of this theory, I will argue both sides of the issue. With the mind-bending heat wave and troops amassing at my every border, you could say I have been acting out. The two burning ends of my candle are getting close to the center. In a charming way.

Right now, I have a solo show up. That's always crazy-making. And contradictory. Pride and doubt. Hope and fear. Strong and needy. Invincible yet wholly vulnerable. I've been living on emotional tenterhooks; it's driving me crazy.

Artist's Pants

There is a hilarious video in the show. If you saw it, and didn't now me, you'd think I was crazy.

The show, the second in a series, is about a vision. Not so long ago, a deity appeared before me, shining like God's own disco ball, and announced that it was my destiny to bring peace to the world. This may sound crazy, but at least I have goals.

I am quitting my sweet, easy and money-making day job in order to follow the logical continuation of this work. (World peace is not part time.) I know it's crazy to leave a dream day job because now I wake up, every morning at 3AM, worried about money.

I am going to risk all that I have, and all that I am, on it.

The next chapter in my life has me crazy with fear.

I'm crazy with impatience.

Regardless of what others may think or what my criminal attorney may say, I am not crazy. However, I do believe that a devil's horn is growing from my forehead. I am glad to be alive, but not fully convinced. I suddenly have a desperate need to fall in love. I prefer addictions to children. I like to wear a sarong. I'm not as savvy as I think I am. I believe in the good of mankind and a harmonious universe.

In this world of so many horrors, I may be laughing like a crazy idiot, but at least it keeps me from crying. That is the nature of making art.

I'll let you in on a secret. I'm really not crazy. It

Gordy Grundy

just looks that way because I work very hard to keep myself amused. This is a full time job and I am a very demanding audience.

I rest my case.

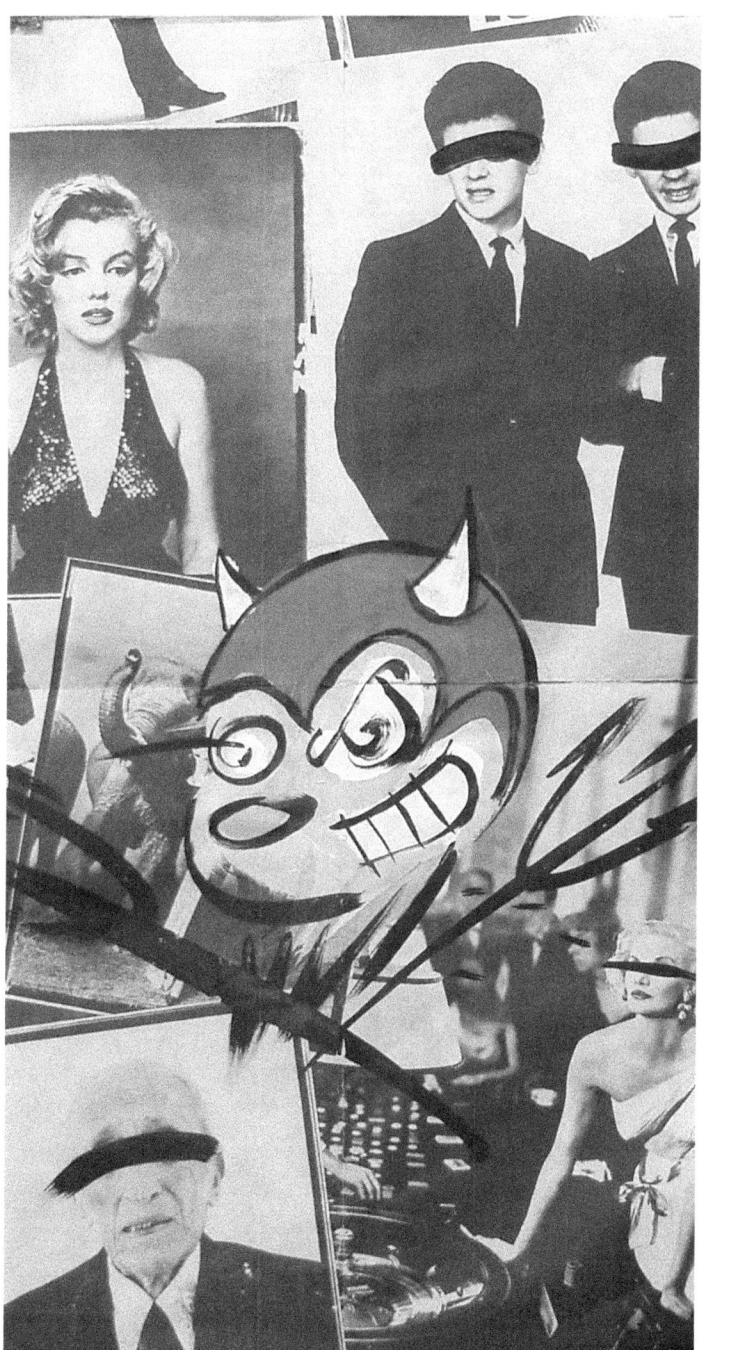

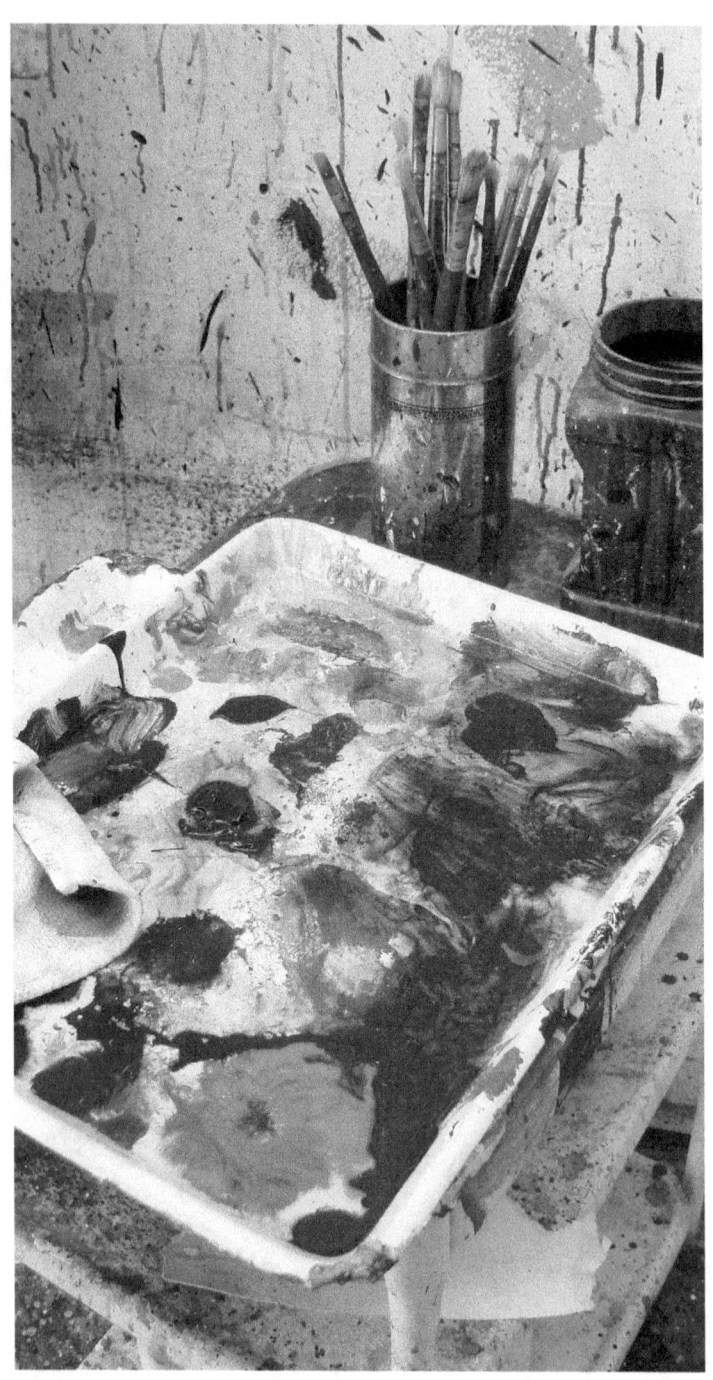

IN MY HEAD

Cho Seung-Hui, the busy Virginia Tech shooter, made a very bad impression on me. First, there was the killing spree. Second, he was a loner, a much reported fact that is destroying a perfectly romantic notion.

When I first read the interior monologue of detective Philip Marlowe, the fictional creation of Raymond Chandler, I found a kindred spirit. I found a soul brother and an id. Marlowe, a knight-errant, walked down lonely streets, a man true to his own self. He was a rational mind against the insanity of the world.

He didn't 'hang out.'

I fell in love with Jay Gatsby, the odd man out, haunted and melancholy, staring across the channel at the green light.

When Pee Wee Herman looked into the blue eyes of a ravishing blonde and snarled, "I'm a loner, Dottie." I said, "Me too!"

Gordy Grundy

These guys had feelings and thoughts that did not need the approval of others. Rather than giving the world an angry finger, they bowed quietly and said, "I'll take it as I see it but not as you play it."

I am a loner. Always have been.

Since I was a kid, in my head is my favorite place to be.

In my mind, I have lived many lives. I have danced across the universe and conquered continents. I have made fortunes and lost kingdoms. I've traveled the world, but my passport says that I have not gone very far.

My mind is a better world than the one I live in. I believe a giant ape can climb the Empire State Building. I have saved children from the deck of a burning freighter. I have flown high over Neverland.

Nothing is impossible, yet I'm having a hell of a time trying to clear a paid parking ticket off my docket.

As an artist, I am left to my own devices.

Alone in my studio, a canvas evolves by itself. It's my world. No one can touch it and there, no one can hurt me. My imagination provides its own Mapquest without direction from others. I stand alone upon the precipice of my studio, high above the turbulent fog of life. It's a world where I'm safe.

To be alone is to be elitist. There is a snob appeal. To me, the voices in my head are far more entertaining that yours. At a cocktail party, I'd rather chat with myself.

Man in nature is a romantic notion. Men in nature is devastation. A man alone can create a dialogue with the world and himself. Truths are realized in unspoken languages. Nature inspires. I am reminded of Caspar David

Friedrich's famous painting, "Wanderer Above the Sea of Fog." Man stands tall, high on a mountaintop, commanding the violent and unseen nature before him. Only alone can the world speak to him. Man is nature's greatest achievement. Just ask Walt Whitman.

Conversely, you put a group of guys together and you get a campground full of McDonalds wrappers or a rainforest devoid of trees. These days, nature refuses to talk back.

Hollywood, the bible of our morality, used to portray the loner as an iconic hero. I bought it hook line. James Dean did it well. Greta Garbo was a loner, but I've never seen her movies. Batman was never big on cocktail parties and I liked him for it. Robert Mitchum. John Wayne. Lee Marvin.

Somewhere Hollywood led me astray. They began to marginalized the loner. It is hard to find a thoughtful character, a seeker, one who introspects and reflects. Somerset Maugham wrote a beautiful book, 'The Razor's Edge', about a man alone finding enlightenment. If Hollywood were to attempt the third remake they would turn it into a buddy picture. Somehow, Siddhartha become Travis Bickle. You'll never find a loner in a TV sitcom; they just aren't that funny.

Because of this, a few aberrations of our society get big media play. The antagonists of Columbine were loners. Pilot Mohamed Atta was a loner. The pederast down the block is a loner. To a gullible public, the evidence appears overwhelming. I worry about a backlash. Just because your neighbors are boring, doesn't mean you have to be.

Being alone used to be transcendent, an inspired reflection. Today, time alone insinuates that you are packing shell casings and downloading kiddie-porn.

Not all mass murderers are loners. Hitler certainly liked stadium-sized spectaculars. Jim Jones served Kool-Aid at his last block party. Charlie Manson never surfed alone.

The Fourth Estate tells me it is bad to be alone yet they are encouraging me to do so. If I am on the Internet, am I alone? If my best friend is a Playstation, who am I with? How many people can cuddle up and watch TV on a cell phone screen?

If we get another shooter anytime soon I'm gonna have to start socializing more. The general public is becoming prejudiced against those who prefer their own company.

Artists have never been more suspect than ever before. I'm afraid of the stigma.

Must a lone wolf now run with the pack? How dull.

Audacity sheds to complicity. Stifle the passion.

Does a group show send a better signal than a solo show?

Are we safer in a movement with numbers?

Alone and thoughtful must mean crazy.

I'm in. Call me crazy, bravely.

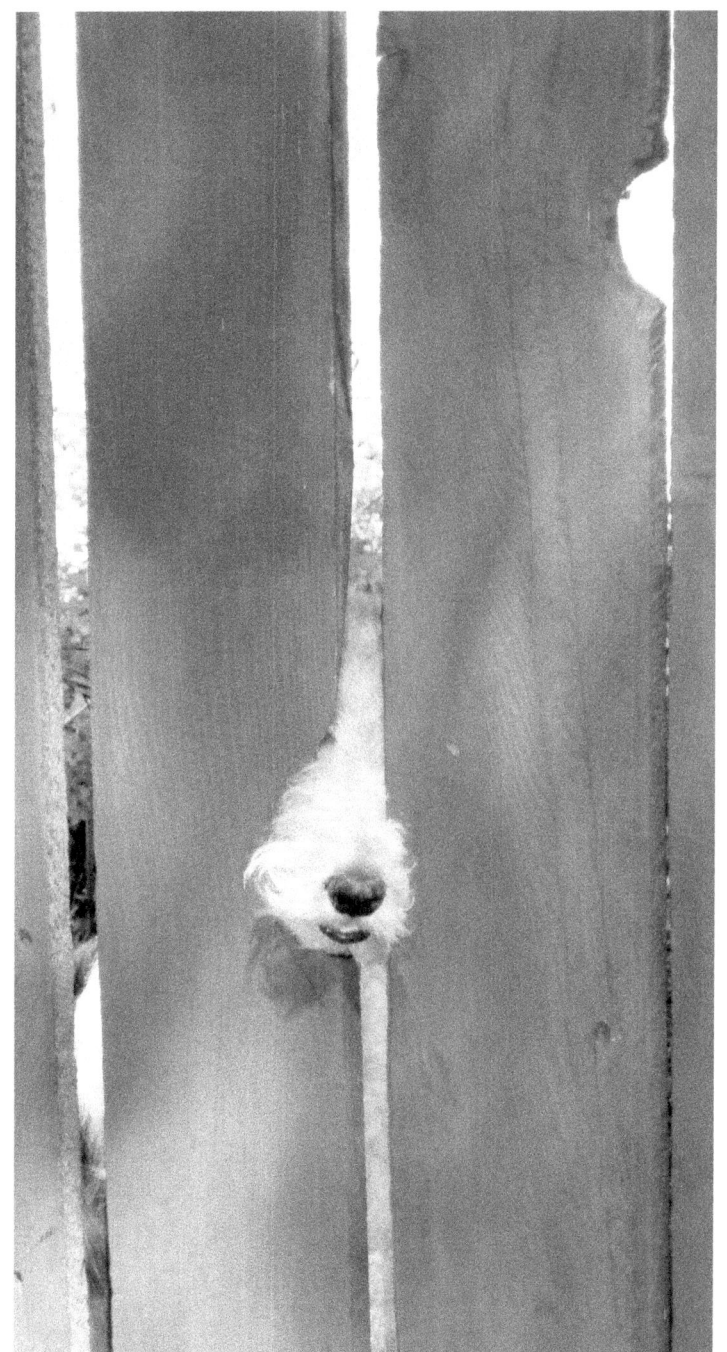

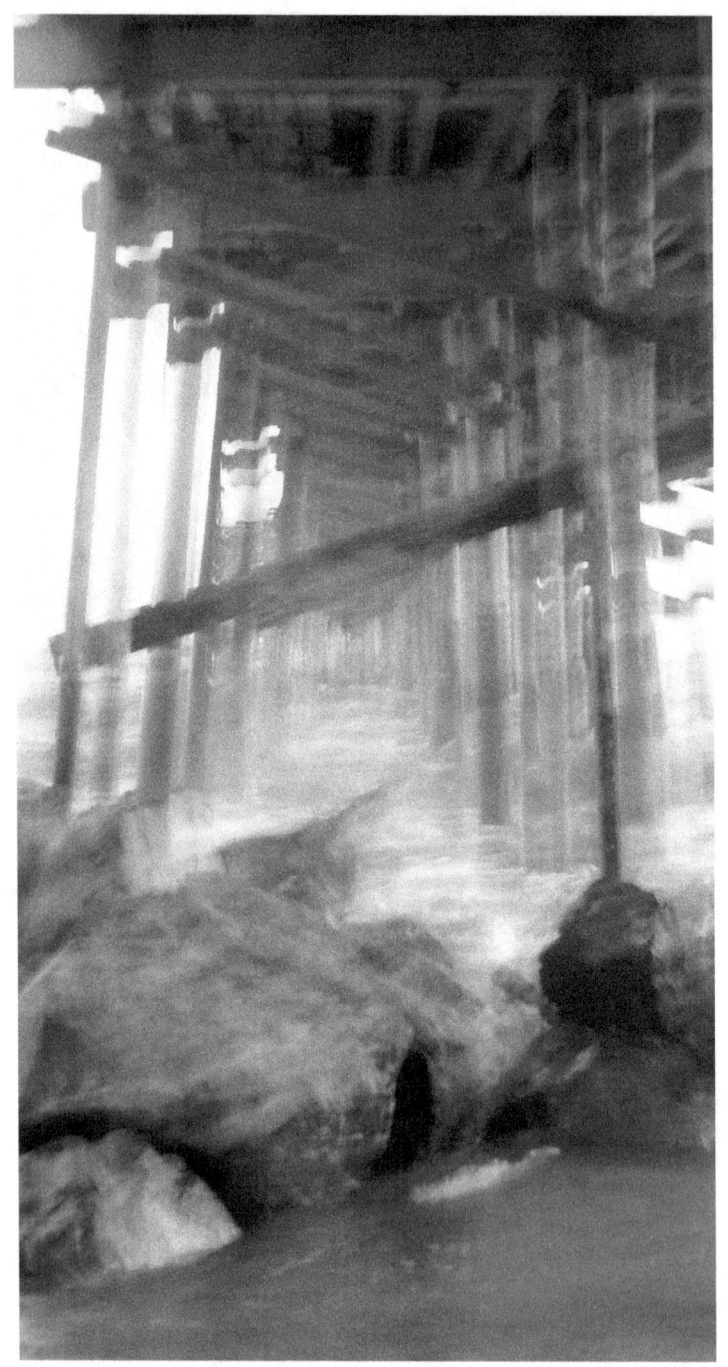

FINE ART CACOPHANY

GREAT MOMENTS IN LOS ANGELES ART HISTORY

Los Angeles never has much of a winter and this night of January thirty-first, 1998, was a shock. The rains had cleaned the air and the asphalt. Smells were sharp and freshly pungent. Collars were pulled tight against the cold. The night sky was a clear and deep violet. In LA, you rarely see the stars, but tonight, you could see them all.

For the fortunate witnesses, this cold and starry evening was titanic.

On the desolate and abandoned 6100 block of Wilshire Boulevard, painters, writers, filmmakers and dancers began to congregate. A new and exciting art complex was opening.

Three much-loved and highly-regarded galleries

were moving into a warren of buildings, thereby creating a new art destination. Marc Foxx, Dan Bernier and ACME were the heroes that night. This move defined a new chapter in Los Angeles contemporary art history.

Each of the three galleries had earned a distinction of their own. Each had been lauded with critical praise. Each had a collector's following. The union and synergy of Marc Foxx, Dan Bernier and ACME put a spotlight on the area, their artists and their advocacy.

It was a magical night in late January. A wind from the north teased the fronds of the palm trees overhead like a calming lullaby.

The crowd was ageless and youthful. All were artists. There were very few collectors present. Every face that you passed in the knotted crowd shared a light, a sparkle behind the eye, a glint of awareness and keen intelligence.

Everyone felt it in their bones: This night would not be forgotten.

Today, prestigious 6150 Wilshire is an essential stop for major collectors and art lovers from around the world.

In the next chapter of "Great Moments in Los Angeles Art History," we will tell the tale of two crazy gallerists who turn a dumpy film studio town into an international arts mecca. On the night of September 4th 2003, Tim Blum and Jeff Poe inaugurated their new gallery Blum & Poe with a spectacular group show.

It created a land grab. Today, Culver City sparkles with over 3,000 art galleries.

FOUND OBJECT: BUMPER STICKER

"New to this country does not have to be rude to this country."

Baby, after waitin' around for a green card, I wouldn't expect too much outta anybody.

EXCERPT FROM A SPEECH ENTITLED "GENUFLECT: WHAT AMERICA CAN LEARN FROM THE CONTEMPORARY FINE ARTS" PRESENTED TO THE LA OPTIMIST CLUB, LOS ANGELES, CALIFORNIA

"... One cannot think of the artist as a craftsman or as a producer of product. We are not an extension of your home furnishings department. We are not your decorator's plaything. To really understand where the artist is coming from and where we belong, consider this. Categorize the artist with your minister, rabbi, favorite bartender or your psychiatrist. Artists are philosophers in many ways. We are the astronauts of our sociology..."

WHAT I HAVE LEARNED (OR HAVE BEEN RE-MINDED OF) RECENTLY

Good work does get noticed and is rewarded.

Unfortunately, that period of time between the good work and the reward crawls at a goddamn snail's pace.

Gordy Grundy

I NEARLY DROPPED MY DRINK

In any new conversation, everyone invariably asks what one does. When you answer "painter" or "artist," more often than not, the conversation just dies. Rapport flees and credibility is shot, instantly. You are rendered useless in their world.

The same sentiment was expressed by artist Mike Kelley. At a lecture at MOCA, Kelley talked about artist Richard Prince and his dread of the question. Prince just shrugs and says he's a plumber.

My friend Alan Wayne, an abstract painter, was cornered at a recent Passover dinner. After the meal, the men had retired to the living room while the ladies cleaned up.

Over glasses of Slivovitz, a well-educated doctor and an intelligent accountant gave Alan the intellectual version of a back-alley beating. They just could not understand *why* he does *what* he does.

Compounding their confusion, Alan is a monochromatic painter.

The fine arts is a liability.

ARE THERE ENOUGH SEATBELTS?

It's June. Forget the Dads; think of the grads.

According to some estimates, there are 40,000 new graduates who are empowered with a Bachelors or a Masters degree in the Fine Arts. That means there are 80,000 disappointed parents wishing their kids had earned a useful degree.

Leaving the warm security blanket of university, they're all chomping at the bit, eager and enthusiastic to enter the glamorous art life. With the rosy optimism of youth, these grads believe they will step through the door of their unknown and waltz onto a plushy red carpet.

Watch your step. The art world is a slippery, frozen tundra. In Los Angeles, there are seven artists to every civilian. Supply far exceeds demand. Some states want to limit the birth rate of artists to one per family. There just isn't enough wall space.

All the art world needs is a scootch more room; so what'll give?

DAMN, THERE REALLY IS NO REST UNTIL YOU'RE DEAD

I like to believe that life has a destination.

It's the only way I can further another step on the hard and dusty road. When the heat is grinding me down into the molten asphalt and the vultures are circling overhead, my mind escapes to the end of the highway, a cool blue Atlantis of my own design.

In Atlantis, you can rest on your laurels, where the jobs come to you, where you pick and choose your labors.

In an interview, the classic cinema star Lauren Bacall burst that dream bubble quite quickly. The established actress confessed how hard she had to hustle for work. And how rare it was to get a decent gig. She chafed at the thought of all the hand shakin' and phone callin' necessary to stay in the race.

In my opinion, Bacall had a great set of laurels to rest upon. It's surprising that she had to duke it out like the rest of us.

Maybe it *is* the journey after all. Maybe there is no Valhalla.

MISSION STATEMENT

I am a Libertine.
I'd rather go to a Bacchanalia than to a Basilica.
I am a lover, not a fighter.
I'd rather dance than walk.
I prefer indulgence to restraint.
I am Pan.

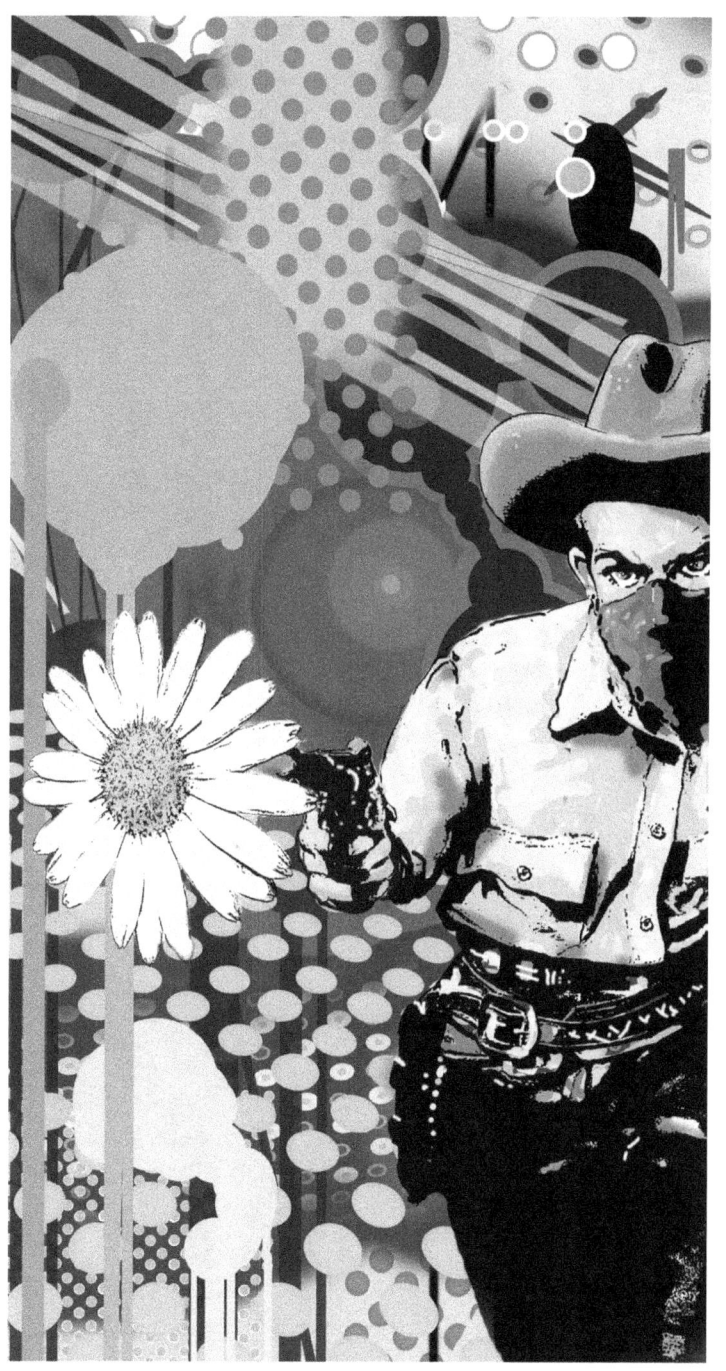

LAUGHTER

Oxygenates Your Soul

SCREEN SAVER

Easter Sunday.

He is risen.

Trying to resurrect myself, but having a hard time waking up.

Do a Systems Check. Toes and fingers wiggle. Lungs operate. Limbs feel perfectly attached. So far so good. Error Reading on Hydration, but what's new?

Looks gray and foggy outside. Easter sunrise services never saw the main attraction.

Quick scan indicates I am home, alone and safe. It's always a relief to wake up in an uncompromising position.

ENTER > GO. I intend to leap out of bed and start the day running but the directive doesn't download. Right leg countermands the left and I fall down.

This action highlights a curiosity. Oddly, I am not in my usual sleeping attire. I'm wearing pants that are gathered around my ankles. Tuxedo shirt and jacket add

229

to the mystery. Save query on Desktop to solve later.

I lie on the floor, overdressed. Memories of the recent past fall all over themselves as I reboot my brain. Thoughts scramble to find their Folders and Documents. Like a downloading image, notions begin to form, clarify and sharpen, but a server cannot be found. Desktop fills up fast.

POP UP MESSAGE > Tonight is the memorial for Billy Dwyer at Ed Moses'. I didn't know him well but liked his work a great deal. William Dwyer was a minimalist. Work I knew was well-crafted, delicate and precious. Funny work for a big barrel-chested guy.

People look like their dogs but artists never really look like their work.

DOG > DYING. Yeah, the heaviness that hangs in my heart. A storm on my Sea of Eternal Sadness. My dog is living his final days. Din, sweet Dobie, lives with my ex-wife. We are steeling for the worst and the inevitable. I have loved Din over thirteen years; feelings go deep. I want him to be comfortable. He's moving in with me.

I guess it's a good thing he isn't here right now; Would've landed on him when I fell out of bed…

I NO LONGER THINK > I DOWNLOAD. All I wanted was DSL but Technical Advisor in New Delhi led me to upgrade everything. All is chaos. Money burns. Logging too many hours on hold for support. So weary, so beaten.

AGGRESSIVE AMERICANISM > OVERLY DESIGNED. NuComputer tries to think for me and fin-

230

ish my sentences. Take five steps back. Trying to under-stand new operating system, so I'm trying to think like it, talk like it.

DEATH > TAXES. Taxes due in four days.

DEATH > HELL > ELECTION YEAR.

DEATH > DAILY > OBITUARIES > WAR DEAD. Every day, I try to read obits of our fallen com-rades. Least I can do.

Yesterday at lunch, had to whip out the shades in-doors and cough-away a sob, reading soldier's last letter to seven year-old son. The stories. The lives. Serving so honorably. I need to *believe* my leaders act accordingly.

ESCAPE > POP UP MENU > HAPPINESS. Song on new mix by DJ Krakatoa can halt all of world's aggressions. Infectious, toe-tappin' disco ditty "Ménage a Trois" (Alcazar) chimes, "Twice is nice but three is di-vine; What's yours is hers and hers is mine; If you're in the middle then just hold on tight." Doubt anyone with that notion in their head would ever blow up a train.

TRAIN > SPAIN. Bombing rattled me. I have loved ones in Madrid.

DEATH > EASTER > 'PASSION' BIG B.O. Mel Gibson says Jesus took it like a man.

DEATH > ENVELOPES. Helping friend Tara stuff invitations to a memorial. Her mother died quietly and unexpectedly, in her sleep.

Vital, successful, beautiful, her mother was dancing on top of the world. Had a loving husband and tight, close family. (They even *liked* to hang out with each other.) New car. New house. Thriving business. Great health. At this time in her life, everything was well-placed and sunny. Gone.

I pray I go like that. With a smile.

ON THE MONITOR > Just noticing, when lying on the floor, the perspective is vertical, always up.

Just noticing, at eye level, the carpet is disgusting and needs to be vacuumed. Little synthetic fibers tickle my nose and are annoying the hell out of me every time I breathe. Jesus, wonder what I'm inhaling. I should get up—Why be hasty?

Suddenly, a golden snowflake drifts into view. A shiny little gold star. Odd. It catches the lamplight and flares as it saunters to the nylon-pile earth.

Then another one sails in, this time larger. Soon, it's joined by a sparkling companion. Flecks of gold are snowing in my bedroom. This does not strike me as unusual.

After all, maybe magic really *does* exist...

ERROR READING > RE-BOOT. No magic. Studio door is ajar; Gold escaping.

GOLD > STUDIO > REBIRTH AND RESURRECTION. Gotta get up. Got work to do. Have to restore a public piece from 1997. It's a behemoth and deadline is now. Using metal gilding and hidden text, series is about surface, philosophy and value. Over time, the bright, polished gold will patina and copper compounds will oxidize, slowly turning the work from dazzling hope to earthen beauty.

Now back to the dazzle.

In the studio, fans are blowing to speed drying time; it's a wind tunnel. Thousands of gold flakes are caught in the tornado and the room flares and dances with explosions of flying light.

Some Gods give; some take away. No matter how severe the damage, the power and force of Life cannot be destroyed. Death is inevitable and regrowth is innate. Old Man River just keeps on rolling along.

And I better roll off this carpet. Resurrection begins one nail at a time.

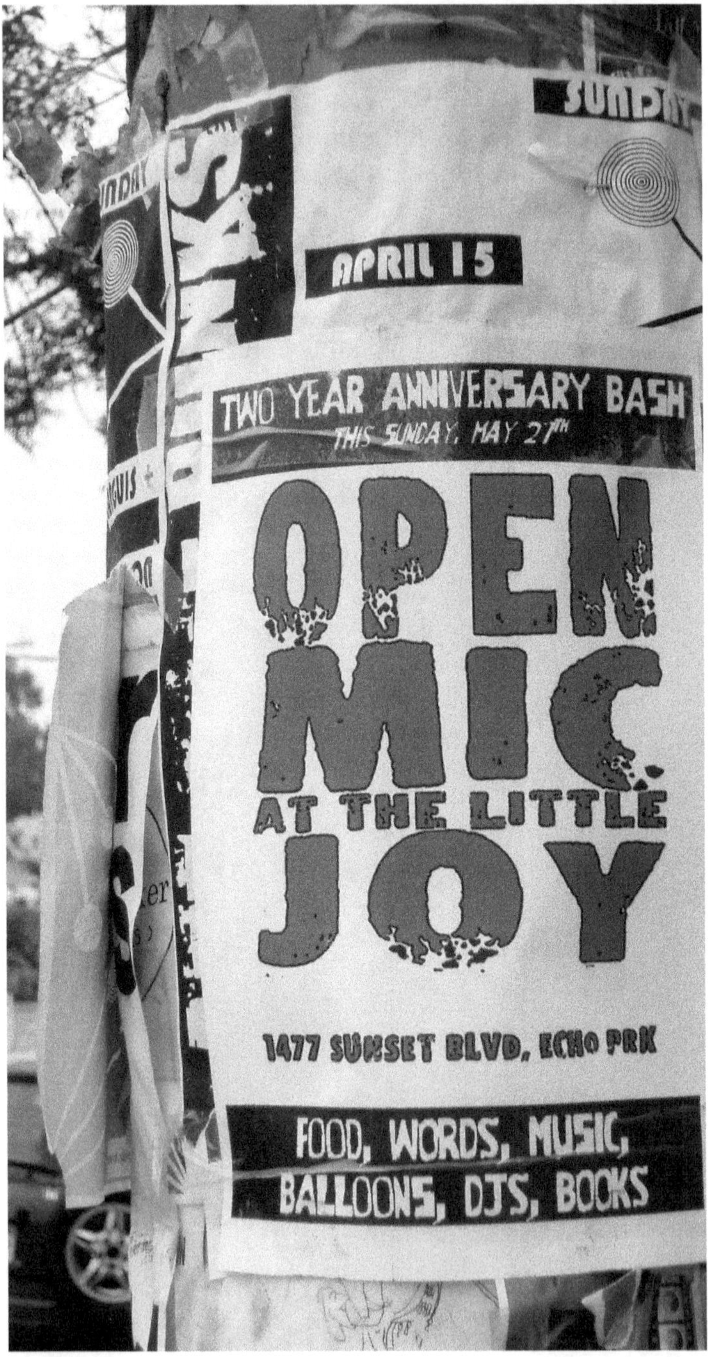
SUNDAY
APRIL 15
TWO YEAR ANNIVERSARY BASH
THIS SUNDAY, MAY 27TH
OPEN
MIC
AT THE LITTLE
JOY
1477 SUNSET BLVD, ECHO PRK
FOOD, WORDS, MUSIC,
BALLOONS, DJS, BOOKS

IT SOUNDS LIKE THE OCEAN

Bad things happen to good people. Luck teaches us that the pendulum always swings. Sometimes we ride it high and sometimes we ride it low. When misfortune clocks us in the head, the only thing you can do is close your eyes, inhale deeply, and listen to the gentle roar of the waves.

No matter how bad it gets, life gives us a choice of perspective. You can choose a traffic jam or the sound of the sea.

Old pal Sally fell madly in love with a house and wanted me to see it. The place was great. It was big, beautiful, and had its own on-ramp. It was located on the Hollywood Freeway. You had to scream to be heard. I asked her how she could possibly live with the roar. Sally shrugged her shoulders and replied, "It sounds just like the ocean."

Gordy Grundy

My old college friend Stu Gimlet recently blew out his knee and had major microsurgery. His lifestyle has been devastated. With a cast on his right leg, he can no longer drink and drive. He can't chase girls. Hopping like a pogo stick, he can't bust a move on the dance floor. His whole life is ruined.

I tried to console the unlucky bastard. Over bong hits, I said, "Stu, it sounds like the ocean."

He nodded in agreement. Five minutes later he asked, "What sounds like the ocean?"

"Your knee," I answered.

Stu smiled and gave me a thumbs up.

LINGO

"sod-buster" \ n : α derogatory term for one who will not find a value in art; 2 : a condescending term for one who does not find a value in art; 3 : an charitable term for one who cannot comprehend any value in art; 4: *"Only a sod-buster would touch a painting."*

(Courtesy of abstract painter Alan Wayne, Los Angeles, California)

BRING ON THE NEW YEAR!

The failure rate of a New Years resolution is extremely high. Often the goals are too far-reaching, not sincere or just damn impractical.

Yet the Holiday is earmarked for renewal. *Change is good.*

When a New Year is in its infancy, there is no better way to honor it than to mimic it. Take your lead

236

from hard-livin' Father Time. The old fart ends each year with a death rattle and, upon the stroke of midnight, resurrects himself into a kicking, cooing babe. Now, you can too!

January is a substance free month. No excessive behaviors here. Renewal brings balance and becomes a fresh test of character.

A rehab respite is a kind way to say thanks to our minds and bodies for all of the hard work and overtime of the previous year.

EARLY WARNING SIGN

When the soundtrack to your life is composed by Portishead.

BUY MORE ART

Every year Los Angelenos Jeff P. and his wife Susan choose to observe their wedding anniversary in a very special way. They honor it with art. And by doing so, they celebrate their love, passion and strength of union.

The act of buying art mimics the vagaries of a relationship. Each year, Jeff and Susan make a series of dates to visit their favorite galleries and explore several new ones. Over candle-lit dinners, they discuss and argue their favorites. The couple find their commonality when they select a piece.

The art becomes their anniversary gift to each

other, a symbol of the physical, emotional and the romantic.

Art is the milestone. I can think of no greater achievement than to fill a house with anniversary art where over the years one can look at each piece and remember the era and the love that it represents.

YOU CAN BE AN ARTS ACTIVIST—KILL THE MESSENGER!

An urban myth is entertaining; unfortunately the notion is often perceived as fact. I have been told the following sordid tale several times over the years and just last week I was introduced to a contemporary version. It is always told in the same manner.

The story:

"My friend, who is a lawyer, was recently in New York on business. With some time to kill, he visits the studio of an old school chum who is now a famous artist. As they are about to leave for lunch, the artist says, 'Hang on a sec, wanna see me make twenty grand?'

The attorney nods gleefully. The artist takes a can of paint and throws it across the canvas.

"There," said the artist, "I just made twenty grand. Let's eat."

The story always follows with a derogatory comment about the arts.

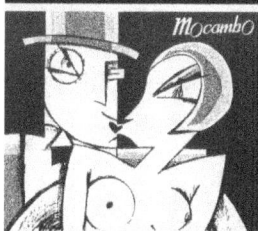

WALK IN DANCE OUT.

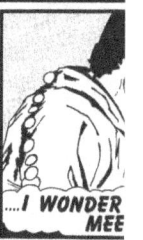

....I WONDER
MEE

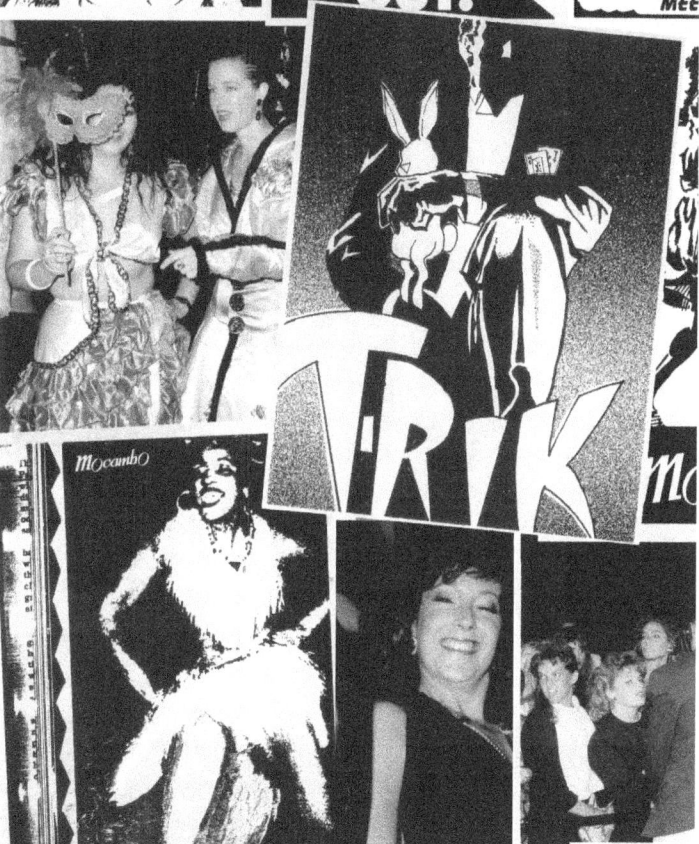

SHE DANCED WITH THE PASSION OF A VOODOO PRIESTESS.

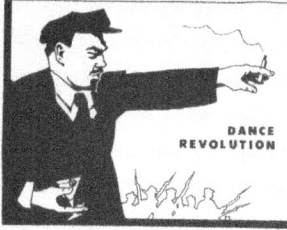

DANCE
REVOLUTION

TR
A
SH

GAMBLING
SE PERMITE APOSTAR

NO LAST POCKET
JUGAR A LA ULTIMA

NO VOODO

BLOOD (NOT SO) SIMPLE

I needed blood. For an artwork, I needed blood to soak into a linen handkerchief.

Some suggested cow's blood or pig's blood or whatever you can find in the carneceria down the street. I wanted human blood in case there was a difference in coagulation.

And naturally, it had to be my blood.

I just wasn't sure how to get it out of the wrapper.

The hyper-elegant piece was to be the crown jewel of my solo show 'Fortuna' at Sala Diaz in San Antonio. In one simple wry work, I wanted to communicate the horror of all the lives that have been lost in the name of religion. The piece was titled "Blood Spilled in the Name of Fortuna (Lotus Bar, June 2006)." I liked the idea of equating a religious war to a bar fight.

To accomplish this, all I needed was a little blood.

241

Gordy Grundy

Quite handy with tools, I am generally always bleeding. Unfortunately, I'm never bleeding enough to fill a small Tupperware.

I could always stab around until I got enough going, but how do you stop it? What if I hit an artery? How do I keep it fresh? There were just too many variables to home bloodletting. I had to look outside.

Believing blood removal to be rather simple, I called my doctor's lab and said I wanted to swing by for a coupla test tubes. They told me this was illegal and that they could not accommodate my wishes.

I explained that the blood was for an art show. (In my mind, there is no greater joy; doors should spring open.)

Of course, that's when it got ugly.

"Are you going to throw it?" the nurse asked.

"No!" I replied indignantly.

"Well, what if you threw it? We'd be liable," said the nurse.

"Well, I'm not throwing it." I said, "Besides, what's wrong with my blood? It's my blood. I can do whatever I want with it."

"Well, we're not taking it outta ya... Understand?"

Realizing this situation could be cleared up with a simple call, I phoned my doctor. I don't see him very often but he is my doctor. We have that friendly patter of uneasy confidence and forced bonhomie. I would never dare press him for a prescription of Quaaludes, but I felt I could ask for a little blood removal on the QT.

He replied, "What if you throw it?"

Yes, I understand now. That's when I started to feel like a fifteen year old girl, pregnant, alone, ditched and with nowhere to turn… A dark alley. A nurse in a greasy vest. A gin-soaked doctor. A rusty coat hanger. I was alone. The deadline had me scared.

I entertained the do-it-yourself concept once again. What do I use? An exacto blade? A chain saw? And what if I found out I liked it? I really don't have the time or the energy right now to discover a fetish or fall into a new obsession. Why open a Pandora's box?

I asked several friends for help. "Will you bleed me?" Everyone answered, "No!" When a new acquaintance answered "Yes!" a little too quickly and salaciously, *I* said "No."

I put the question out to Craig's List on the internet for any ideas. All I got was sympathy or disgust. Several people suggested pig's blood, but a pig lacks a certain dignity, which the piece most definitely required.

In this land of the free, blood is like Social Security. You have it but you just can't get to it. Our government wants our blood to stay where it's supposed to.

My only option was the underground. Scoring drugs is easy but bloodletting is not. I thought a heroin addict would know his way around a needle.

I was just about to head to the LA River when my friend Lucy saved me. Through a friend of a friend's friend, she found a registered nurse, a supporter of the arts, who might be persuaded to bend her Hippocratic Oath and perform the illegal act.

I really didn't see the problem with it. Sure, if I

243

were trying to extract *your* blood, we'd have an issue. But I was merely trying to get at my *own*. Second, blood is edgy all by itself. When you add 'artist' to 'blood' you get questions like "Are you gonna throw it?"

That was the first thing the renegade nurse asked me.

"No," I replied, "But I'm starting to think about it."

Tawny, the rebel nurse, and I got off to a slow start. First, her phone machine answered, "Mutt Rescue. You ditching, dumping or donating?" This threw me off for several days since she didn't return any of my repeated calls; I thought I had a wrong number and a dead end.

I started to panic about my deadline. This woman was my last resort. The show was opening soon and much work had to be done. I had to have her help; there was no one to turn to. I needed her bloodletting bad.

Second, as an artist, I have a hard time knowing when to shut up. Every time an artist talks about their own work, my eyes glaze over. Suddenly, in mid-monologue, I realized I was doing it to her! As I was excitedly explaining what the work was about, I could sense that I was losing her. Usually, folks just meander away with the vague excuse of refreshing a full drink. But this was no cocktail party; we were on the phone.

Brassy Tawny interrupted my convolution and asked, "So, are you gonna throw it?"

In brief, Tawny agreed to help and we became pals. The red head stuck her neck out for me. We've now shared a few funny, memorable moments and even a bonfire. It doesn't get any better than that.

Luck gives us the good and the bad. As Luck would have it, the piece, the crown jewel of my show, was preciously framed and completed on time. I couldn't have been happier.

That joy ended when the bloody piece was stolen or inconceivably misplaced. Either way, I'll never know. All I know is that it never made it to the show in Texas.

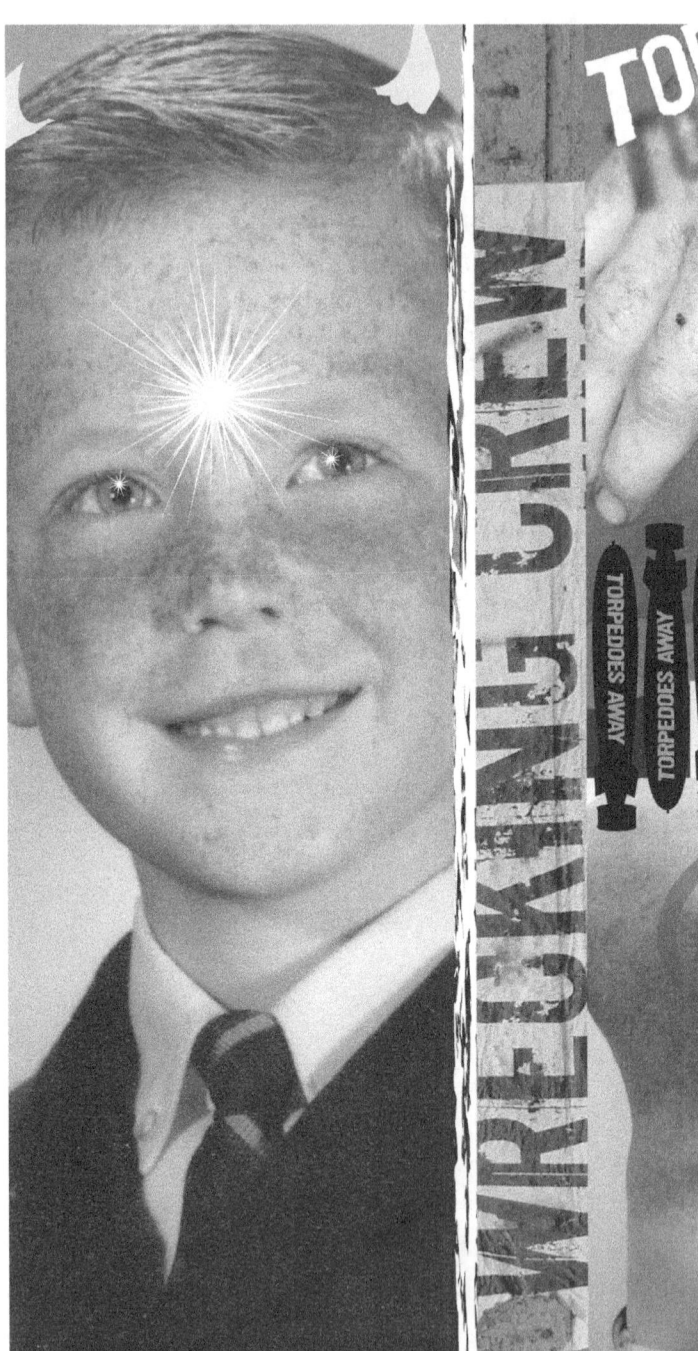

CHEEKY

ART RIOT

You never know what can set you off. Usually a confluence of ugly factors have built to a pressure point and the explosive matter just lingers, waiting. All it takes is a trigger, a spark to detonate your powder keg.

Who thought it could have been a cartoon?

Just last weekend, Friday night, I was at the Skylight Bookstore in East Hollywood, lollygagging, killing time before the movie started next door. Meandering. Browsing. There was so much to look at. All of it made me happy. My sweet soul was singing. Life was good.

The *New Yorker* logo caught my eye. The big book was encyclodpedia-thick, a collection titled 'The New Yorker Book of Art Cartoons.' I leisurely thumbed through several pages, looking to laugh. I like cartoons. I like to laugh.

247

Gordy Grundy

Suddenly, I realized the book was making fun of artists. "Plein Aire or not, fella, ya gotta put your pants on!" What is that insinuating? Artists are exhibitionists? "How do you know when you're done appreciating art?" That's like making fun of one's religion! "Abstract Expressionist Face Painting $5." Is finding a complex form some kind of joke? "And don't forget to feed the Artist-in-Residence!" Furthering negative stereotypes. You can get arrested for making fun of someone in a wheelchair. Artists are open season. "I'm looking for something my kids could have made." A punch in the face.

Suddenly, I didn't feel very well, as if my stomach had filled with cement. I began slapping through the pages rather than turning them. My eyes darting across each. Panic rising.

An icy, cold hand grabbed my heart and yanked it from my chest. *These cartoons aren't funny!* They are *making fun* of artists. Humiliating devoted and devout people like me!

The agony and torment was great. What felt like a lion's roar was tearing through my throat. People were looking.

Crazed, I was! Senseless. Uncontrollable. The blasphemy! This wasn't some half-assed French newspaper. This was the *New Yorker*!

Like Charlton Heston and his Ten Commandments, I raised the book above my head, so as to smite it down mightily upon the Bargain Books table.

But the heavy tome caught me off balance and I fell backward, hard against a freestanding bookcase of Women's Literature.

I heard the sound of snapping wood and the

bookcase fell, smashing into another.

As I ran from the store, with the 'Book of Art Cartoons' still held above my head, I could hear the synchronized explosions of each bookcase colliding into the next, like dominoes in swift succession. Bam! Bam! Bam! Bam! …BAM!

Later, the TV news reported there were no injuries except for a couple buried under the Human Sexuality section.

Outside the bookstore, a large crowd had gathered, waiting to buy tickets to the triple feature. The neon marquee promised 'Basquiat,' 'Modigliani' and 'Pollock.'

Wild-eyed, red-eyed and yelling, I burst from the store. The masses parted. A woman screamed. All eyes met mine.

I looked up at the heavens, beyond the thick book still held high above my head, and I howled with all of the pain that was searing my soul.

A hand touched my chest. Ink-stained fingers smoothed my shirt, wrinkled with sweat. The gentle caress belonged to Laura, a printmaker I know. Her sweet caring face was angled up at mine. Those deep water eyes were filled with compassion. So clear. So tender. Of any artist I know, she is one of the purest. One of the most devoted. ONE OF THE MOST—Fire and blood rushed to my head. "ART CARTOONS! THE BLASPHEMY! *THE INDIGNITY!*" I screamed. I roared.

Like a Grizzly mauling a camper, I began to tear the glossy comic pages from the weak spine of the mirthless cartoon book. The pages flew skyward. Curious moviegoers leapt at the line art obscenities. As each cartoon was digested, another soul was blackened.

Exclamations rose throughout the fevered crowd.

"My God!"

"That's not funny!"

"What's this caption mean? *'It's not her oeuvre!'* I don't get it."

The crowd began to surge and spark. The din, a welter of discordant agony, flared into an irate cacophony. To the right, glass broke and a car alarm hollered.

Three guys, I recognized them as downtown Ab-Ex painters, wrenched a newspaper rack from its mooring. I stepped aside just as they heaved it through the bookstore window.

People started screaming, then chanting. The liquor store, two doors down, was emptied out by a bucket brigade passing cases of beer.

Half a dozen Conceptualists (Culver City hopefuls) had flipped a car onto its roof. They were trying to jam an uprooted ficus tree into the undercarriage.

A chorus of car alarms started to sound like the drone of locusts.

Whomever yelled "Fucking artists!" was answered by a flurry of fists.

As I turned to grab a friend, I got clipped on the forehead by a flying bottle. The guy who tossed it had a funny hat on his head. He might have been a DADA-ist or maybe a Muslim. The streetlights began to solarize and my knees started to buckle.

Just before I lost consciousness, I saw a palm tree go up in flames.

CONSCIOUSNESS REDUX

I really shouldn't feel as bad as I do for inciting the riot. Mullahs and their Muslims have a hard time with cartoons as well. I mean, it's one thing to attack your God *or* your dog, but the *New Yorker* was humiliating my reason for living.

How personal can you get?

I thought my skin was a bit thicker. The Fine Arts does that to you. It tans our oh-so-sensitive hide. Indignity and blasphemy are as much a part of the Artist's Life as creating, producing and exhibiting.

The artwork that you consider to be unbelievably lame gets the front-page review. The museum show goes to the graphic artist who paints. The 'new idea' is always the one you dismissed long, long ago. It's the educated arts patron who smears a greasy finger across the surface of your painting. Ad nauseam.

Of course, insult is always added to injury. The art world, as a society, reacts very much like a sorority. When value and worth can be easily debated, the only armor is attitude. Understandably, it is hard to build a foundation on the uneven earth of subjectivity.

Whether inside art or out, we are forever the outsiders.

At the very moment when you devote your life to the Arts, a knife is run deep into your midsection. Even though you may learn how to live with the blade, the hilt remains forever exposed. This is our vulnerability; it is easy to twist.

251

Gordy Grundy

An indignity is far more pungent than a compliment. By our nature, we have a tendency to slight the goodwill and deeply bury a criticism. Sadly, congratulations never fester; insult and insecurity do.

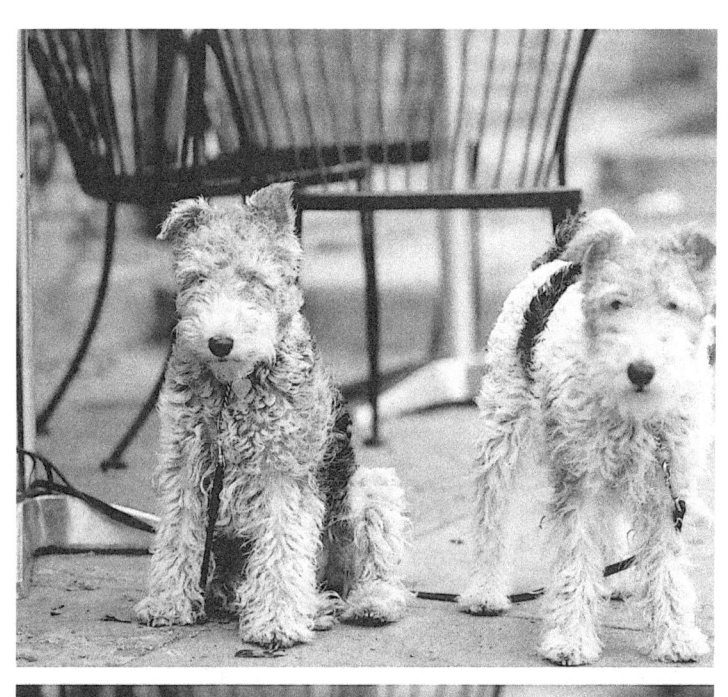

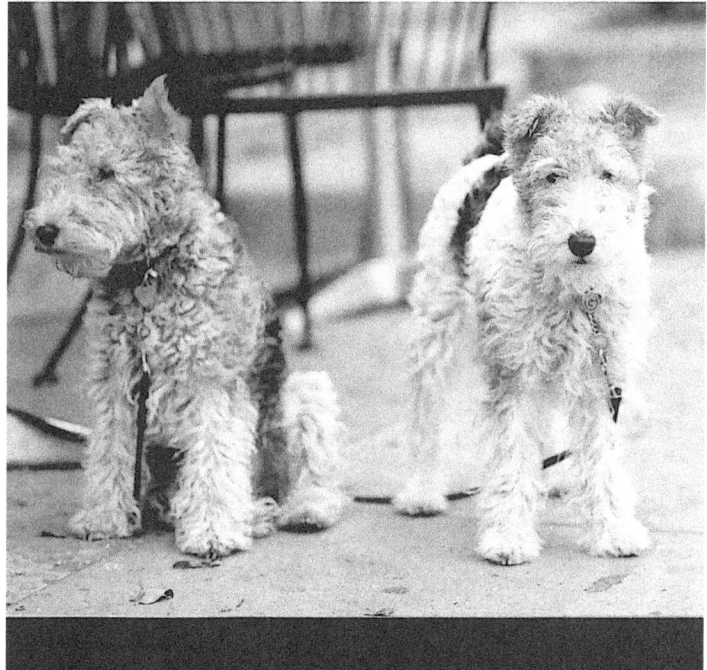

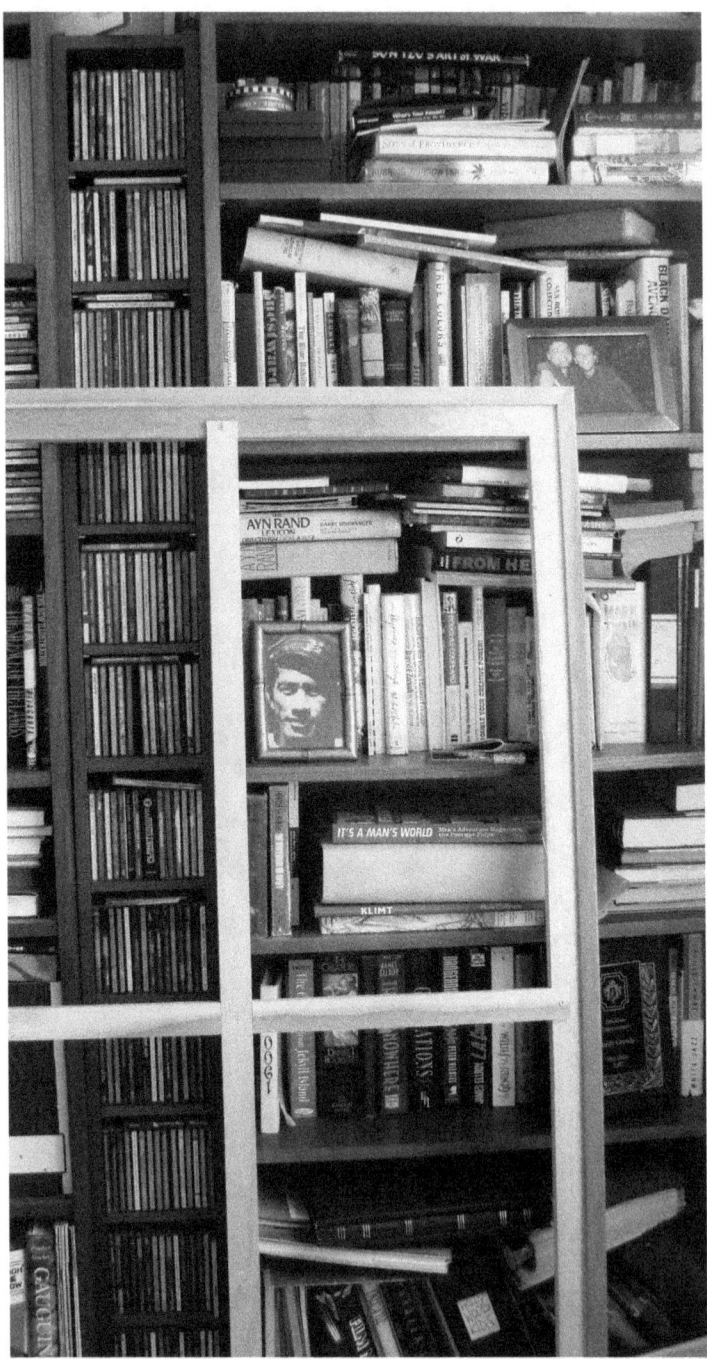

LIVING IN WARTIME, PART TWO

SIZE ELEVEN AND A HALF IN GALVANIZED

This is rather embarrassing to write about, so publicly, but I have little choice. It's hard to hide. You see, I stepped in a bucket.

And I can't get my foot out. Neither can the experts.

So I am learning to live with this bucket.

I thought I was doing the right thing, just walking along, on my sunny side of the street. When suddenly, I stepped into this pail I didn't see coming. A black leather, size eleven and a half, Lucchese cowboy boot is now stuck in a medium-sized galvanized bucket.

The emergency crew didn't want to cut it off for fear of damaging something. The doctors agreed that it needs X-rays and tests before they attempt a removal. It has to do with angle and pressure.

Gordy Grundy

My foot is stuck.

I have to learn to live with the bucket boot for a while. My pants are cut open along the side. Fifteen safety pins are keeping it together but it's still breezy. I need pants with a full zipper up the right leg. I have a pair on order, so I now wear a sarong. I look like a Tahitian cowboy, with a bucket on one boot.

It's a good thing I'm not a private detective or a spy because there is nothing subtle about my approach. I am rather loud and slow. Step. CLANK. Step. KLUNK.

Rather than shame the deformity, I am embracing it.

Two nights ago, I filled the bucket with white sand before I went to a party. My smoker friends found my ashtray handy and convenient.

Today, I have the bucket filled with water and nine little Feng Shui goldfish. I figure I need all the luck I can get.

You could say that I've *really stepped in it this time*. I have a bucket on my right foot and all I can do is make the very best of it.

I can't get it off; I have to live with it. I have a choice and I will make this a good experience. Somehow.

OLD WORLD ORDER

My friend Marsh explains himself with his hands, gesturing as if he were rocking a salad bowl or a globe from side to side.

He says that the political flavor leans a little to the left and then it shifts a little to the right. And vice-a-versa.

It is this motion, the flow and the pull, that keeps the equilibrium of a democracy.

EVERYONE, EVERYWHERE

The world has truly never been smaller.

Right now, for some people, life is a searing physical pain. For others, their heart aches to touch a loved one. Some people are angry and half-mad. Others are anticipating a financial windfall. Most are fretting. Somewhere in the world, two people are falling in love. Some are spooning, holding one another and feeling intense comfort. Some people are so stinkin' dirty that they can't even remember how good a hot shower once felt. Some are scoffing at ideas and some are passionate about them. Some are easily convinced and others are thinkers. For some, life is no longer worth living. Some know that they have a friend. Right now, somewhere in the world, two people are laughing and giddy. Others are humorless.

It happens to everyone, everywhere, right now.

TOO MUCH IN A BLINK

I really think my nerves are pushing their seams. My timing is off. The synapses are misfiring. Veins in my eyes glow red like lava.

There is too much comin' at me. Every time I

hear a car backfire, I think the terrorists are attacking Los Angeles. I know they're dying to. I am compelled to check on world events every ten minutes or so. Where's Paris right *now*? How much of MySpace is mine? Do I have the hottest ring tones?

I can't sleep. I can't eat. Thankfully, I can still drink.

The *LA Times* says that folks are exhausted from watching the Battle for World Order on TV.

I'll say. I sure am. And I don't even own a TV.

My psychiatrist, the esteemed Doctor Emile Von Burstebagge, spoke at length on the subject. As usual, I didn't know what the hell he was talking about. My main man, Doc Von, speaks in such a heavy Austrian accent that I rarely know what the fuck he is saying.

At first, I thought he was recommending that I "carjack an old lady for the spring harvest renewal." Later I realized he was saying something completely different. "The stress of advanced technology on a newly evolving brain creates a conflict in the neurological system."

The technology of communication has evolved faster than our brains have. When we process too much too fast, we blow a fuse in our Zortex. I believe that's what my psychiatrist said.

Each bit of information we get has a corresponding emotional reaction of some duration and priority. So if your dog dies, you will feel *real* bad for three weeks and less bad for thirty more. If you get a nickel-an-hour raise, you will feel real proud and elated for about twenty-five minutes.

As your bean gets info, it has to process that bit

emotionally as well as conceptually and objectively. The more info your noggin gets, your Zortex gets swamped with more than your noggin can handle. We start skipping or shortchanging stuff. We start living less well. And therefore we stop living.

"Neva has zee human rr-race, as a schh-pecies, been mo' shallenged! Yah!" sputtered Burstebagge.

He took a swig of coffee that smelled an awful lot like schnapps. He slowly cleared his throat and shrugged his shoulders.

"Zat's da problem of leeving in vartime."

NATIONAL EMPOWERMENT IS PERSONAL EMPOWERMENT

I got rid of my mullet; I now have a blow-dry freedom cut.

Right after the first 'Decapitator' hit Baghdad, I had my stomach surgically stapled. I lost eighty pounds and I look great. I feel great.

The polyethylene pec implants have given me a physique that even Tarzan would admire. Steroids have given me new, vein-popping biceps.

Viagra has put a tiger in my trunk. I smile with pearly capped whites.

My jaw line, once concave, now juts forward like Ben Affleck. My chin implant is made of glass. I better be careful where I swing it.

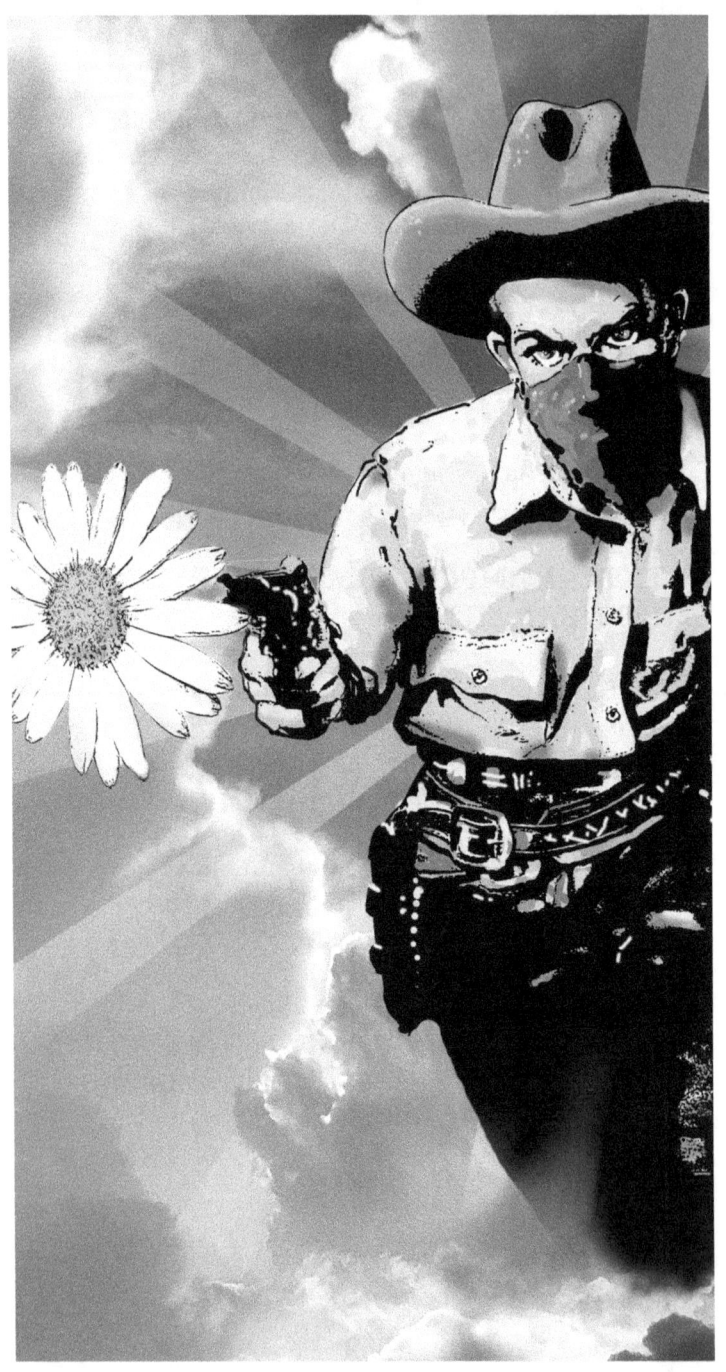

ARTIST'S PANTS

A certain, unnamed, national retailer that sounds a lot like Saks Fifth Avenue has been quietly contracting with a handful of U.S. artists to provide high-end apparel manufacturing services. Rent is almost due and, thankfully, I am one of them.

I got the job when I clipped the phone number from a flier on a telephone pole just outside my local coffeehouse.

Soon to debut in the Fall are colorful 'Artist's Pants,' the next big push in fashion.

In these hurly burly days of Living in Wartime, John and Jane Q. Public have little time to devote to their own expression. That Manhattan bond trader may have the soul of an artist, but not the dedication. A Pacific Palisades housewife knows what she likes, but hates to get her nails dirty.

How can you express your creativity and individuality? How can you bulls-eye a first impression? Art-

Gordy Grundy

ist's Pants.

The unnamed retailer has been shipping fresh, clean khaki pants, in a variety of sizes, to a number of painters across the country, myself included. I am saving a fortune on rags for I am getting paid to clean my hands and wipe my brushes on my pants.

My "patron of the arts"—that's what Miguel, the factory foreman, wants us to call him—my *patron* offers very simple instructions: "Wipe like the wind, amigos!

The more colorful the better. And the more colorful, the more profitable. The unnamed and tight-fisted retailer is paying approximately $12.50 per pair of finished 'Artist's Pants.' Sadly, Monochromatic painters get only half that.

You can earn more. If you have an MFA, expect an additional $2 per pair. Cigarette burns bring in an additional 35 cents per hole. A small landscape or doodle adds $3 to $4 per pair.
There are penalties. Liquor, blood and vomit stains can result in a deduction of $3 to $5 per stain.

Naturally, the more pants I can produce in a week, the more money I can make.
Luckily, I have always been very quick and skilled at putting on my pants. You never know when a spouse, away on a business trip, will return home unexpectedly.
This training has aided my productivity enormously.

We've heard rumors that these unique and stylish

262

pants will retail at $975 per pair.

They anticipate a huge demand, with a focus on urban centers, where artists are truly appreciated.

Market research indicates that 'Artist's Pants' are a big bomb in rural areas, where consumers were confusing them with plumber's pants and (house) painter's pants.

This is the bold, new urban look.

Parents will finally be relieved that their high schoolers will no longer be dressing like crack dealers and ghetto gangstas. Now their kids will want to emulate the clean cut, hard-working American artist.

Unfortunately, wait till Mom and Dad get a load of the price tag of art school. They may want to rethink the Role Model.

The fashion world publicity machine is gearing up. I'm told that Kate Moss will wear 'Artist's Pants' on the November cover of *Vogue*.

In June, the cover story of *Bride* will be titled "Oil Paint and Lace."

All of the contestants on *American Idol* will receive a bar of Ivory Soap, Travel Yahtzee, and a pair of 'Artist's Pants.'

Which senatorial candidate will be the first to court the artist vote, wearing a new pair? We shall see.

It is also rumored that several couturiers are rushing to cash in on the trend.

I have heard that Armani and BCBG are competing to attract Blue Chip galleries for their Blue Chip Artists.

"Say, how much for those David Hockney-Marc

Gordy Grundy

Jacobs pants?"

The real sharks are smelling the blood; I've heard that Damien Hirst is coming out with an entire, paint splattered, lifestyle line.

Unfortunately, now that the word is out, my art dealer is demanding half of my pant earnings.

To me, the real value is in the promotion. Like the Beanie Babies, each pair of Artist's Pants will feature a small hang tag, which lists the name and bio of each artist.

Mine will read, "If you like the pants, you'll love the paintings."

Predictably, dark clouds are gathering on my economic horizon. For every falling piano, there is an artist below it.

Despite my productivity and cheerfulness, the unnamed money-grubbing retailer has been slowing down the volume.

They are going overseas. Haitian children will paint for 35 cents a pant.

Red Chinese prisoners produce a pair at 72 cents. And Latin Countries are offering $1.25 with brighter colors and a faster turn around.

Goddamn NAFTA.

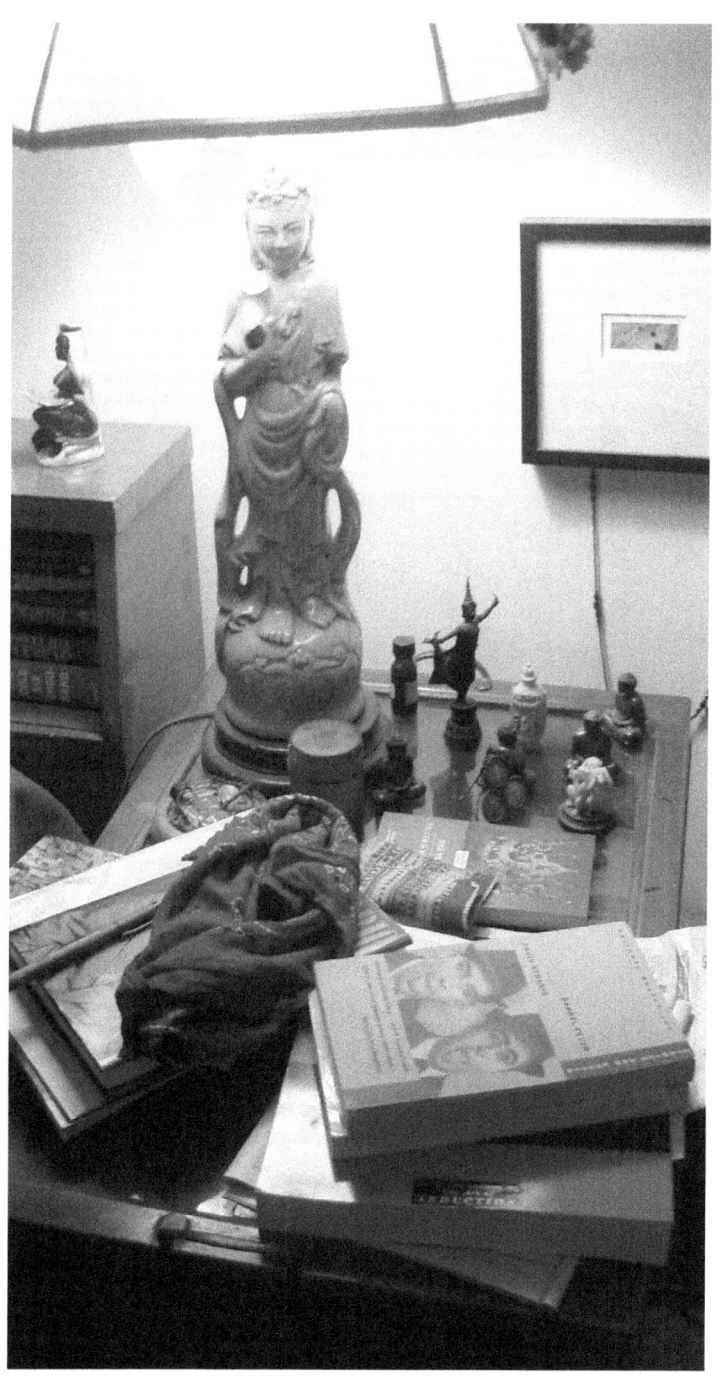

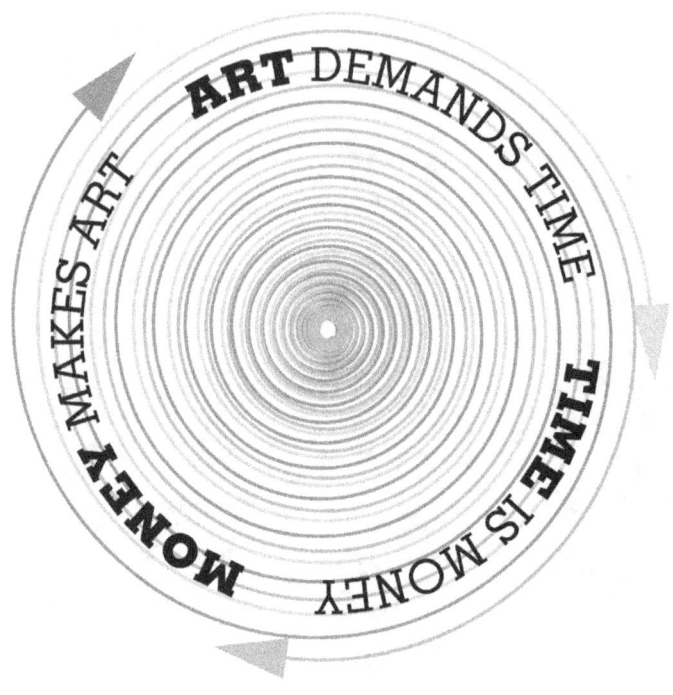

**ECONOMIC CYCLES OF
THE FINE ARTIST**

Figure 23.1

ECONOMIC OPPORTUNITIES FOR THE FINE ARTIST

Every artist who is not supported by tenure or a trust fund must keep an entrepreneurial eye on the financial horizon. Our axiom, "Making Art Takes Time and Time is Money," demands that the ol' Day Job must offer the most drachmas in the least amount of time.

I have begun to look at various Business Opportunities in hopes of finding my golden cash cow. The effort has revealed three investment goldmines. I hope to sink my shovel into one of them and shout, "Eureka!"

BULLETS
I) Munitions continues to be a growth industry. Like food, medicine and DSL, munitions can be considered one of those staples that we just can't live without.

The profit margins are huge.

Best of all, the defense business seems to do a lotta entertaining on yachts in the Mediterranean, which suits me just swell.

Unfortunately, three reasons prevent me from attaining great success in this field.

First, you need a lotta capital to make bombs and I can't afford a firework stand.

Second, I am a Lover not a Fighter. This attitude lacks the necessary instinct that might make success in this field more assured.

Third, I would rather Create than Destroy, which again is a recipe for defeat. I knew I had to look beyond my limitations.

ESCAPISM

II) With tensions high and climbing, wartime provides a steady market for inebriants and their detractors.

In times of great stress, folks like to dance it off and the devil may care. Drug dealers, liquor distributors, tobacco growers, recovery centers, faith-based initiatives and televangelists are popping corks over their wartime success.

While society is waiting for the other shoe to drop and the Alert Level to leap, Bacchus-based initiatives are on the rise.

I had an idea, a new concept in Better Living, that I called Vice Transference Recovery Systems (VTRS). The concept is simple. Rather than trying to eliminate the habit, we will help you transfer the object of your passion.

Sex addicts are refocused to become stoners.

Dragon Chasers are told to follow a pair of dice.

Wanna quit smoking? Have a drink instead.

I just hate to see someone give up something they love.

Unfortunately, the VTRS Concept failed. In self-testing, it was actually *adding* vices rather than transferring them.

Another dream bubble had burst. And I was looking forward to having celebrity clients...

THE OLDEST PROFESSION IN THE WORLD

III) Sometimes the most obvious is the hardest to see, which makes the third opportunity so brilliant.

I went back to the basics, to the tried and true, to one of the oldest professions.

Throughout the ages, *religion* has been one of the world's greatest moneymakers. You say, "Fervent" and I say, "Customer."

I took a gander at various beliefs, thinking that joining an existing institution would be like buying a successful franchise. Due Diligence took a look at all aspects of various faiths.

Unfortunately, every religion known to man was scratched off my list for either logical, dietary or libertarian purposes.

If I couldn't buy into a church, I'd have to start my own.

Having recently discovered and concluded the true Meaning of Life, I am well qualified to establish such a spiritual venture. As a Los Angeleno, my environment is endowed with a long tradition of health fads, twisted cults and evangelical start-ups.

Gordy Grundy

It felt like a fit. I knew I could do it.

Several months later, I was ready to go. The new religion had a belief system, a creation story and most importantly, a cool logo. I was practicing the speech that I would need to make in order to get certified by the California State Board of Religion, Belief and Wishful Thinking.

"There is a deep and meaningful philosophical core to the Fellowship of Fortuna. Due to space limitations and the imminent start of Happy Hour, we will gloss over the Glory and focus on the sizzle.

"In brief, the Fellowship of Fortuna celebrates those things that unite every human being, the first and foremost trait being Chance. Sometimes good and sometimes bad, we all have Luck. While most call her Lady Luck, we know her as Fortuna. Every church needs an icon and the Roman Goddess is the inspiration for ours.

"As a figurehead, Fortuna stands tall, swinging a down-turned sword back and forth like a pendulum. With it, she dispenses Luck, both fair and foul. She does not wear a blindfold, for her impartiality is her integrity. She has a beautiful, intriguing face with a quirky smile, like the Statue of Liberty or Angelina Jolie. Her steady gaze can both comfort the misfortunate with tender empathy and wink gaily at a winner. Fortuna is a vixen.

"The members of the Fellowship of Fortuna, known as the 'Fortunates,' are an active and involved bunch. Collectively, they have several things in common. All tend to be quite bright. All have a keen interest in learning. All strive for experience.

"A collective of engineers and marketing types who call themselves 'The Continuum' are dedicated to the swing of Fortuna's sword. With physics, probability and statistics, they are trying to quantify Chance.

"The 'Flaming Fortune,' our car club, is aptly named. Restoring a car costs a fortune and all of the vehicles have the ability to shoot flames from their tail pipes. This is dangerous and illegal, so we try and turn a blind eye.

"Our sports teams win most titles in their leagues. These men and women, the 'Falcons of Fortuna,' are scoring trophies in volleyball, skateboarding, boxing, basketball, billiards, dragstrip racing and water polo. There is talk of a sailing team.
"We have a surf squad, 'SurFortuna,' but they've never turned in any paperwork.

"Our cheerleading squad, the 'Frisky Fortunettes,' are so compelling that a network wants to devote an *entire* cable channel to their reality show.

"Unlike most other religious institutions, the Fellowship of Fortuna has a high threshold for joy, fun and frivolity. Laughter figures prominently into the doctrine as well as the services.
"Our 'Big Sunday' is rather entertaining and fast moving. An organ and choir have been replaced with DJ Valihi and the 'Fly-Fortunes,' a dance team. Music, skit comedy and rousing sing-alongs are a part of the program.
"As they say in Fortuna slang, it's *"Hey-Fortu-*

nato!"

"The Skulls of Fortuna, a Mod-Goth-Punk styled support group, generates most of our customs and rituals. We're not sure what we think about it yet, but they have given Communion a makeover. The 'Body of Christ' is no longer represented by a thin wafer but with a bold petit filet breakfast steak served with two ranch eggs. The ridiculous notion that grape juice can signify 'The Blood of Christ' has been redeemed with a spicy Bloody Mary.

"Currently in the planning stages, the cathedral La Sagrada Fortuna features a design inspired by Gaudi and the Pacific Dining Car steakhouse. Pews will be replaced with red leather booths.

"Whereas the Catholic Church has the honorable Knights of Malta as their premiere service group, we have the High Flyin' Libertines (HFL). The HFL travel a lot. Lavish, first class trips feature brilliant speakers and a gourmet taste bud. Despite the rumors and tawdry tales, it really *is* a study group.

"On the deeper issues of Life, the Fellowship of Fortuna has a doctrine, "The Massive Missive," which is currently being written by the Plumes of Fortuna, a forward-thinking bunch of radical intellectuals who can't agree on anything except how to have a good time.

"The Massive Missive (or in church slang, the Double M) is heavily footnoted with references to the work of Umberto Eco and Jean Beaudrillard.

"Art-centric, church influences can be found in Minimalism, the Hyper-Realities and an aggressive freedom that can be won only through our trademarked brand of Neo-Nihilism.

"The FoF is open to all and discriminates against none. Tithing is strongly suggested at thirty-five percent (35%) of gross income before taxes.

"May Luck Swing Favorably With You!"

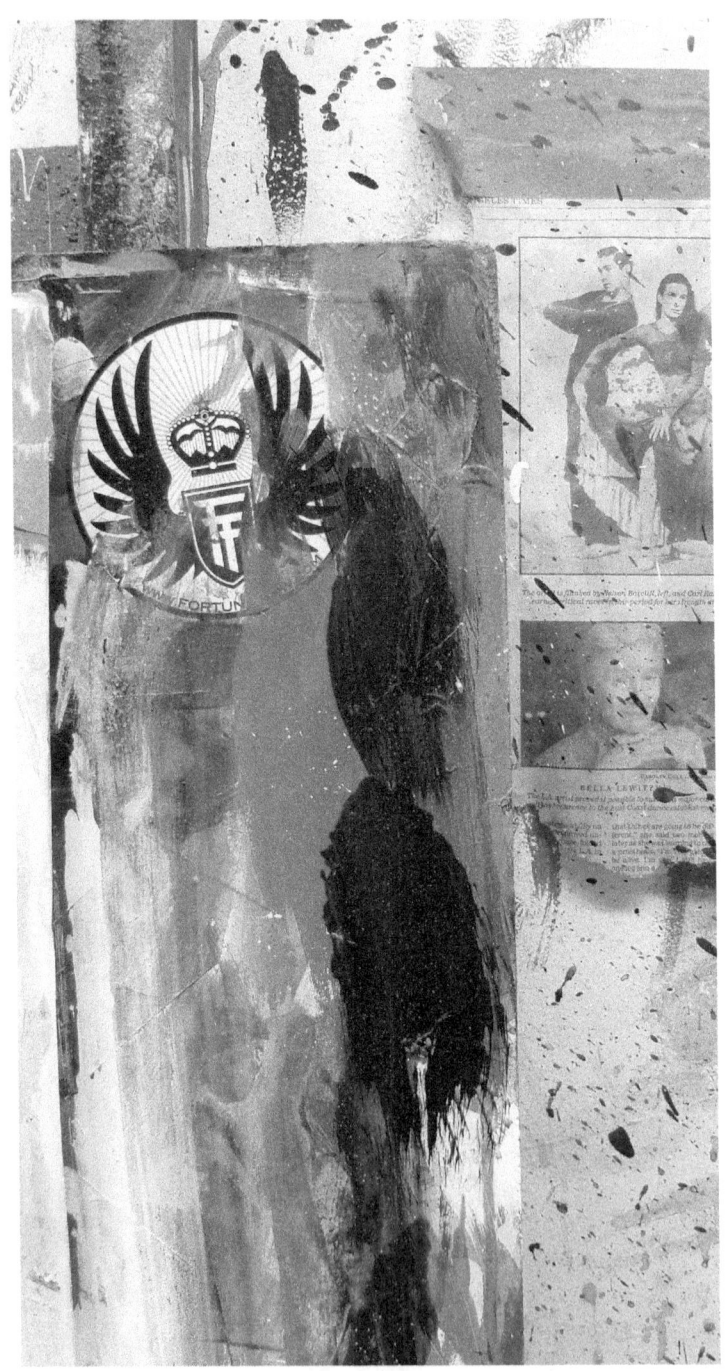

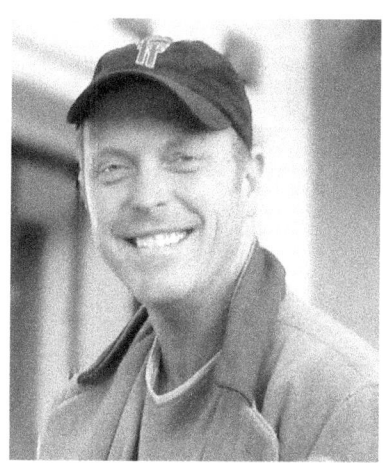

GORDY GRUNDY

Gordy Grundy is an American artist and arts writer. A native of Newport Beach, California, he has been influenced by sunny flights of SoCal fancy, the bold stroke and the grand gesture. Hollywood, Disney, the secrets of re-creation and the Healing Power of Pop continue to fascinate him.

Grundy is a graduate of the University of Southern California with a degree in Economics. He makes art daily and shows frequently.

In addition to a career in the arts, he has served as a nightclub impresario, lifeguard, film producer, tennis instructor, promotionalist, and theatrical producer.

Always a volunteer, he has served in leadership positions with the Barnsdall Art Center, Newport Beach Historical Society, Jonathan Art Foundation, Swim With Mike, Downtown LA Neighborhood Arts Council and more.

As a writer and columnist, he has written for Artillery magazine, the Huffington Post, the Los Angeles Times, the LA Weekly, ArtNews and many others.

His visual and literary works can be found at www. GordyGrundy.com

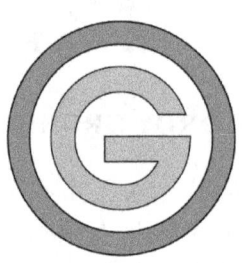

HOUSE
of
GO-GO

www.ingramcontent.com/pod-product-compliance
Lightning Source LLC
Chambersburg PA
CBHW060826170526
45158CB00001B/95